Library of
Davidson College

ESSAYS IN
EUROPEAN
LITERATURE

for Walter A. Strauss

Edited by
Alice N. Benston
Marshall C. Olds

STCL 1

ESSAYS IN

EUROPEAN LITERATURE

for Walter A. Strauss

Edited by
Alice N. Benston
Marshall C. Olds

Copyright © 1990 by Studies in Twentieth Century Literature, Incorporated, Manhattan, Kansas 66506-1003.

All rights reserved, including the right to reproduce this book, or parts thereof, in any form, except for the inclusion of brief quotations in reviews and scholarly publications.

Library of Congress Catalog Card Number 89-062858

ISBN 0-9624892-0-4

Printed in the United States of America

Acknowledgements

The Editors extend their warm thanks to Case Western Reserve University for so generously supporting the publication of this volume.

complexus hominem congratulatusque

Mircea Eliade

Wallace Fowlie

H. E. Francis

Erich Heller

Mark Irwin

Marie-Pierre Le Hir

Odette Petit-Morphy

Inge Schmidt

Gary Lee Stonum

CONTENTS

Acknowledgements   v

Tabula   vi

Portrait, by Mariana Carpinisan   vii

Foreword, by Alice N. Benston   xi

Changing Attitudes Toward Popular Culture in Aretino's *Sei Giornate*
    Richard M. Berrong   1

The "Oblique Gaze": Some Evidence of Symmetry in Montaigne's *Essais* (1:1–6, 57–52)
    Randolph Runyon   13

"Si la mer bouillait...": Repetition, Conjecture and Error in *Jacques le fataliste*
    Dalton Krauss   27

Phenomenology Strictly Exercised: Love and Truth in Jane Austen's *Pride and Prejudice*
    Edouard Morot-Sir   41

Possible Witnesses: The Hypothetical Characters in *La Comédie humaine*
    Maryann Weber, SND   63

"Paris change!": Perception and Narration
    Lilian R. Furst   73

From Stage to Page: The Impossible Theaters of Flaubert and Mallarmé
    Marshall C. Olds   85

From Chateaubriand to Proust: Or are Diegetic Images Metonymic?
    Marcel Muller   99

Proust: *Mise en Question* of the Myth of Orpheus
    Germaine Brée   115

Valéry's Degas and Rilke's Cézanne
    Ursula Franklin   125

Pirandello's Anti-Aristotelian Move: Character as Text
    Alice N. Benston   147

From *Marianne* to *Vendredi*: Two *Hebdomadaires de Gauche* of the Popular Front
    Steven Ungar   161

Habermas's Thesis of Internal Colonization: Reconstructed or Deconstructed Marxism?
    Wolfgang Sohlich   179

Scheherazade and Nozdref's Cook: The Role of the Female Storyteller in Isak Dinesen's *Seven Gothic Tales*
    Tiina A. Kirss   193

Psychoanalysis and Female Identity: The Adolescent Diaries of Karen Horney
    John Neubauer   215

A Contemporary Quest for a New Kabbalah
    Thomas J. J. Altizer   229

Walter A. Strauss, *Bibliography*   239

Contributors   243

FOREWORD

The large oak tree is still there, a wonderful relief to the plain stucco facade of Fishburn Hall on Emory University's campus. When I returned to Emory two years ago, I was grateful that this part of the grounds had not yet been redeveloped since my student days. This place is the haunt of Walter Strauss in my memory, for it was under that tree that Walter would hold his classes on pre-air-conditioned days in warm Atlanta. Dante, Manzoni, Leopardi, Baudelaire, Mallarmé and others all emerge from that tree when I glance at it, voiced through Walter's readings and comments. Further down the lawn, his figure will appear at the spot where I so often encountered him as he came out of the building. I can see him so clearly: the bulging briefcase, short sleeved shirt, beads of sweat on his upper lip and, at that time, the inevitable Gauloise dangling from the corner of his mouth. His puckish upturned smile might have a touch of irony about it, but never mockery. He would stand there, mindless of the heat, and, rocking on the heel of one foot, engage in conversation. The range of topics of those talks would surprise none of Walter's students or friends. It might be Goethe or Grabbe, Piero or Picasso, Wagner or Mahler, Fellini or Chaplin. In fact, in those days, when few understood what Comparative Literature was as a discipline and none could fathom the then new Institute of Liberal Arts, a fledgling adventure at Emory, I would simply say, "I'm majoring in Walter Strauss."

Over the years the conversation continues, at MLA meetings, in letters and in occasional visits. In fact, there was no perceptible transition from student to colleague, for Walter was never an "advisor," but a true "mentor." Always generous with ideas, he is also warmly receptive of one's own thoughts. The excitement of the exchange will frequently lead him to interrupt your sentence, never to erase your idea, but rather to corroborate it by playing with it. Talking with Walter is an act of thinking together, a mutual rumination and exploration. When you give him a paper to read, whether as a student or colleague, you can count on a careful reading. He will not flatter you, but his firm comments are always encouraging. His own works are to many of us the model of a combination of critical insight and felicity of expression.

The variety of the essays in this volume is something of a reflection of Walter's breadth of interest. Early on, Marshall Olds and I discovered that no theme, century, genre or language would pull Walter's admirers together. Hence we all offer this eclectic group of essays as a continuation of our conversations. We wish to honor more than his contribution to our profession or the intellectual camaraderie he has given us. We also write in affection, for Walter is, above all else, a warm and generous friend. Whether as former students, or past or present colleagues, we each have experienced his caring for us as people.

Alice N. Benston

CHANGING ATTITUDES TOWARD POPULAR CULTURE IN ARETINO'S *SEI GIORNATE*

Richard M. Berrong

The sixteenth century witnessed a marked increase in social unrest throughout western Europe. The most famous manifestations, such as the Peasants' War in 1524–25 and the Anabaptist seizure of Münster in 1534–35, occurred in northern Europe, but the rest of the continent was certainly not immune to what was often described as an ever-spreading plague.

The causes of this unrest were many and varied. Certainly the most obvious was the birth and growth of the Reformation. As recent historians have shown, however, economics and demographics played extremely important roles as well.[1] By the time the Black Plague and the Hundred Years' War subsided in the fifteenth century, Europe's peasant population had been so badly decimated that agricultural production was able to meet the nutritional needs of the survivors abundantly and relatively cheaply. As a result this peasant population, able to eat well and not hindered by disease or warfare, began to enjoy a comparatively prosperous existence.

It did not last. The peasants' comfort and prosperity led to a steady increase in their population. As a result, by the opening of the sixteenth century agricultural production on the continent was no longer able to meet the peasants' nutritional needs, shortages began to occur, and the cost of food started to rise. Inflation stemming from a variety of factors aggravated the problem until, by the 1520s and 30s, continental European peasants found themselves in a state of misery only highlighted by memories of material comfort in the previous century.

They did not sit at home quietly crying in their beer. They rioted. In city after city they rose up, breaking into food warehouses, murdering officials who tried to stop them and aristocrats who had flaunted their own material comfort. In 1524–25 tens of thousands of such angry peasants swept across the German states with all the violence of unpaid mercenaries, who in this might have served them as behavior models.

The aristocracy, seeing the threats posed by the starving, angry peasantry, began to distance itself ever more from a group whom it came to see increasingly not simply as different but as inimical. Capital punishment was decreed for vagabonds and the unemployed were literally thrown out of some cities. Popular culture, previously engaged in by all members of society, was methodically excluded from or repositioned in the lives of the upper estates.[2]

This exclusion and repositioning of popular culture did not result solely as a reaction to peasant revolt, however. As recent Early Modern European social historians have discovered, this change operated on two fronts.

On the one hand, the establishment churches, and especially the Roman Catholic church, attacked popular culture both because they saw it, quite correctly, to be a repository of pagan beliefs and because they regarded it to be an indulgence in licentiousness.[3] The first of these reasons must have had something to do with the Renaissance rediscovery and awareness of antiquity; the more scholars learned about the cultures of past civilizations, the more sixteenth-century men, including clerics, would have seen the similarities between popular culture and pagan civilization. The second reason must have owed more to the Renaissance's chronological sibling, the Reformation. One of the main issues on which Luther, Calvin, and other Reformers attacked the Catholic church was the immorality of its prelates. As a result much of the Counter-Reformation, as well, of course, as the Reformation, involved the condemnation and expulsion of hitherto tolerated moral license.

Both of these objections to popular culture appear in the Roman Catholic church's treatment of festivals. As Robert Muchambled has shown, the Catholic church went so far as to convert popular festivals into religious processions,[4] striking from them in the process the paganism and licentiousness which sixteenth-century Reformers had condemned as having no part in the Christian sacred.[5]

The other front on which the rejection of popular culture operated during the sixteenth century was the aristocratic, that of the secular upper estates. The writing of Castiglione and other Italian humanists had a real influence on the economic and political elite, who did indeed reject the universal participation in popular culture of their ancestors in order to adhere to and develop a separate, "refined" culture of their own.[6] Peter Burke offers one possible explanation for this change: "as their military role declined, the nobility had to find other ways of justifying their privileges: they had to show they were different from other people. The polished manners of the nobility were imitated by officials, lawyers and merchants who wanted to pass for noblemen. The withdrawal of all these groups from popular culture was more complete because it included their wives and daughters, who had long performed the function of mediators."[7]

Different historians stress different factors to explain why this two-fronted rejection of popular culture was carried out so thoroughly during the sixteenth century but not before. Muchambled emphasizes that before 1500 neither the state nor the church had sufficient power, was sufficiently centralized, to impress its will to any great extent on the populace.[8] Burke acknowledges that some sporadic attempts at rejection or at least modification of popular culture were made by church and state during the Middle Ages,[9] but stresses that these reforms were not undertaken in a systematic and thus effective fashion until the sixteenth century because the views and values that lay behind them were largely the result of Renaissance and Reformation.[10] If the power establishment began to reject and condemn popular culture in the sixteenth century, it was out of disdain and disapproval as much as out of fear.

It should come as no surprise that the changing relationship of the upper estates toward the peasantry affected the literature written for and by these upper estates. In the first half of the sixteenth century one can find the problem treated in works of continental literature such as Ariosto's *Orlando furioso* (1516, last revision 1532), Castiglione's *Cortigiano* (1528), and Rabelais's *Pantagruel* (1532) and *Gargantua* (1534 or 1535). In the case of the last two works especially it is not simply a question of the passive literary reflection of a *Zeitgeist* or estate mentality, but rather an example of what might almost be termed an active writer-reader dialectic. Rabelais undoubtedly wrote his initial narrative work with a concern for and supposed awareness of his presumed audience's values and expectations. As the changes he made in later editions of this and subsequent works demonstrate, however, he continued to be aware of, responsive to, and sometimes critical of these values and expectations as he came to understand them better through reader reaction focused directly on his own work. I have discussed this phenomenon in Rabelais's work extensively elsewhere, however.[11] Here I would like to present an analogous case, that of Rabelais's Italian contemporary, Pietro Aretino.

In April, 1534, while Frenchmen—or at least some Frenchmen—were enjoying *Pantagruel*, and possibly *Gargantua*, a new work of fiction appeared from the Parisian press, though the printer himself was Venetian and the text in Italian. It was entitled *Il Ragionamento della Nanna e della Antonia*, and it was followed by a sequel, *Il Dialogo nel quale la Nanna insegna a la Pippa* (Venice, 1536). Together the two works have become known as *I Ragionamenti* or *Le Sei Giornate*, in English as the *Dialogues*. Their author, Pietro Aretino, was Rabelais's almost exact contemporary (1492–1556) and his most famous, or infamous, literary work is worth a moment of attention in the context of what has been discovered by Early Modern European social historians regarding the upper estates' shifting attitude toward the people and popular culture during the sixteenth century.

Aretino was of humble origins, although he did his best to disguise the fact. Born in Arezzo, whence his name, he was the son of a shoemaker. By dint of his intellectual talents, his will to "be somebody," and his almost complete indifference to the moral objections that could be raised against his methods of attaining this goal, Aretino worked his way to the top of the social and political hierarchy of his day. At his peak he carried on conversations and correspondence with princes and prelates, even to such figures as Francis I and Charles V.

When not busy living a life that even Benvenuto Cellini would not have found boring, Aretino wrote. His output was as diversified in subject matter, genre, and style as it was plentiful and included plays, among them some of the best Italian Renaissance comedies, epic poetry (evidently some of the worst), religious prose and poetry, the famous published correspondence, and the *Dialogues*.

In the first three *Dialogues*, those published in 1534, Nanna discusses the advantages and disadvantages of the three possible careers to which she could direct her daughter Pippa: the convent, marriage, or prostitution. At the end of the third day, Nanna and her friend Antonia decide that Pippa would be best off as a whore. As a result, in the second three dialogues, published in 1536, Nanna explains to her daughter how best to succeed in the oldest profession.

As one biographer of the author has phrased it, "there is much in [the *Dialogues*] to test broadmindedness."[12] It is not simply that they treat of prostitution, wifely infidelity, and clerical licentiousness. That much Boccaccio had done two hundred years before. It is that they do so with a "disturbing sense of realism,"[13] i.e., with considerable crudity of vocabulary, much specific detail and, in the first dialogue, with an imagination involving permutations, combinations, and devices that even Sade would not surpass two centuries later. Though they are certainly much else besides, the *Dialogues* are quite definitely quite pornographic.

In certain ways they also make considerable use of popular culture. Aretino or his speakers constantly employ short similes drawn from the everyday life of the common man: people haggling in the marketplace, pickpockets moving among the crowds, fullers fulling cloth, etc. There are continual references to the various bodily functions, to disease, including "the French disease," to popular songs, etc. Members of the Catholic clergy are frequently ridiculed, often by juxtaposition with aspects of the "natural bodily lower stratum."[14]

The book clearly is not written for "the people" but for the upper estates, whose patronage Aretino was always courting, and among whom he prided himself on being able to move. There are a sufficient number of allusions to the classics, classical history and mythology, as well as negative remarks about peasant crudity, to demonstrate that Aretino had no thought of writing for the common man, or even for a general audience (had such a thing existed in the sixteenth century). Yet it is quite clear from the language he employs and the subject matter he treats that he felt the inclusion of popular culture in his work would not turn away the audience for whom he was writing.

Or at least should not. In the second dialogue Antonia mentions a woman who "has discovered a new way of speaking." When Nanna asks for details, Antonia explains:

> She mocks at anyone who does not talk in accordance with the rules ["alla usanza"]. She says that one should say "aperture" ["balcone"] and not "window" ["finestra"], "portal" ["porta"] and not "door" ["uscio"], "soon" ["tosto"] and not "hurry" ["vaccio"], "countenance" ["viso"] and not "face" ["faccia"], "heart" ["cuore"] and not "ticker" ["core"], "harvests" ["miete"] and not "crops" ["mete"], "knocks" ["percuote"] and not "bangs" ["picchia"], "hoax" ["ciancia"] and not "jape" ["burla"]. . . .

Nanna objects and declares: "I want . . . to talk as they do in my home town" (*Dia* 94, *SG* 82).[15]

The conversation between Antonia and Nanna at this point would certainly seem to be an allusion to the very lively discussion about the proper Italian for literary and courtly discourse, "la questione della lingua," that had been underway in Italy since the beginning of the sixteenth century. The vernacular tongue which has evolved into modern standard Italian made a glorious literary debut in the late thirteenth and early fourteenth centuries at the hands of such giants as Dante, Petrarch, and Boccaccio, but by the fifteenth century it had gone into decline as a literary language. Caught up in the fevered excitement that accompanied the rediscovery of classical Latin texts, most Italian writers of the fifteenth century abandoned their native tongue as a medium of important literary discourse and turned more and more exclusively to Latin. When this trend was reversed in the early sixteenth century Italian writers found themselves confronted with a major problem: they no longer had at their disposal a living, contemporary literary Italian. The vernacular employed by the fourteenth-century masters, principally Boccaccio and Petrarch, though the object of much praise and admiration, seemed to many unacceptably old-fashioned and hence ridiculous.

As a result several possible solutions were proposed, often in discussions among courtiers such as those idealized by Castiglione. Some Italians, such as Romolo Amaseo, supported a continued use of Latin on the grounds that it was the language of gentlemen whereas the vernacular was the speech of the lower estates. "A language of the plebs is a plebian language," wrote the humanist Francesco Bellafini in 1530.[16] Unlike the discussions in France several decades later, however, the language debate in Italy did not generally center on whether the vernacular was as deserving as Latin to be used in serious intellectual and literary discourse; most of the disputants were willing to accept it as a medium capable of expressing elevated thought and great artistic inspiration.

The argument, instead, revolved around what type of Italian was to be employed. Mario Equicola (d. 1525), a learned courtier and secretary to the marchesana of Mantua, proposed that writers should draw upon the most cultivated usage at the papal court and considered the living Tuscan dialect to be a plebian language. "As in political life, so also in speaking," he wrote, "we should distinguish ourselves in some fashion from the ignorant multitude." Castiglione's principal speaker on this topic, Count Ludovico da Canossa, proposes much the same solution: literary and spoken Italian should be derived from the best of what was currently spoken at the various princely courts.[17] Others such as the humanist and poet Pietro Bembo, who figures as one of the interlocutors in Castiglione's dialogues though his real-life position on this issue is advanced not by the character with his name but by Federico Fregoso, argued in favor of continued usage of the Italian of Petrarch and Boccaccio despite the obsolescence of some of its vocabulary and forms. In his *Prose della volgar lingua*, completed c. 1512, Bembo criticized Dante for using "crude, filthy, ugly, and very harsh" words. Still others, mostly Tuscans, maintained that the contemporary Tuscan dialect should be the language of choice, claiming that it was the direct and improved descendant of the language of the fourteenth-century masters. Eventually it was Bembo's viewpoint that won out, but as is quite evident, "in this debate, it was impossible to obfuscate the social core of the question."[18]

Aretino was obviously aware of the changes in upper-estate discourse underway in the courts of his native Italy. He was familiar with the Papal court in Rome and the ducal court in Mantua, and must have seen first-hand the development of a courtly speech that was designed to be different from the common, popular tongue that had sufficed for all in previous centuries. And it is also obvious that Aretino does not approve of this development and, as the first three dialogues make quite clear, that he had every intention of including popular discourse in his own work even though the work was written for the dominant estates, written by someone who was very intent upon being seen as a member of those estates.

Though we have nothing in the way of contemporary book reviews to gage the reactions of his intended audience, Aretino makes certain remarks in the second half of the work that suggest his public's reaction to the first. In the fourth dialogue, by the composition of which Aretino had had a chance to sample his readers' response to the first three, the characters return to the subject of popular discourse, though this time they extend the topic somewhat. Speaking of the public reaction to the publication of her conversation with Antonia, Nanna tells Pippa:

> They've kicked up such a fuss, the fools, as if they did nothing but criticize those who speak in the style of their native

dialect! ["ciò che si favella a la usanza del paese"]. Why, they slice away at their own expressions as a housewife slices a radish. I beg you, please, my dear daughter, do not forsake the speech which your dear little mother taught you; leave all "in such manner's" ["in cotal guisa"] and "directly's" ["tantosto"] to affected courtiers, and cry quits when these dames, using certain new, penetrative terms, say: "Go, that the Heavens may be propitious for you and the hour propinquious," just so they can look down their noses at those who speak plainly ["a la buona"] and say "hurry" ["vaccio"], "soon" ["a buonotta"] . . . "blockhead" ["sciabordo"] . . . "gloomy" ["cupo"], "dark" ["buio"], and a hundred thousand other unaffected expressions of everyday speech. . . . They want us to say "forthwith" ["tosto"] and not "right away" ["presto"], "moisture" ["in molle"] and not "wet" ["in macero"], and if you ask them why, they'll answer that "he carries" ["porta"] and "he fetches" ["reca"] do not come under the same rule, so that from now it is even dangerous to open your mouth. (*Dia* 182–83, *SG* 165)

Aretino makes it quite clear that in his eyes courtiers were developing their new language so that they could distinguish themselves from, "look down their noses at," those who still spoke as of old. His adamant refusal to give up the vocabulary of common, universal (or at least previously universal) speech is all the more striking given his own particular situation. The son of a cobbler who enjoyed being admired and treated as an equal by the great, Aretino was certainly in a position in which many another would have been quick to adopt the new courtly language in order to facilitate a distancing from or even a denial of earlier, less courtly origins. In the 1530s Aretino's true parentage was not generally known; it seems that, before it was revealed by an enemy in 1550, Aretino had passed himself off as the illegitimate son of a provincial nobleman. Still, unlike the "affected courtiers," Aretino refused to exclude common, everyday, universally employed terms from his written discourse.

In the second set of dialogues it is not just a question of the defense of general, common language as opposed to a courtly speech, however. In the same passage of the fourth dialogue previously cited, Nanna tells her daughter that people became very upset upon reading the licentious tales she told about nuns in the first dialogue. "The world isn't what it used to be," Nanna sighs, adding: "nor can a person who knows how to exist live in it any longer" (*Dia* 181, *SG* 164). If the readers became upset at what she told Antonia, Nanna continues, what would they say if she recounted some of the even more outlandish activities she has seen nuns engage in? Here it is no longer a question of common speech vs. courtly speech. Evidently there was a negative reaction to the content of the first dialogue, which portrays nuns and monks as anything but celibate. And yet this was nothing that Boccaccio had not depicted to great and lasting acclaim two centuries before. (Or almost nothing—some of Aretino's variations on positions, devices, and couplings go rather beyond anything I remember in the *Decameron*). Nanna makes the temporal change in reader tolerance clear: "The world isn't what it used to be." It gets upset now at things that did not upset it before.

Aretino's interlocutors return to this moral change in the sixth and last dialogue. At the end of one of her digressions the Midwife says: "but I was starting to tell you about the man who clutched the hope aroused by the stain of the swallow that shat on my shoulder." The Wetnurse interrupts her: "That word 'shat' ["carcare"] ill becomes your mouth, and it seems that in these days one must spit manna if one does not want to attract the curses of those harpies who stun the bakeshops and markets with their carping. It's a strange thing that one cannot even say ass ["cu' "], cunt ["po' "], and prick ["ca' "]" (*Dia* 325, *SG* 298). Again the same lamentations. "In these days" one can no longer make mention of bodily functions or of the parts of the body associated with the "material bodily lower stratum." There has been a change in what is acceptable subject matter and vocabulary, a reduction of possibilities and scope. Aretino, if one can extrapolate his opinion from those of his characters, is not pleased with the change. Not pleased at all.

Aretino's contemporary, Rabelais, became aware of the shift in his audience's attitudes toward popular culture at least in part as Aretino did, through their reaction to his first volume, *Pantagruel*. He took this shift into account as of his second narrative, *Gargantua*, and his narratives continued to be reprinted throughout the rest of the century.[19]

Aretino did not. Though there is no equivalent for the first dialogue in the three published in 1536, i.e., nothing quite so free in its permutations and combinations or its ridicule of the clergy, the second set is still as filled as the first with popular—including scatological—vocabulary, details of everyday life, etc. And despite what Brantôme reports concerning the success, at least in Paris, of the first edition,[20] the work was not published again until 1587.[21]

Why? Certainly not because of censorship. It is, rather, very tempting to suggest that it was because Aretino had misjudged his market, to use modern business terminology. His use of popular language and his defense of it, his refusal to include more upper-estate discourse and his ridicule of it, his reliance on popular culture as a source of similes and his unrestrained references to sex and the "material bodily lower stratum" may simply have resulted in a work that was not to the taste of the upper estates of the 1530s and later, the audience for whom Aretino wrote. Though the element of literary quality certainly also enters the picture—the *Dialogues*, though entertaining and well crafted, do not begin to measure up to *Gargantua and Pantagruel* in richness and complexity—one cannot help but wonder to what extent the commercial failure of Aretino's work was a result of the fact that he was unwilling to take into consideration the changes in manners of the learned and dominant estates of his time.

NOTES

1. The bibliography on popular unrest in Early Modern Europe is already immense and continues to grow rapidly. Among the works relevant to this discussion are: Yves-Marie Bercé, *Croquants et Nu-Pieds: Les Soulèvements paysans en France du XVIe au XIXe siècle* (Paris: Gallimard, 1974); Natalie Zemon Davis, *Society and Culture in Early Modern France* (Stanford: Stanford University Press, 1975); Bernd Moeller, *Imperial Cities and the Reformation*, ed. and trans. H. C. Eric Midelfort and Mark U. Edwards, Jr. (Philadelphia: Fortress Press, 1972); Robert Muchambled, *Culture populaire et culture des élites dans la France moderne (XVe-XVIIIe siè*cles) (Paris: Flammarion, 1978).

2. The bibliography on the shifting attitudes toward popular culture in the sixteenth century is also substantial. The interested reader should start with Peter Burke's seminal *Popular Culture in Early Modern Europe* (New York: New York University Press, 1978), which has a large bibliography. Also: Norbert Elias, *The Civilizing Process*, trans. Edmund Jephcott (New York: Urizen Books, 1978), vol. I; Carlo Ginzburg, *The Cheese and the Worms*, trans. John and Anne Tedeschi (Baltimore: The Johns Hopkins University Press, 1980); Lauro Martines, *Power and Imagination: City-States in Renaissance Italy* (New York: Alfred A. Knopf, 1979); and

Muchambled's above-cited study. For modifications of Burke's thesis on the shift in the upper estates' attitude toward popular culture at this time, see David Warren Sabean, *Power in the Blood: Popular culture and village discourse in early modern Germany* (Cambridge: Cambridge University Press, 1984).
3. Muchambled, 209.
4. Muchambled, 158.
5. Several historians have noted the development of a definitely sharper distinction between sacred and profane during the sixteenth century. See Muchambled 209, Burke 211.
6. Burke, 271.
7. Burke, 271–72.
8. Muchambled, 22.
9. Burke, 218.
10. Burke, 271.
11. *Rabelais and Bakhtin: Popular Culture in "Gargantua and Pantagruel"* (Lincoln: University of Nebraska Press, 1986).
12. Thomas Caldecot Chubb, *Aretino, Scourge of Princes* (New York: Reynal and Hitchcock, 1940), 356.
13. Chubb, 356.
14. Mikhail Bakhtin's famous term, from his study of popular culture in Rabelais, available in English as *Rabelais and His World*, trans. Hélène Iswolsky (Bloomington, IN: Indiana University Press, 1984).
15. Quotations from Aretino's work are taken from Raymond Rosenthal's English translation (New York: Stein and Day, 1971). Page numbers are also given for the original Italian text, taken from: *Sei Giornate*, ed. Giovanni Aquilecchia (Bari: Laterza, 1969).
16. Quoted in Martines, 319. My discussion of "la questione della lingua" is taken from his section entitled "The Language Question," 317–22. The standard work on "la questione della lingua" remains Thérèse Labande-Jeanroy's *La Question de la langue en Italie*, Publications de la Faculté des lettres de l'Université de Strasbourg, 27 (Strasbourg and Paris: Istra, 1925).
17. Baldassar Castiglione, *The Book of the Courtier*, trans. Charles S. Singleton (New York: Anchor Books, 1959), 47–64; *Il Libro del Cortigiano*, in *Opere di Castiglione, Della Casa, Cellini*, ed. Carlo Cordie (Milan: Ricciardi, 1960), 51–69.
18. Martines, 317–18. As of the final, 1532 edition of his epic romance, Ariosto in his last canto momentarily leaves the medieval world of knights and fair ladies to sing the praises of Bembo, "who rescued the purity of our gentle idiom from the drabness of common usage [the *volgare uso tetro*] and gave us an example of how it ought to sound [*quale esser dee*, "how it should be"]." See: Ludovico Ariosto, *Orlando furioso*, trans. Guido Waldman (New York: Oxford University Press, 1983), 558–59; *Orlando*

furioso, ed. Lanfranco Caretti (Milan: Ricciardi, 1963), canto 46, stanza 15, lines 2–4.

19. On the shifting attitude toward the people and popular culture in Rabelais's narratives see the study cited in footnote eleven above. The standard bibliography of the early editions of Rabelais's works is the *Bibliographie Rabelaisienne* compiled by Pierre Paul Plan (Paris: Imprimerie nationale, 1904).

20. Cited in Chubb, 342.

21. On the editions of the two sets of dialogues published during the sixteenth century see Aquilecchia's bibliographical essay in his edition of the *Sei Giornate*, 359–417.

THE "OBLIQUE GAZE": SOME EVIDENCE OF SYMMETRY IN MONTAIGNE'S *ESSAIS* (1:1–6, 57–52)

Randolph Runyon

"Mes fantasies se suyvent, mais par fois c'est de loing, et se regardent, mais d'une veuë oblique," Montaigne writes in "De la vanité" (3:9, 973b). One of the ways his fantasies look at each other in that oblique way, and at times over considerable distances, is through what I believe to be a symmetrical arrangement of the chapters of his *Essais*. Each chapter has a double, equidistant from the center of the book in which it appears (the three central chapters 1:29, 2:19 and 3:7), in which certain words and turns of phrase are repeated, and consequently certain images and opinions are taken up for discussion once more, from a different perspective. Roy Leake's *Concordance de Montaigne* facilitates the task of finding these textual echoes, and has made it possible to prove that in many instances certain words and combinations of words make their only appearance in a given book (or sometimes in all the *Essais*) in two such symmetrically placed chapters. The first six such pairs in Book 1 of the *Essais* offer a convenient way to sample the fifty-two chapter symmetries in Montaigne.

1:1/57

Montaigne's first chapter opens the *Essais* with an unacknowledged contradiction that grows more paradoxical the longer one looks at it. "Par divers moyens on arrive à pareille fin" (1:1) is a title that is in retrospect only halfway accurate, if not in fact misleading, for as the essay took shape in its successive editions from 1580 until 1595, it became nearly as much a collection of instances in which the same means led to diverse ends.

La plus commune façon d'amollir les coeurs de ceux qu'on a offensez, lors qu'ayant la vengeance en main, ils nous tiennent à leur mercy, c'est de les esmouvoir par submission à commiseration et à pitié. Toutesfois la braverie, et la constance, moyens tous contraires, ont quelquefois servi à ce mesme effect. (1:1, 11a)

Even this opening declaration is contradicted by Montaigne's examples, for of the seven stories of victors and vanquished that the first edition recounted, in only one instance did groveling submission (what Montaigne calls "La plus commune façon") lead to mercy; in five cases mercy was achieved through brave defiance (relegated in his opening statement to what happens only "quelquefois"), while in one case defiance led to death. Of the ten stories the chapter had accumulated by 1595, the odds had become nearly even between the *fin* of death (four instances) or that of survival (five instances) for those who chose the same *moyen*, brave defiance. And the discrepancy between the title and the essay had become even greater.

If the title of the first essay is only halfway relevant to that essay, it may be because the other half of its relevance belongs to the essay with which this one is symmetrically paired in Book 1—to the last essay, "De l'aage" (1:57). In the beginning of that essay Montaigne argues that to die of old age is extremely rare (it happens, he says, about once every two or three centuries); what we really die of is a great diversity of mishaps, "un si grand nombre d'accidents ausquels chacun de nous est en bute par une naturelle subjection" (1:57, 312a). He cites a few: one man breaks his neck in a fall, another drowns in shipwreck, another is struck by the plague, still another by pleurisy. "Par divers moyens," in other words, "on arrive à pareille fin"—and not, as we might tend to think, by the single *moyen* of old age. A natural death is in fact an accidental one: "on doit, à l'aventure, appeller plustost naturel ce qui est general, *commun* et universel" (1:57, 312a), he writes, echoing the "plus *commune* façon" that was at issue in 1:1. "Mourir de vieillesse, c'est une mort rare, singuliere et extraordinaire, et d'autant moins naturelle que les autres" (1:57, 312a).

Old age, he continues, is "la borne au delà de laquelle nous n'irons pas, et que la loy de nature a *prescript* pour n'estre point *outre*-passé...." If we have reached old (or even middle) age "nous avons passé les limites accoustumez... nous ne devons esperer d'aller guiere *outre*..." (1:57, 312a). In the heart of "Par divers moyens..." is a story of what happens when one does precisely this—when, that is, one overstays one's allotted time (and it is told with the same words: *outre*... and *prescrit*): The Thebans put their generals Pelopidas and Epaminondas on trial for their lives "pour avoir continué leur charge *outre* le temps qui leur avait esté *prescrit* et preordonné" (1:1, 12a). Both got off—Pelopidas, though just barely, by groveling and Epaminondas by brave defiance.

The question of how long, in the ancient world in which these two lived, one should hold military office is, in turn, an issue Montaigne takes up in "De l'aage." "Servius Tullius dispensa les chevaliers qui avoient passé quarante sept ans des courvées de la guerre; Auguste les remit à quarante et cinq" (1:57, 313a). Montaigne himself was not in favor of such early retirement: "Je serois d'advis qu'on estandit nostre vacation et occupation autant qu'on pourroit, pour la commodité publique...."

Thus does Montaigne begin (and end) the first book of the *Essais* with two parallel chapters—parallel because they both speak of arriving at the same end (death) by diverse means (the various accidents that end our lives, of which old age is the rarest), and because they both speak of going beyond (*outre*) the prescribed *(prescrit)* time—that may themselves enact the truth of the first's title, arriving at the common end of a symmetrical structure through the means that are themselves, at first glance, diverse.

1:2/56

Diodorus the dialectician met a horrible fate for finding himself unable to work his way out of an argument—he "mourut sur le champ, espris d'une extreme passion de honte, pour *en son eschole* et en public ne se pouvoir desvelopper d'un argument qu'on luy avoit faict" (1:2, 17a). Though not meant as a cautionary tale but rather as yet another example of "l'imbécilité humaine" near the conclusion of "De la tristesse," the second chapter in Book 1—a compilation of examples of extreme death—it could nevertheless serve as one for someone who tries to develop an argument for reading Montaigne that, to work, must be universally true. What if I came across a pair of chapters equidistant from the center of one of the *Essais'* three books that had absolutely nothing in common?

No danger of that here, at least for Montaigne who opens chapter 56, "Des prieres," with a passage that is likewise about debating in schools (and debating highly unlikely arguments, at that): "Je propose des fantasies informes et irresolues, comme font ceux qui publient des questions doubteuses à debattre *aux escoles* . . ." (1:56, 302a). From 1582 (when Montaigne inserted this new beginning for "Des prieres") until 1588 (when he added one more sentence to the end of "De la tristesse") the end of 1:2 (Diodorus's end) thus anticipated the beginning of 1:56—as if the two chapters in fact formed a single text.

I would like to argue, as indeed I would for all the other such pairs in the *Essais*, that they do form such a unity. And I believe this can be demonstrated by pointing out that while in "De la tristesse" Montaigne accumulates examples of grief (and other emotions) so great that it cannot be expressed in words—Psammenitus, for example, who "se tint coy sans mot dire" (1:2, 15a) when he saw his daughter taken prisoner and his son put to death but who did weep when a mere servant had been led away captive, and who, when asked why, said that "les deux premiers surpassans de bien loin tout moyen de se pouvoir exprimer" (1:2, 16a)—in "Des prieres" the essayist presents another subject for which which human language is totally inadequate: talking about God. "*Chi puo dir com'egli arde é in picciol fuoco*," he argues in "De la tristesse," quoting Petrarch on the subject of passion. Likewise, in "Des prieres," he contends that God is too great a subject to be bandied about by all and sundry. He says, for example, that the Church was right to forbid the Psalms of David to be sung by the laity (it was a distinguishing mark of Protestant religious practice): "Cette voix est trop divine pour n'avoir autre usage que d'exercer les poulmons et plaire à nos oreilles; c'est de la conscience qu'elle doit estre produite, et non pas de la langue" (1:56, 306a). He argues that the prayer we should most often pray (i.e., "sinon seulement, au moins tousjours" [1:56, 303c]) should be the Lord's Prayer, since it has been "dictée mot à mot par la bouche de Dieu" (1:56, 303a) and is therefore free from the imperfections of human language. He speaks with some hint of approval of "ceux mesmes qui ne sont pas des nostres [qui] defendent pourtant entre eux l'usage du nom de Dieu . . ." (1:56, 309a).

"Des prieres" is to a considerable degree an argument for silence in the presence of mystery too great to be spoken, even at the risk of silencing itself:

Et ne diroit-on pas aussi sans apparence, que l'ordonnance de ne s'entremettre que bien reservéement d'escrire de la Religion à tous autres qu'à ceux qui en font expresse profession, n'auroit pas faute de quelque image d'utilité et de justice; et, à moy avecq, à l'avanture, *de m'en taire?* (1:56, 309b)

As such, its continuity with "De la tristesse" 's accounts of emotions too great to be expressed is evident: the ancient painter's depiction of the grief of Iphigenia's father for his sacrificed daughter—"il le peignit le visage couvert, comme si nulle contenance ne pouvoit representer ce degré de dueil" (1:2, 16a)—or the way the poets pictured Niobe, who had lost all her children, transformed into a rock, "pour exprimer cette morne, *muette*, et sourde stupidité qui nous transit, lors que les accidens nous accablent surpassans nostre portée" (1:2, 16a).

1:3/55

"Nos affections s'emportent au delà de nous" (1:3) is a collection of posthumous effects. Bertrand de Glesquin died at the siege of Rancon, whose inhabitants were later compelled to carry the keys to the city on his corpse. It was decided not to ask for safe-conduct to carry the body of Barthelemy d'Alviane back to Venice through hostile territory, since he should not show less courage in death than in life. Edward I of England, dying, instructed his son to carry his bones into any future war with the Scots, since his physical presence on the battlefield had led to such great success in the past. The Protestant Jean Vischa wanted his followers to make a drum out of his skin to carry into battle against his enemies for the same reason. Likewise certain Indians carried with them the bones of one of their captains when they fought the Spanish conquistadors. Our affections carry themselves (or are thought to) beyond ourselves in this sense, beyond our physical, living presence.

To these posthumous effects "Des senteurs" (1:55), in its 1580 version, responded with an address, in its closing lines, to a certain Posthumus:
Posthume, non benè olet, qui benè semper olet (1:55, 301a). Smells are a particular instance of what "Nos affections s'emportent au delà de nous" in a more general way describes, for they carry themselves away from our bodies all on their own. How smells transport themselves, how they are *carried—portées—*is in fact specifically addressed in "Des senteurs":

> Quelque odeur que ce soit, c'est merveille combien elle s'attache à moy et combien j'ay la peau propre à s'en abreuver. Celuy qui se plaint de nature, dequoy elle a laissé l'homme sans instrument à *porter* les senteurs au nez, a tort; car *elles se portent elles mesmes*. (1:55, 301b)

Those last five words come quite close to echoing the title of 1:3, with the interesting difference that here in 1:55 smells are carried *to us* while in 1:3's title our affections are carried *from us*. those instances I cited above from 1:3 of posthumous effects were themselves in each instance echoes of the same *s'emportent* in that title: the besieged were "*obligez de porter* les clefs de la place sur le corps du trespassé" (1:3, 20a); the body of Barthelemy d'Alviane had to be "*raporté à Venise*" (1:3, 20a); as for Edward I's bones, "il les reservast pour les *porter* avec luy et en son armée" (1:3, 21a); Jean Vischa wanted his skin to be made into "un tabourin à *porter* à la guerre" (1:3, 21b); and the Indians "*portoient*" their leader's bones into battle (1:3, 21b).

A 1588 addition to "Des senteurs" echoes 1:3's *raporté à Venise:* "Ces belles villes, *Venise* et Paris, alterent la faveur que je leur *porte*, par l'aigre senteur, l'une de son marets, l'autre de sa boue" (1:55, 302b). And the echoes perpetuate themselves, like *senteurs* that have a half-life of their own: the "*faveurs* celestes nous accompaignent au tombeau, et continuent à nos reliques" (1:3, 21a); while the *alterent* just before in these concluding lines from 1:55 is itself echoed in a post–1588 addition that becomes the new conclusion to 1:3:

> Tout ainsi que nature nous faict voir que plusieurs choses mortes ont encore des relations occultes à la vie. Le vin *s'altere* aux caves, selon aucunes mutations des *saisons* de sa vigne. Et la chair de venaison change d'estat aux saloirs et de goust, selon les loix de la chair vive, à ce qu'on dit. (1:3, 24c)

While a post-1588 addition to the last page of 1:55, inserted just before the passage about Paris and Venice, answers this talk of wine that changes according to the *seasons* and venison that changes its taste when salted (though not just because of the salt) with talk of other foods that change their taste with the addition of *seasonings:* "l'art de ces cuisiniers qui sçavent *assaisonner* les odeurs estrangeres avecq la saveur des viandes" (1:55, 302c). Like the celestial *faveurs* that accompany us beyond the tomb, and linger around the relics of our bones, the marvelous (I almost said "heavenly") *saveurs* that the king of Tunis's cook concocted survived the peacock and pheasants he knew so well how to prepare, lingering in the halls of the palace long after their carcasses were carved: "et, quand on les despeçoit, remplissoient non seulement la salle, mais toutes les chambres de son palais, et jusques aux maisons du voisinage, d'une très soüefve vapeur qui ne se perdoit pas si tost" (1:55, 302c).

It is strange how those passages in the *Essais* that appear most actively to take part in the symmetrical relations between the chapters at the same time also seem to hint at, to wink slyly at, the very existence of those parallels, as if to acknowledge the secret. Thus here the venison and wine that appear to respond in occult ways to events taking place elsewhere to which one would have thought they had no connection could be a figure for the essays themselves as they seem to change (particularly as they accumulated more and more additions from 1580 to 1595) in response to what changes were being made elsewhere—in the other essays that, like our affections and like smells, provide a ghostly accompaniment.

1:4/54

In "Comme l'ame descharge ses passions sur des objects faux, quand les vrais luy defaillent" (1:4) Montaigne asserts that when the soul is agitated, by anger for example or by love, it must either have an object to vent its passion on or invent one: "plustost que de demeurer en *vain*" it "s'en forge ainsin une faulce et *frivole*" (1:4, 25a). "Des *vaines* subtilitez" (1:54) presents itself, from its very first sentence, as just the kind of vain and frivolous invention that the soul would concoct in the absence of a proper object: "Il est de ces subtilitez *frivoles* et *vaines*..." (1:54, 297a). Although Montaigne warms to the task with a list of other vain subtleties such as poems each of whose lines begin with the same letter, poems that form pictures on the page from the lengthening and shortening of their meter, the man who tried to calculate how many words the letters of the alphabet could form, or the man who could throw a grain of millet through the eye of a needle, he goes on to propose one of his own: "Nous venons presentement de nous jouër chez moy à qui pourroit trouver plus de choses qui se tiennent par les deux bouts extremes" (1:54, 298a). Such are the titles *Sire* and *Dame*, which are applicable only to the highest and lowest classes of society; or *dez (dais)*, canopies which can be spread over tables only in the houses of royalty and in taverns; or the fact that the ancient Romans wore the same costume for days of mourning and of celebration; or that lead ingots will melt in both extreme heat and extreme cold.

In the end he concludes that this pastime was all the more vain for being too easy: "nous avions pris pour un exercice malaisé et d'un rare *subject* ce qui ne l'est aucunement; et qu'après que nostre *invention* a esté eschaufée, elle descouvre un nombre infiny de pareils exemples" (1:54, 300a). The mind, once it has chosen a subject that calls for some invention, is apt to perform this task all too well—as Montaigne also found when he spoke in 1:4 of how the soul "en ses passions se pipe plutost elle mesme, se dressant un faux *subject* et fantastique" (1:4, 25a) and when he complains as well of too great a power of invention: "Quelles causes *n'inventons nous* des malheurs qui nous adviennent?" (1:4, 26a).

Several verbal echoes emerge when we compare these two chapters that, unlike certain others, already appear to be talking about the same thing. An example of extremes that touch is "Les *dez* qu'on estend sur les tables" (1:54, 298b) that can be legally found in palaces and taverns but nowhere else, while homonymic *dets* function in 1:4 as a false object upon which passions are discharged: "Qui n'a veu ... se gorger d'une bale de *dets,* pour avoir où se venger de la perte de son argent?" (1:4, 26a). "Aristote dict que les cueus de *plomb* se fondent et coulent de froid et de la rigueur de l'hyver, comme d'une chaleur vehemente" (1:54, 298a) in "Des vaines subtilitez," while lead serves in 1:4 (in its only other appearance in Book 1 of the *Essais*) to provoke a misaimed discharge of passion: "Ce ne sont pas ces tresses blondes que tu deschires, ny la blancheur de cette poictrine que, despite, tu bas si cruellement, qui ont perdu d'un malheureux *plomb* ce frere bien aymé" (1:4, 26a). The man in 1:54 who could throw grains of millet through a needle's eye could do it "sans *faillir*" while 1:4 is about what happens to the soul and the objects of its passion "quand les vrais luy *defaillent*." One of the vain subtleties cited is that of "celuy qui *s'amusa* à conter en combien de sortes se pouvoient *renger* les lettres de l'alphabet" (1:54, 297a), while one of those guilty of discharging their passions on false objects is Cyrus, who "*amusa* toute une armée plusieurs jours à se venger de la riviere de Gydnus" (1:4, 26a), and another is the Thracians "qui, quand il tonne ou esclaire, se mettent à tirer contre le ciel d'une vengeance titanienne, pour *renger* Dieu à raison, à coups de flesche" (1:4, 26–27c). These *coups de flesche* will hardly make an impression on their target, which Montaigne in the line just before implies could as easily be fortune as the deity: "qui s'en adressent à Dieu mesmes, ou à la *fortune*, comme si elle avoit des oreilles subjects à nostre batterie, à l'exemple des Thraces qui . . ." (1:4, 26ac). Now arrows and outrageous fortune crop up as well in 1:54 when Montaigne speaks of how both the wise and the stupid are impervious to misfortune because the latter are unaware of it while the former have "une ame forte et solide, contre laquelle *les traicts de la fortune* venant à donner, il est force qu'ils rejalissent et s'émoussent, trouvant un corps dans lequel ils ne peuvent faire impression" (1:54, 299a). The arrows that in one chapter are shot at a God who is another name for fortune are in the companion chapter launched by fortune, with the same inability to hit their intended target in either instance.

1:5/53

"Si le chef d'une place assiegée doit sortir pour parlementer" (1:5) is a problem characteristic of our times, Montaigne writes, since we do not fight war as honorably as did the Romans, whose observance of ancient mores forbade them from taking unfair advantage of the enemy. "Et pour cette cause, c'est une reigle en la bouche de tous les hommes de guerre de nostre temps, qu'il ne faut jamais que le gouverneur en une place assiegée sorte luy mesmes pour parlementer" (1:5, 28a). To this contemporary military proverb the symmetrical arrangement of the *Essais* invites us to compare an aphorism from the mouth of a military man of that more ancient, and perhaps nobler, time—Caesar: "Il se faict, par un vice ordinaire de nature, que nous ayons et plus de fiance et plus de crainte des choses que nous n'avons pas veu et qui sont cachées et inconnues" (1:53, 1518n [this translation of Caesar's Latin lasted until the 1595 edition {1580:1, 475}]). It all the more specifically invites us to do that because the title of 1:53, "D'un mot de Caesar" makes that sentence its ostensible subject.

The context developed for that word of Caesar's in 1:53 is that of our incessant desire to go beyond our present state. "Quoy que ce soit qui tombe en nostre connoissance et jouissance, nous sentons qu'il ne nous satisfaict pas, et allons beant après les choses advenir et inconnuës, d'autant que les presentes ne nous soulent point" (1:53, 296–297a). Yet it is peculiarly apposite as well to the military situation 1:5 presents for our consideration, where it is there very much a question of both placing one's trust in and yet fearing what is not yet known—and a question too of leaving a place of safety for one of danger in the hope of bettering one's condition. For Montaigne does not entirely agree with those who say that the governor of a besieged city should never venture forth to parley with the enemy. "Si est-ce que encores en y a il, qui se sont très-bien trouvez de sortir sur la parole de l'assaillant. Tesmoing Henry de Vaux", who decided to "sortir à parlementer pour son profict" (1:5, 29a). For once he had, the enemy pointed out to him that they had mined the walls of his castle,

> et son evident ruyne luy ayant esté monstrée à l'oeil, il s'en *sentit* singulierement obligé à l'ennemy; à la discretion duquel, après qu'il se fut rendu et sa trouppe, le feu estant mis à la mine, les estansons de bois venus à *faillir*, le Chasteau fut emporté de fons en comble. (1:5, 29a)

Until two more sentences were added in 1588, 1:5 concluded with this disintegrating structure—and thereby formed a context of continuity with the first sentence of 1:53:

> Si nous nous amusions par fois à nous considerer, et le temps que nous mettons à contreroller autruy et à connoistre les choses qui sont hors de nous, que nous l'emploissions à nous sonder nous mesmes, nous *sentirions* aisément combien toute cette nostre contexture est bastie de pieces foibles et *defaillantes*. (1:53, 296a)

If we were, that is, to turn around and look at the structure of our own life as Henry de Vaux was encouraged to come out and see with his own eyes how fragile was the state of his castle, we would be surprised. But the irony of it is (and there is, perhaps, always irony in Montaigne) that it appears that the only way we are going to discover this is to stop going outside of ourselves (*hors de nous*)—while in de Vaux's case the only way the discovery could be made would be for him to do precisely the opposite.

The two sentences added in 1588 are nevertheless germane to Caesar's talk of fear and *fiance*: "Je me *fie* ayséement à la *foy* d'autury. Mais malaiséement le fairoy je lors que je donnerois à juger l'avoir plustost faict par desespoir et faute de coeur"—that is, from *crainte*—"que par franchise et *fiance* de sa loyauté" (1:5, 29b).

I:6/52

"De la parsimonie des anciens" (1:52) is itself parsimonious, being so brief that in the Pléiade edition it amounts to less than a full page. In 1580 it was composed of only two anecdotes (in addition to a listing of the small number of servants hired by Scipion Aemilianus, Homer, Plato and Zeno); after 1588 of three. Given so small a space in which to speak of ancient thrift, it is somewhat puzzling that Montaigne should be so wasteful as to spend almost the half of it (42% in 1580), and the first half at that, telling a story that has little, if anything at all, to do with parsimony. It is an account of how the Roman general Attilius Regulus, while winning victories in Africa, wrote to the Republic that a farm laborer he had left in charge of his seven-acre farm back home had absconded with the farming tools and asked permission to return so that his wife and children would not suffer. The Senate found a replacement to oversee the farm, restored what had been stolen, and ordered his family to be cared for at the public expense. The only hint of a connection with the declared subject of the essay is the fact that his farm was so small as to have only seven acres. Indeed, that the Senate decided to feed his wife and children out of the public purse rather goes against than supports the argument of the chapter that the Roman Republic was tight with its money. In the light of the fact (added in 1588) that Tyberius Gracchus, who was a very prominent figure ("estant lors le premier homme des Romains" [1:52, 296b]), was allowed only five and half *sous* a day for business expenses when he was on official state business, it seems something of a public extravagance.

Such puzzles as these in the *Essais*—intensified in Books I and II by the extreme brevity of many of the chapters—can sometimes be helped toward a solution by taking a look at the essay that secretly accompanies the one that poses the problem. "L'heure des parlemens dangereuse" (1:6), on the other hand, is puzzling for another reason. Why did Montaigne divide his consideration of the danger of going out to parley into two succeeding chapters? Their continuity is apparent from the first word of 1:6—"*Toutes-fois*..." (1:6, 29a)—and from a parenthetical expression in that first anecdote of treachery during parley time—"*comme je viens de dire*..."—which refers to what he had just said in 1:5 about how such behavior is characteristic of the *reigles* (1:6, 30a; cp. 28a: "c'est une reigle en la bouche...") of war we observe in our times. The answer I would like to propose to this question is that the same issue is examined in 1:5 and 6 from two different aspects, each of which is drawn out by certain echoes in chapters 1:53 and 52, respectively. The way 1:53 parallels 1:5, as we have just seen, emphasizes the danger *to the negotiator* of venturing forth from the castle walls, both from the manner in which the saying of Caesar's reiterated the way we respond to the unknown beyond with both *crainte* and *fiance*, and from the way the opening of 1:53 with its warning to take a look at how close our own structure (*contexture*) is to collapse reflected the way Henry de Vaux was urged to come out and observe how close his castle was to disintegration (emphasizing in his case not the danger to the negotiator but the salvation that will come to him for having dared to venture forth). One might, of course, have noticed this from a close reading of 1:5 itself, as well as its title, which emphasizes the danger to the negotiators, not to the inhabitants of the city. Count Guy de Rangon, for example, did well to stay close to the fort when he went out to parley with the Seigneur de l'Escut, for when some trouble started up among the troops it was de l'Escut who, finding himself the weaker, was constrained to seek shelter in the city (1:5, 28–29a).

"L'heure des parlemens dangereuse" (1:6), by contrast, emphasizes the danger *to the beseiged*: it wasn't just the negotiators, but the inhabitants themselves of Mussidan who were *mis en pièces* (1:6, 30a); it was the inhabitants of Phocaea who suffered when L. Aemylius Regillus's soldiers broke discipline and pillaged the town he had entered by negotiation (1:6, 30c); the Argiens were all slaughtered when Cleomenes attacked them at night during a seven-day truce, alleging that the truce didn't cover evening hours (1:6, 30a); it was during a parley that the town of Casilinum was taken by surprise (1:6, 30c); likewise Capua, Yvoy, Genoa, and Ligny-en-Barrois (1:6, 31a). In fact in some instances the negotiator himself is not under attack, but only the citizens he left behind: "à Yvoy, le Seigneur Jullian Rommero, ayant fait ce pas de clerc de sortir pour parlementer avec Monsieur le Connestable, trouva au retour sa place saisie"

(1:6, 31a); "en Ligny en Barrois... Bertheuille... estant sorty pour parler, pendant le marché la ville se trouva saisie" (1:6, 31a).

Now this difference in emphasis between 1:5 and 6 may allow us to make sense of why it is that "De la parsimonie des anciens" (1:52) starts with an anecdote that doesn't quite fit. What happened there to Attilius Regulus, who left his wife and children behind at home while he went off to fight the Carthaginians in Africa, was rather like what happened to Rommero and Bertheuille in "L'heure des parlemens dangereuse" (1:6): the inhabitants of his estate were subjected to treachery behind his back, when he was away, unable to defend them. In both chapters it is those back home that one must worry about, not, as was the case in 1:5 and 53, those who venture forth from domestic safety. The treachery in question was theft—the farm laborer "ayant *desrobé* ses utils de labourage" (1:52, 295a) and the Senate "luy fist restablir ce qui luy avoit esté *desrobé*"—while 1:6 concludes with the characterization of treacherous victories as, likewise, theft: " «Point, fit-il, ce n'est pas à moy d'employer des victoires *desrobées*...»" (1:6, 31b). And Æmylius Regillus—whose name faintly echoes Attilius Regulus's (as does, too, that of Scipion *Æmilianus*, who is cited in 1:52 for the parsimony of going on a diplomatic mission with only seven servants [l:52, 296a])—found that he could not keep his men from stealing: "Il ne fut en sa puissance, quelque effort qu'il y employast, de tenir la bride à ses gens; et veit devant ses yeux *fourrager* bonne partie de la ville, les droicts de *l'avarice* et de la vengeance suppeditant ceux de son autorité..." (1:6, 30c).

The other major portion of "De la parsimonie des anciens" (1:52) is the account of the thriftiness of Cato the Elder, citing two instances in which he went on foot to save money—selling his horse so as not to have to pay for its passage when he returned from Spain and making all "ses visitations à pied" (1:52, 296a) when he was governor of Sardinia. This, in turn, echoes the way that, as Thomas M. Green has remarked, in "L'heure des parlemens dangereuse" "the terrible problem of the siege has been elided into a metaphorical *foot*race" (8 [my emphasis]). It happens when Montaigne cites, approvingly, Chrisippus:

Fu il vincer sempre mai laudabil cosa, Vincasi o per fortuna o per ingegno, disent-ils. Mais le philosophe Chrisippus n'eust pas esté de cet advis, et moy aussi peu: car il disoit que ceux qui courent à l'envy, doivent bien employer toutes leurs forces à la vitesse; mais il ne leur est pourtant aucunement loisible de mettre la main sur leur adversaire pour l'arrest, ny de luy tendre la jambe pour le faire cheoir. (1:6, 31a)

The pedal contamination of these scenes of siege, by the way, was already afoot when Montaigne decided to use the colorful verb "sup*ped*itant" (trampling) to describe how Æmylius Regillus's soldiers disobeyed his orders in order to make off with what they could in Phocaea.

To read the *Essais* is to be confronted, as Richard Sayce has put it, by two contradictory impressions: one of "disorder, formlessness, contradiction, and eclecticism; and an equally or more powerful impression of overriding unity, both in thought and form" (327). These six examples will, I hope, suggest just how well-founded that second impression is—the extent to which order lies hidden within Montaigne's apparently disorderly creation. In particular, the hidden symmetry of the *Essais* will allow us to find how each essay, complete or incomplete as it may seem to be in itself, has another half—a secret sharer, a ghostly double, a partner in conversation.

WORKS CITED

Greene, Thomas M. "Dangerous Parleys—Essays 1:5 and 6." *Yale French Studies* 64: 3–23.
Leake, Roy E. *Concordance des Essais de Montaigne*. 2 vols. Geneva: Droz, 1981.
Montaigne, Michel de. *Oeuvres complètes*. Ed. Albert Thibaudet and Maurice Rat. Paris: Gallimard (Pléiade), 1962.
Sayce, Richard. *The Essays of Montaigne: A Critical Exploration*. London: Weidenfeld and Nicolson, 1972.

"SI LA MER BOUILLAIT...": REPETITION, CONJECTURE, AND ERROR IN *JACQUES LE FATALISTE*

Dalton Krauss

> How seriously does Mallarmé take the "jeu"? And how real or unreal is the fiction? How literally does he mean "la gloire du mensonge"?
> —Walter A. Strauss. *Descent and Return: The Orphic Theme in Modern Literature.*

How difficult it is for a *dix-huitièmiste* to pay tribute to Walter Strauss in a way that will somehow appear relevant to those themes and concerns which have dominated his long career as a scholar and a critic. At first glance, the eighteenth century seems conspicuously absent from his two principal works: reduced to a single sentence in *Proust and Literature* and looming over much of *Descent and Return* as the spectre of a non-Orphic literature against which the lyric poetry of the early nineteenth century, particularly that of the Novalis and Nerval, was to rebel.

Of all eighteenth century literary figures, Diderot undoubtedly finds himself at the greatest distance from the inward-directed poetry of romanticism, a poetry which descends toward a center that does not exist for Diderot, in order to effect a reconciliation between opposites—life/death, presence/absence, reality/dream, Apollo/Dionysus. Indeed, none of the mythological figures evoked by nineteenth and twentieth century poets appears to concern the *philosophe*: neither Apollo nor Dionysus nor especially Orpheus with his song, nor even Prometheus, Icarus or any of the other emblems discussed by Professor Strauss in his studies of lyric poets. The landscape of *Jacques le fataliste* is as flat and lacking in depth as that of Samuel Beckett. No direction is discernible as the narrative unfolds, and no truth is to be discovered at the conclusion of the journey. This juxtaposition of *Godot*'s post-modern bleakness and

Diderot's ironic games serves moreover to emphasize the point to which our era has returned to the literary concerns of those Enlightenment writers for whom form and language were the focus of their literary efforts. The concerns of pre-Orphic literature are thus again to be found in the works of those recent prose writers, Kafka and Beckett in particular, for whom the figure of Orpheus is no longer relevant.

It is with this in mind, and particularly in light of the illuminating studies of Mallarmé and Blanchot in *Descent and Return* that I offer this essay on Diderot's most playful and disjointed work in honor of my friend and former colleague, Walter Strauss.

It is somewhat surprising that, of all of Diderot's problematic texts, it should be *Jacques le fataliste* which has attracted the most intense critical interest—surprising, not because the work itself is not immensely seductive, but rather because it is precisely this seduction which has lured many readers into the devious labyrinth of traps and pitfalls which have been set in their paths. Not the least of these traps is the impression of even the most innocent of readers that *Jacques* is a text which defies interpretation just as it defies classification in any of the traditional literary genres. It is a work whose meaning is to be found entirely on its surface, a work that says everything about itself that needs to be said, and yet it is a work forever in motion, constantly slipping through the reader's fingers. As the "reader" is reduced to a submissive acceptance and the "author" crows his triumph on every page, *Jacques* becomes a work whose true goal is merely the assertion of the superiority of the latter over the former, a work in which both reader and author are at once outside of the text and creations of it.

In the large body of critical writings which *Jacques* has inspired, the most successful are those which have attempted to view this work as a textual apparatus whose dynamics derive from a number of processes which may or may not prove to be closely related to one another. I shall discuss, without pretending to exhaust the possibilities of the narrative machinery in this brief paper, three of these processes, which I shall call *repetition*, *conjecture*, and *error*.

Among the several ways in which repetition informs this text, the most obvious one is the one which interests me the least: I shall not deal except in passing with the thematic networks whose recurrent figures have provided a number of critics with keys to the "secret unity" of a work which appears to defy all efforts to view it as a totality. The chain (*la gourmette*), the gag (*le baillon*), the flask (*la gourde*), and even the great scroll itself—all these have been read as metaphors whose insistence in the dialogue has served to alert the perceptive reader to the existence of a level of meaning beyond the actual signifiers.[1] The types of repetition which I would consider pivotal *processes* in *Jacques le fataliste* are not, however, those tropes which play on the variety of signified floating beneath a single signifier; they more resemble those figures which Fontanier classified as "figures of elocution," based not on a change in "meaning," but rather on an accumulation of like elements whose function is "merely" decorative and serves as a shifter-like device which calls attention to the act of narration rather than to the content of the narration. The most frequent manifestations of this type of repetition take the form of refrain-like utterances, sometimes scattered throughout the work ("écrit là-haut"), sometimes appearing in clusters in paragraphs or other brief segments of the text. An example of this latter procedure can be found in the "et ils avaient tous deux raison" (42)[2] which punctuates the argument between Jacques and his master concerning women, and which has, incidentally, become for some readers an emblem of the non-disjunctive logic which they see as governing the text.[3] Another passage in which the figure of repetition manifests itself occurs in the tale of Jacques' adventure with Suzon and Marguerite, marked at brief intervals by a "le fait est" whose accumulation produces a comic effect, especially when the final element of the sequence is entirely outside of the context of the discussion. And of course we should not overlook the series of "c'est X qui me donna" which is the formula central to Jacques' recounting of the history of his life as a valet, and the insistent repetition of which accentuates the desolate repetitive cycle of bondage and servitude that has characterized his life.

Whether the result of this "special" use of language is ironic or comic, or merely representative of the monotonous and repetitive quality of the events recounted, it is clear that the use of this figure in *Jacques le fataliste* is not the peripheral and decorative function described by Fontanier. This becomes particularly clear when one examines the connection between the process of repetition at the level of the paragraph and the thematization of the concept when the question of narrative structure is raised. For just as each new episode in the story of Jacques' relationship with his employers repeats an initial event, so too do most *récits* consist of a repetition of some initial event or situation. Like the master-servant relation of subject-object which repeats itself in a number of episodes, the duel forms the basis of a group of interspersed tales in *Jacques*. Most striking of the actual duels in *Jacques* are the interminable series of encounters between the two captains and the recurrent duels of Desglands with his anonymous adversary. As the "author" observes, "les duels se répètent dans la société sous toutes sortes de formes, entre des prêtres, entre des magistrats, entre des littérateurs, entre des philosophes" (89).

Another striking example of the device of repetition is to be found in the Master's reaction to his valet's account of his amorous adventures; for what are love stories, but the repetition of an initial event, always the same?

Le maître:	...j'ai toujours été friand du récit de ce grand événement.
Jacques:	Et pourquoi, s'il vous plaît?
Le maître:	C'est que de tous ceux du même genre, c'est le seul qui soit piquant, les autres n'en sont que d'insipides et communes répétitions. (209)

Repetition is not, however, an innocent device, whose usage leaves the text unmarked; just as each seduction after the first is somehow inferior to its model, just as Desglands' bandage shrinks from duel to duel, so any repetition inevitably wears away at the fabric of the original text. The first time, as the Master implies, is always the best. The message becomes, like a coin, with the passage of time and reiteration, less readable as it passes from narrator to narrator: "ces pièces d'argent qui à force de circuler perdent leur empreinte" (254).

Of course, what occurs in *Jacques*, and what constitutes one aspect of that work's uniqueness when compared to conventional narratives, is that the supposedly original event is put off, placed beyond the text itself. Thus there is no origin in the saga of Jacques' loves, only endless repetition of events which at the same time are assumed always already to have happened and are displaced from their privileged position as generators of the text to a realm of silence which the narrative reaches for but never attains. The "meaning" of the work, once again, is not to be found in the reconstitution of an original coin, but rather in the description of its passing from hand to hand, in the narrating of the events rather than in their content, in the process of *énonciation* rather than in the *énoncé*.

Such an approach to the textual elements, whether one considers merely individual words or expressions, or instead expands the field of inquiry to encompass entire narrative chains, implies, as Thomas Kavanaugh has demonstrated in his excellent study, an approach to writing which is markedly at odds with the traditional view of *mimesis* which has exercised such a determining function throughout the history of the novel.[4] If it is, indeed, the act of narrating which, in *Jacques*, becomes the essential question governing the text, this would indicate that the notion of representation has been replaced by the process of repetition which structures the work by the re-writing or reinscription of a pre-existing text.

Here I refer, in addition to the passages which we have been discussing, to the importance of intertextual materials in Diderot's work. The generative role of *Tristram Shandy* in the inception of *Jacques le fataliste* comes immediately to mind, although recent criticism has tended to reduce the emphasis placed on the "influence" of Sterne on Diderot. But when viewed as a part of a network of explicit references to other works and authors—from Aesop to Jean-Jacques, passing through Dante, Rabelais, Molière, Aristotle, Horace, and many more—the decisive role of such allusions and cross-references becomes apparent. The result is always to render impossible any claims of originality, although the precise value of the intertextual borrowing depends upon the voice which introduces them into the text. In the case of the Master, they tend to underscore the derivative nature of his discourse, thus rendering him pompous, confused, and even ridiculous. His quotations and borrowings are, in fact, often flagrantly inappropriate, as in the anonymous lover's complaint that he transforms into a parody of a funeral oration for Jacques' captain; and even his erudite references to Dante or his critique of the hostess's tale which summons up the authority of past theoreticians of rhetoric prove to be irrelevant or trivial. On the other hand, when it is the "author," who, in his dialogues with an imagined "reader," has recourse to quotations, this serves frequently to explain and justify the words and actions of his characters, as in the discussion of the use of profanity following the "Bigre" story, or to guarantee the veracity of his own discourse, as in the following passage: "Vous allez prendre l'hisoire du captaine de Jacques pour un conte et vous aurez tort. Je vous proteste que telle qu'il l'a racontée à son maître tel fut le récit que j'en avais entendu faire aux Invalides . . ." (81).

It should come, therefore, as no surprise that *Jacques le fataliste*, reduced to the "proverb," "Jacques mène son maître," becomes the source of future borrowings, finds its true destiny in an interminable series of repetitions from generation to generation.

Jacques: ... que le reste de notre vie soit employé à faire un proverbe.
Le maître: Quel proverbe?
Jacques: Jacques mène son maître. Nous serons les premiers dont on l'aura dit, mais on le répétera de mille autres qui valent mieux que vous et moi. (185)

But that which will be repeated of these *mille autres*, the *text* from which will be culled their proverb, is itself a repetition of another "manuscript." The work that we call *Jacques le fataliste* is nothing more than an imperfect copy ["il y a ici une lacune vraiment déplorable dans la conversation de Jacques et de son maître"] of an invisible original, somehow more complete, closer to the truth (234).

Often the layers of fiction overlap one another to form an intertextual web in which the origin disappears from sight. Thus a seemingly casual comment with little direct bearing on the text ("mais la vérité, c'est que l'*Engastrimute* est de moi, et qu'on lit sur le texte original *Ventriloque*" 234), can, when properly read, reveal a startling complexity. Here, the fictitious "author" has substituted for the direct language of an equally fictitious "texte original" a learned expression which leads us back, through Rabelais, to Greek mythology. Moreover, what emerges from this play of signifiers is also a metalinguistic commentary on its own discourse: the voice of Jacques, as well as all of the other voices in *Jacques le fataliste* are, in fact, nothing but dummies, empty receptacles of the discourse of other texts, which, in turn, replace other invisible ventriloquists beyond them, and so on, in a forever receding play of mirrors in which the images reflected are at once present and absent.[5]

II

There is, in *Jacques*, a group of figures which recurs with a particular insistence, and which, while not unrelated to that aspect of repetition which consists in the multiple enunciation of identical elements, occupies a position apart in the machinery of the text. This device, which I shall call *possibility*, and which consists of the accumulation of unlike and seemingly contradictory elements the choice among which, normally necessary to the forward movement of the narrative, is either postponed as long as possible or suspended entirely. When the choice among possible solutions is left to the "reader," this is tantamount to leaving the question forever undecided. "De ces deux versions, demain ou après-demain, vous choisirez, à tête reposée, celle qui vous conviendra le mieux" (175). For even if it is assumed that the *lecteur* so frequently addressed by the "author" represents Diderot's efforts to account for the collective voice representative of the conventional wisdom of his contemporary readers of the novel, this plural *destinataire* remains a fiction, merely one pole in the process of enunciation whose other pole is the *je* of the (equally fictional) "author;" for this *sujet d'énonciation*, in other words, there is no "tomorrow" or "the day after," but only a discursive present tense, a narrative past, and a problematic conditional.

On other occasions, the elements are presented hypothetically, in "if" clauses, subjunctive clauses introduced by *que*, or in situations preceded by *peut-être que*. Although many of these conjectures are rendered inoperative, either because the question asked has no answer, or because the answer has already been given, the very presence of the impossible alternatives in the text works to undermine the linear clarity of the narrative. And while the countless segments which begin with such expressions as "qu'est-ce qui m'empêcherait de dire ... ?," "quel parti un autre que moi n'aurait-il pas tiré ... ," or "un autre que moi ne manquerait pas ... ." frequently conclude with the announcement of an arbitrary selection from among these possibilities based on something called "truth," such constructions seem more revealing of the process of narration than of the truth or falseness of the events narrated. Just as what is repeated is less important than the fact of repetition, the nature of the choice eventually made is less important than the inscription of the possibilities in the text, for, once again, it is the process of enunciation which is called to our attention rather than the *énoncé*.

The problematics of the text are, at least as I read it, rooted in its manipulation of language: on the one hand, repetition manifests itself initially in the form of a discursive figure whose function is to transfer the emphasis from the purely communicative aspect of language, that aspect which assumes a directly perceivable link between signifier and signified, to one of the non-communicative functions which do not suppose a transparency of the signifier. Possibility, on the other hand, or choice, or conjecture, is generally expressed most clearly through the use of certain grammatical categories, especially by the choice of verb tenses. Indeed, it is the overwhelming presence of the conditional tense that is responsible for much of the indefinite and even experimental quality which characterizes this text. For the ultimate effect of the simultaneous presence of all of these elements is to make manifest the logical framework which underlies the text, to underscore the reluctance to resolve contradictions which would enable the unfolding of a linear narrative, and to insist on the refusal to establish a dialectical process in which the opposites would be subsumed in a single entity on a higher plane in order to permit the *truth* of the text to be revealed.[6] Lecointre and Le Galliot, and later Huguette Cohen have analyzed this process, which they have called "non-disjunctive." According to their analyses, the principal pairs of opposites which structure *Jacques le fataliste* remain irreconcilable throughout the text, neither one succeeding in its efforts to achieve domination in this text "où tout est affirmé *et* niè la fois."[7] Thus non-knowledge never becomes knowledge, but rather exists simultaneously with it; and, perhaps even more explicitly, since Jacques himself is aware of the problem, cause and effect are present to each other at the same instant in the Great Scroll:

Le maître:	Je rêve à une chose, c'est si ton bienfaiteur eût été cocu parce qu'il était écrit là-haut, ou si cela était écrit là-haut parce que tu ferais cocu ton bienfaiteur.
Jacques:	Tous les deux étaient écrits l'un à côté de l'autre. Tout a été écrit à la fois. (10)

III

The unusual relationship between certainty and uncertainty in *Jacques* is mirrored in another seemingly irreducible opposition, that between truth and error. In the conventional novel, when truth is an issue, it is normally associated with the true "meaning" of the text, a meaning revealed at the conclusion of a gradual process of stripping away of layers of error. *Jacques*, too, is about truth, but here the relation between truth and non-truth is much more elusive. We are told over and over again, not only by the "author," but also by the narrators of the various narratives and sub-narratives, that what interests them is merely *la vérité*; what we have here is not, after all, a *conte* or a *roman*, but rather *l'histoire*. And while it is true that most of the sub-plots end when a truth, hidden from one or more of the protagonists throughout the tale, is revealed, the work as a whole seems obsessively, even perversely concerned with mistakes, misrepresentations, errors, deceptions, or, in a word, *quiproquo*.

Not only is deception central to the Madame de La Pommeraye and the Père Hudson stories, to Jacques' adventures with Suzon and Marguerite as well as with his friend Bigre, but also an error of judgment or interpretation is crucial to the tale of the Master's victimization by Saint-Ouin, to the account of the adventures of Gousse and his clever mistress, to the tale of the baker and his unfortunate rival, and to many other episodes of the work as well: "Jacques et son maître se mirent au lit en riant du quiproquo qui leur avait fait prendre une chienne pour la fille ou la servante de la maison..." (108). As Jacques points out, the mistaking of one thing for another is an essential process of life: "Mon cher maître, la vie se passe en quiproquos. Il y a les quiproquos d'amour, les quiproquos d'amitié, les quiproquos de politique, de finance, d'église, de magistrature, de commerce, de femmes, de maris..." (76).

In a broader perspective, of course, the ultimate truth of Jacques' tale is not revealed at all, and it is this displacement of the truth, this postponing of its unveiling which never will, never can occur, which makes error, not truth, the fundamental driving force at work in *Jacques le fataliste*. Error is thus essential to this work not only as a recurrent theme, but also as a *process* which, together with repetition and conjecture, informs and structures the text simply by allowing the discourse to continue its interminable flow. For if, as the Master asserts, the content of his conversations with his servant is inconsequential, "pourvu que tu parles et que j'écoute" (60), then the more necessary of the two interlocutors is not necessarily the one who does the most talking. Indeed, it is the *destinataire*, the object of the recounting, the Master or the fictional "reader", who, by demonstrating his inability to piece together the narrative, to determine by himself the logical sequence of events, provides the work with its very peculiar dynamics. He is "le souffleur" (106), the eternal questioner, lacking knowledge or information, condemned, as in the Master's abortive attempts to complete the tale of Jacques' amorous adventures prematurely, to constant error, faux-pas, and misjudgment: "— Et pourquoi (le maître) questionnait-il?—Belles questions! Il questionnait pour apprendre et pour redire, comme vous lecteur . . ." (67). Although the impatience with which such displays of lack of comprehension are frequently greeted would seem to indicate a petulant dismissal of these interjections as unwelcome disruptions of the linear narrative—"Mais si vous m'interrompez, lecteur, et si je m'interromps moi-même à tout coup, que deviendront les amours de Jacques?" (56)—it would seem, paradoxically, that it is Jacques, quick to grasp the correct solution to the problems posed, who creates an obstacle to the attainment of the real goal of this text. Jacques' precipitous foreclosure of the narrative, resulting as it does in the cutting off of contact between the interlocutors, is therefore roundly, and correctly, chastised by the Master: "Tu vas anticipant sur le raconteur, et tu lui ôtes le plaisir qu'il s'est promise de ta surprise; en sorte qu'ayant par une ostentation de sagacité très déplacée, deviné ce qu'il avait à te dire, il ne lui reste plus qu'à se taire, et je me tais" (252).

Thus it is the Master, whose curiosity is treated so contemptuously by the servant, who permits the operation of the redundancies, the hypotheses, fatuous and wrong-headed as they may be, and the mistaken conjectures which are at the heart of *Jacques le fataliste*.

Le maître: S'ils avaient refusé de se coucher?
Jacques: Cela était impossible.
Le maître: Pourquoi?
Jacques: Parce qu'ils ne l'ont pas fait.
Le maître: S'ils se relevaient?
Jacques: Si . . . si . . . si . . . et . . .
Le maître: Si, si la mer bouillait, il y aurait, comme on dit bien des poissons de cuits. (31)

Without error, the story would be over as brusquely as the final sentence in this exchange; without error, the telling of the tale would be but an all-too-brief pleasure, if that. For repetition prolongs desire, and possibilities which may or may not be realized transform communication into play.

The voice at the beginning of Robert Pinget's novel, *L'Inquistoire*, demands "Oui ou non, répondez:" four hundred pages later, the reader understands that this initial question will never receive an answer. Likewise, in the final work of Diderot's to be published in his lifetime, *L'Essai sur les règnes de Claude et de Néron*, four hundred pages of "history" are not adequate to guarantee the veracity of the information communicated. "Qu'en savez-vous?" asks the author. "Rien."

In the same way, the response to the questions with which *Jacques le fataliste* begins never is, never can be forthcoming.

And even the truth which we are assured exists at the origin of the text is truth only insofar as we are *told* that it is. If we accept the importance of the process of repetition in wearing down the very concept of origin in this work, however, this claim of truth must be treated with some skepticism. What counts, after all, is not that an event have its source in the truth, but that we believe it to be true: "on ne peut s'intéresser qu'à ce qu'on croit vrai" (288).

History and fiction thus carry on a tantalizing flirtation with each other, while we the readers, moths attracted to the flame of uncertainly, are caught between fable and truth: "De quelque côté que vous vous tourniez, vous avez tort" (230).

The ubiquitousness of error moreover transforms this text into a subversive machine in which Jacques' *quiproquo* (mistaking one thing for another) disrupts and wears away that other, more traditional *quid pro quo*—the exchange of signifying values that forms the linguistic network upon which communication takes place. Without such an implicit contract, language becomes, as Pierre Saint-Amand has pointed out in a recent and very important article, mere noise.[8] The contract between the players sets up the rules of the game; the code enables the interlocutors to engage in meaningful discourse. Without this structure, the carefully maintained hierarchy between Master and servant, reader and narrator, dissolves, as it does at the conclusion of *Jacques le fataliste*, into anarchy.

Any reading of this text, especially my own, thus becomes a potential victim of its decoys, its deceptions, its illusion, its *quiproquo*; every interpretation of this work, especially my own, is thus, potentially, a mistake. "Quoi! c'était un jeu?—Un jeu" (286).

Thus more than a century before *Un Coup de dés*, Diderot had taken the *jeu* very seriously indeed. The game had become, in the form of the duel, the desire for unattainable mastery and conquest in political and social contexts, and in the tropic forms of error, repetition, and conjecture, the dissolution of the linguistic contract upon which communication is based. While Diderot never approaches what Walter Strauss has referred to as Mallarmé's "saintliness," his *quiproquo*, as integral to his theoretical framework as the poet's "glorieux mensonge," was to be on the threshold of the twentieth century. Our modernity owes much to both the faun and the Janus-faced weathervane, particularly since both revel in ambiguity: "The ambiguity of Mallarmé's spirit is, in the final reckoning, the ambiguity of the modern spirit in the face of chaos and meaninglessness, but raised to the ultimate degree."[9] Cannot much the same be said of *Jacques le fataliste*?

NOTES

1. On *la gourmette* and, especially *le rouleau*, see Stephan Werner, *Diderot's Great Scroll: Narrative Art in Jacques le Fataliste* (Banbury: The Voltaire Foundation, 1975) 95.
2. Denis Diderot, *Jacques le Fataliste et son Maître*, in *Diderot: Oeuvres Complètes*, 23 (Paris: Hermann, 1981) 3–291.
3. Simone Lecointre and Jean Le Galliot, "Pour une lecture de *Jacques le Fataliste*," *Littérature* 4 (1971) 22–31, and Maurice Roelens, "Jacques le Fataliste et la critique contemporaine," *Dix-huitième siècle*, 5 (1973) 119–137. See especially page 132: "le roman obéit à une logique et à une dynamique de la non-disjonction: l'ignorance *et/ou* la connaissance. Logique de *double*, par quoi toute lecture univoque est interdite . . .".
4. "If the word 'literary' is to have any meaning at all, it must be as a language totally aware of its power as language. The history of Western realism can be seen as the concealment of language's performative power behind the mask of constative mimesis." Thomas M. Kavanaugh, *The Vacant Mirror: A Study of Mimesis through Diderot's Jacques le Fataliste* (Banbury: The Voltaire Foundation, 1976) 130.
5. "Le dialogue, cher à Diderot, confrontation d'opinions, de paroles, ne vise pas à faire triompher la 'bonne parole' mais à désigner le fonds d'écriture sur lequel toutes s'élèvent." Serge Baudiffier, "La Parole et l'écriture dans *Jacques le fataliste*," "*Studies on Voltaire and the Eighteenth Century*, 185 (1980) 295.
6. I must take exception with Erich Köhler's description of the Master-Slave dialectic outlined in Erich Köhler, "Est-ce que l'on sait où l'on va? L'Unité structurale de *Jacques le fataliste et son maître* de Diderot," *Philologica Pragensia* 13 (1970) 186–202.

7. Huguette Cohen treats the question of author/reader, master/slave relationships extensively in *La Figure dialogique dans Jacques le fataliste* (Banbury: The Voltaire Foundation, 1976). Using as her point of departure Lecointre and Le Galliot's analysis of the non-disjunctive structure of Jacques, Cohen speaks of "ce roman où tout est affirmé *et* nié à la fois" (167).

8. Pierre Saint-Amand. "*Jacques le fataliste* ou Jacques le Parasite." *Stanford French Review* (Spring 1987) 109.

9. Walter Strauss, *Descent and Return: The Orphic Theme in Modern Literature* (Cambridge: Harvard University Press, 1971) 135.

PHENOMENOLOGY STRICTLY EXERCISED: LOVE AND TRUTH IN JANE AUSTEN'S *PRIDE AND PREJUDICE*

Edouard Morot-Sir

The following lines of William Cowper, the favorite poet of Jane Austen, will serve as exergue to my study:

Now truth, perform thy office, waft aside
The curtain drawn by Prejudice and Pride (*Hope*)
God made the Country, and man the Town (*The Sofa*)
To find the medium ask some share of Wit (*Conversation*)

In our neopragmatic time when theoretical truth is reduced to its own successful applications, when literary criticism is invaded by hermeneutics of all sorts, and when history of literature attempts a sober return to Lansonism, one may wonder what went wrong with the dream of Husserl who believed in Phenomenology as a *rigorous science*. . . . One thing is sure: the basic phenomenological concepts, elaborated by the author of *Logical Researches* (1900) and *Méditations cartésiennes* (1931), were dropped by his followers, or converted into psycho-sociological schemes. Without discussing the legitimacy of such a historical development, I would like to come back to the fundamental Husserlian concept of *Transcendental Intentionally* and measure its efficacity in literary criticism. I choose to apply it to a well-known literary text—Jane Austen's *Pride and Prejudice*.

I. The Methodological Decision

In this return to phenomenological sources, four main options are at hand: 1) Phenomenology as the new *psychological approach* to literary works: early examples of this approach were given by Bachelard, Sartre, the Geneva School, the hermeneutic criticisms. They are Husserlian offshoots, but not Husserlian at all. They reject traditional psychology which in a very eclectic way, intervened in Lansonian criticism, such as the psychology of faculties, associationism, behaviourism, etc.[1] I call it *magic phenomenology* because it tends to be interpretative criticism, and it believes that with some tricks applied to spatial, temporal and stylistic forms, the critic-conjurer will be able to expose the most intimate parts of any literary work and become the lucid mirror of a work and, through it, of its era. 2) Phenomenology as *theory of works of art*, especially the literary works: Roman Ingarden's books are the best examples of this sort of phenomenological research. I admire him. However, I am not sure I can agree with his description of the constitutive elements of the work of art. Furthermore, Ingarden has been rather shy in applying his theory to the actual analysis of literature. Without belittling his contribution to the philosophy of literature, I do not feel ready to discuss his theoretical views or to apply them to any literary text. 3) Phenomenology as leading to a new *metaphysics of language*: Heidegger would be our guide. It is the most tempting venture. It still attracts today some of the dominant critics in this country with Derrida as Intercessor and his deconstructionist technique. 4) However, I decide in favor of a fourth option: *to follow strictly in Husserl's steps*. I know the basic objection well: which Husserl? The first Husserl? The later one? I do not want to enter into these controversies, all the more as I am not sure there are so many Husserls. To me, Husserl remained faithful to himself from the *Philosophy of Arithmetic* to the last papers: he obstinately dug deep and deeper in the same ground.

Be that as it may, here are, for me, the capital Husserlian prerequisites: a) Phenomenology hopes to become a *rigorous science*; without this requirement, phenomenology has no right to exist; b) Phenomenological methodology belongs to epistemology. Its sole objective is the founding of knowledge and truth. Any conscious operation—cognitive, emotional, volitional—implies a *Transcendental Intentionality* that relates the subject and the object of consciousness, the Ego and the World. Such a concept has nothing to do with the psychology of authorial intentions. It is a search for the a priori meanings or *essences*, the system of which "constitutes" simultaneously the Ego and the World, or, if one prefers, consciousness and reality.

Now I can formulate my own axiomatic limits: a) I will look at *Pride and Prejudice* (P and P) as a cognitive product. b) I will look for the Transcendental Intentionality (from now on designated as T. I.) that is, according to the phenomenological hypothesis, subjacent to Jane Austen's novel. By that, I do not claim to explore Austen's dispositions, frustrations and subsequent talents. I strictly apply Husserl's existential and transcendental epochè or suspension. In *Ideas for a Pure Phenomenology and Phenomenological Philosophy*, Husserl remarks: "Fiction is the vital element of Phenomenology, as of all eidetic sciences."[2] Thus the typical phenomenological process which gives access to the essences and to intuiting them consists in the modification of the object of consciousness by imagination. It is a *phenomenological fiction*, which, if done properly, should lead to a better understanding of any regional ontology—in the present case, the regional ontology is *P and P* in its total existence and being. Let us remember also that the three phases of the phenomenological reductive process (*epochè*) are *eidetic* reduction (separation of essences from facts); *philosophical* reduction (separation of essences from ideologies and systems); and *phenomenological* reduction proper (access to the Transcendental Ego). The three levels of "bracketing off" correspond to three levels of experience by the imagination: a) experiences of the sense-realities in themselves; b) experiences of Ideal essences; c) experience of the Transcendental Ego. I plan to remain at the first and second level for the analysis of *P and P*. I reserve the last phase for the conclusion as the uncovering of the ultimate meaning of the coessential tension between Love and Truth.

II. General Hypothesis

Following Husserl in the exploration of Transcendental Intentionality, we have to distinguish its *noematic* and its *noetic* sides—i.e. intentionality apprehended in its necessary objective and subjective aspects. T. I. can be intuited as *noema* or as *noesis*. In more general terms, it is the well-known opposition between content and form, but at the sophisticated level of Husserlian epistemology.

After many readings of *P and P*, I saw that among the few possible a priori constituents of *P and P*, the two dominant essences were, on the objective side, Love, and on the subjective or noetic side, Truth.

A purely formal and fictive analysis shows immediately that the intentional field of *P and P* will be activated by four fundamental tensions: *truth of love, love of truth, love of love,* and *truth of truth.* It is clear that the basic and permanent conflict will be between the *love of truth* and the *love of love,* conflict which is for me the deepest constitutive structure of *P and P's* linguistic coherence and originality.

III. Love as Transcendental Noema

The analysis should be a balanced movement between what love as essence requires and what the actual *decisions* made in *P and P* are. Let us explore the potentialities of the essence of love: 1) *Love implies lovers.* Love could not exist without lovers, and there are good and bad lovers, anti-lovers, a-lovers. In each case, there are qualitative differences (there are, for example, many ways to be a bad lover). If it is true that love is for all seasons, it has essential connections with *time*: beginning(s), history(ies), stabilization(s), end(s). It has also essential connections with *space*. 2) *Love has its friends and its enemies* (among the essences). Friends can also be substitutes. Love is at the center of a very complex co-essential network of "possibles" or "compossibles" or "impossibles." For example, admiration, esteem, happiness are compossibles of love; egotism, scorn, indifference are among its impossibles; jealousy, hatred, sexuality are impossible-compossible. There are also social structures, such as marriage, home, country, town. 3) *Love in its unity and unicity remains a mystery* as the ultimate relation between human beings, or between them and God. Love in its essence is the final form of existence beyond biological individuality and anonymity.

After this brief formal exploration, let us see how the essence of love is incarnated in *P and P*, without considering the psychology or the sociology of the facts of love, ignoring also for the moment the noetic aspect of the novel.

P and P offers a coherent sampling of lovers or candidates for love: eight (with equal sexual distribution) potential lovers. Each of them is in a relation of complementarity and of contrast with the others. There are four couples, four marriages, two potential successes, two ambiguous failures. There are also older couples and married people who seem to be out of love, or to have replaced love by friendship. Elizabeth and Darcy correspond to an idealization of love; they are ideal heroes, romance-lovers while the other matchings are closer to real lovers and couples. I do not mean that with these two characters *P and P* is contributing its share to the sentimental novel. It is simply confessing that there is no love-language without a concession to romance, to the dream of ideal love and eternal happiness. Elizabeth and Darcy are heroic models fighting for their loves against themselves. External obstacles are superficial. They are also the best expression of masculine and feminine idealized characters, although they remain psychologically probable.

In *P and P*, love is sudden, irresistible; but it has a history, full of external and internal obstacles and difficulties. Will and reason have nothing to do with the advent of love. However, love has its ethics and its esthetics, which can be summed up in a unique concept: *propriety*. There is a proper manner to love and an infinite number of improper ways. Lydia and Wickham are examples of improper conduct within love. It is why their love story will be short. Collins and Charlotte are improper too because they marry without love.

Duration is uncertain. The novel never commits itself except for the future of Wickham and Lydia. A look at the mature couples is not encouraging. At its best, love turns into reciprocal esteem and warm friendship (the Gardiners).

What are love's main obstacles? *P and P* is the story of the difficulties that love has to face and of the awareness of the relative improbability of good matchings. The economic and social obstacles are the least serious of all. Real problems are within persons, especially when the predestination of love is clear. Here come pride and humility. Humility is the weakness of Jane and Charlotte, and of Bingley, too. Pride, as is well known, is the distinctive trait of Elizabeth and Darcy. For both, prejudices are linked to their pride, although pride is not responsible for all prejudices. Other causes can be intellectual or emotional limitations, lack of information, "precipitation of judgment."

It is significant to note that in David Hume's *Treatise on Human Nature*, pride and humility are the two basic passions of the self.[3] In *P and P*, pride has the same definition as in Hume's *Treatise*. It is the main obstacle inside the self itself. For each individual, pride is a permanent threat to any kind of love. So is humility, although it does not receive full treatment in *P and P*, as it does in most of Jane Austen's other novels. However, there is a "proper" pride. And it is the paradox of love: it requires simultaneously self-respect, the other's respect, and respect of the other. It is a very delicate harmony: too much pride, not enough pride, and the propriety of love is never reached. In brief, love, by the fact of its appearance, cannot grow and live without the presence of pride and humility, because they are the passions of the self for itself, always present, each one in some way destructive of love which is the passion of (for) the other.

What are the causes of love? We are approaching its essence as T. I. of *P and P*. There are many catalytic causes that are not the true cause of love, but without which it would be impossible. They are mainly moral causes: esteem, admiration, gratitude, respect, and finally, happiness. I hesitated a long time to put happiness among the occasional causes, first tempted to see it as the sign and the end of love. Happiness is clearly the most universal instinct of human nature. For *P and P's* characters, even in the negative case of Charlotte, to be in love is at the same time to be conscious of the mutual chances of happiness with the beloved, and the spontaneous desire to contribute to his/her happiness. But the instinct of happiness is not enough to explain the existence of love. *P and P is the dramatization of love as psychological predestination.* As in the myth older than Plato, each individual life is a tense search for the other as ideal matching. Immediate recognition is the awareness of a deep psychological and partly social agreement. This recognition is often noticed by everyone, except in the exemplary case of Elizabeth, since nobody, not even she, knows that she is in love with Darcy upon their first meeting and that this is no less true for Darcy. Denials are symptoms of their attempts to fight an inevitable matching.

Is love the imperious psychological need for a unique somebody else? Yes, but it is much more. There is no direct analysis of the essence of love in *P and P*, nor in any other novel of Jane Austen. The rare commentaries cannot be taken at face value since they are reactions to feelings or expression of feelings, and they have nothing to do with truth-language. For example, Elizabeth's constant hostile statements against Darcy are direct proofs that she is caught and that Darcy is constantly present in her mind, especially at the time she fancies herself attracted by Wickham.

Then comes the unavoidable question: is there any possible sexual attraction discreetly suggested by frequent and varied adjectives qualifying the prettiness and the handsomeness of the young people? I do not think so. Even for the couple Wickham-Lydia, it is far from certain that their common attraction is physical. Their respective temper and character is really responsible for their eloping. More generally, I suppose that *P and P* concurs with Adam Smith's *Theory of Sentiments*, for which too strong a physical attraction is judged improper and indecent. Physical attraction and physical acts of reproduction are part of married life. Even the esthetic attraction of human bodies and faces is not sexual; it is just the beginning of the complex and rich experience of life. In *P and P* (and it is true for the other works of Jane Austen), I found only one passage which is a small and indirect vista to the most important but secret experience of human life. Elizabeth is speaking with her aunt, Mrs. Gardiner, who is trying to guess her feelings after Wickham has dropped her, and she asks the direct question: is it true love that you feel for Wickham? Elizabeth answers: "I am convinced, my dear aunt, that I have never been much in love; for had I really experienced that *pure and elevating passion*, I should at present detest his very name, and wish him all manner of evil" (chapter 26; italics mine).

There is also this very curious comment by the author on Elizabeth who has just learned about Lydia's eloping and has met briefly with Darcy. The narrator comments: "If gratitude and esteem are good foundations of affection, Elizabeth's change of sentiment will be neither improbable nor faulty. But if otherwise, if the regard springing from such sources is unreasonable or unnatural, in comparison of what is so often described as arising on a first interview with its object, and even before two words have been exchanged, nothing can be said in her defence, except that she has given somewhat of a trial to the latter method, in her partiality for Wickham, and that its ill-success might perhaps authorize her to seek the other less interesting mode of attachment. Be it as it may . . ." (chapter 46). Here the narrator passes the responsibility for the decision to the reader.

Elizabeth is not a sweet creature. Her aggressivity is an important part of her temper, a violent temper well hidden and controlled by wit and manners. The reference to love as "that pure and elevating passion" means that love in its extreme form is a passion, the only passion which takes possession of a mind, physically and spiritually, more spiritually than physically, if one gives to the adjectives "pure" and "elevating" their full meaning. Is not this text contrary to my hypothesis that Elizabeth has been in love with Darcy since their first meeting? Many answers are possible. Elizabeth has always tried to hide her feelings from herself and her family. Her sincerity is doubtful. Having in mind the text quoted above, one can come to another solution: the narrator is not committed in this question of the nature of Elizabeth's love for Darcy. It could be admiration or esteem, but it could be something deeper. Elizabeth, unaware of her own feelings, looked for this experience with Wickham, then with Darcy. If the reader says finally with the narrator, "Be it as it may . . ." he is invited to conclude that the superficial signs of human love are very difficult to decipher and that their deepest sources are obscure.

Thus, at our present analytical level of the T. I. of *P and P*, love appears to be the ultimate and unique human experience, the highest form of life, a passion harmonizing beauty and happiness: it belongs to the "order" of predestination; in its ideal form it is rarely experienced. It has diverse qualities and styles. Elizabeth's and Darcy's loves are qualitatively different from those of Miss Bennet and Bingley or a fortiori of Wickham and Lydia. I am tempted to complete Cowper's line quoted at the beginning by saying, God gave love to Humanity, and man invented social relations and marriage. Let us not forget also that for Elizabeth and Darcy more than for other couples, the *Country* is the Transcendental Setting, in Husserlian terms, for the idealization of love.

Before taking the second step, may we stop for a moment and reflect on the methodological techniques which have been used for the analysis of love as the noematic polarization of *P and P*? My analysis has not been an empirical exploration of a given text, followed by a few generalizations. Husserl condemns this method which nevertheless has been practiced by the various defenders of phenomenological psychology applied to literary criticism. On the contrary, I practiced, successfully or not, a sort of *analytical shuttle* between a pure, abstract exploration of the concept of love, and the limited concretizations (not in Ingarden's meaning) or illustrations of the concept by *P and P*. The transcendental analysis shows first the relations within the a priori potentialities of an essence, patterns of virtualities; then *in the confrontation with the actual text it uncovers its paradigmatic choices*. This complex process derived from Husserl's methodological requirements strictly obeyed offers two prime advantages for literary criticism: 1) it is a technique for solving the almost unsolvable problem of the paradigmatic choices made by a given text, and 2) it sheds some light on the mysterious passage from epistemology to esthetics: the positive and negative choices made by the text among the essential potentialities reveal the final strength and weakness of a text for the reader whose expectations are at the transcendental level.

IV. Truth as Transcendental Noesis: Noetic Paradigmatic Choices

As already seen from the noematic side, the Transcendental Ego, in a given world—here, *P and P*, a self-sufficient textual world—supposes an a priori balance between potentialities and choices, both related to a dominant essence, love, in the present case. It would be a serious mistake to believe that the phenomenological fictive exploration has done its work, and that from now on the critic can return to his usual empirical, impressionistic craftsmanship. The activities thanks to which the noematic system comes into existence originate in a priori dynamic structures made of potentialities with invitations to choice controlled by a dominant intentionality. I have already formed the hypothesis that for *P and P* the noetic intentionality which organizes its activities is Truth.[4]

The essence of Truth is immediately connected with a few typical intentionalities: truth as *representation* (the well-known *adequatio rei et mentis*), truth as *coherence*, truth as *persuasion*. Each of these intentionalities is linked to a definite epistemology—realist, idealist, pragmatic. Then there are truth-conducts, like pure description, deduction, induction, experimental proof, probability, etc. There is also the awareness of the so-called Aristotelian principle: there is science but of the general; and the problem which haunts modern epistemology: is the science of individuals possible?

I confess the enormous difficulty of a paradigmatic evaluation when one tries to play a priori with all the possible choices that any text rejects by the fact of its actualization. Here I can but sum up long and patient analyses.

P and P implies a few epistemological options: the human world is made of individuals and their relationships. As in the Lockean-Humean theory of knowledge, human substance, if it exists, is inaccessible. Individuals are known by their appearances and conducts. The self (a word that is rarely used) is the unity of a typical psychological diversity of dispositions. *P and P* supposes that there is a human nature. Individuals follow certain patterns: they can be grouped under certain types of characters.

P and P being a novel, that is, a totality of linguistic signs referring to imaginary people living in imaginary settings, the a priori problem of truth cannot take the patterns of the social sciences. Novelistic characterization could be absolutely arbitrary and submitted to the noetic requirement of romance: then the work's T. I.

would no longer be truth but loyalty to romance as a literary genre. Our text rejects romance coherence; it is based upon another coherence—that I propose to call the *epistemological coherence of love* that is *the submission to Truth*, all the truth about love, whether we like it or not.

A lexical analysis based on my approximate quantitative research shows the high frequency of words used by the 17th and 18th-century philosophers in search of the human knowledge that would be parallel to Newton's "natural philosophy," such as character, temper, humour, disposition,—then more specialized moral words referring to sensibility, understanding, and will,—and the complex vocabulary for the description of moral and social conducts. It is easy to observe the following uses of this vocabulary: individuals are described, characterized and explained through the appearance of their diverse behaviors with the help of this basic philosophical vocabulary; its words are applied in an impersonal way, the narrator's way, or are used by characters directly when they speak of themselves or more often about their friends or relatives. These varied lexical applications are coherent; they constitute the typical coherence of every individual. In my judgment, the lexical applications in *P and P* are made with the greatest accuracy of meaning, with an extraordinary psychological verisimilitude and characterological rigor.[5] Among modern novels, *P and P* gives us one of the surest presentations of human intersubjectivity and of its social correlations.

Truth Intentionality is not limited to rigor and accuracy in the use of psychological lexemes for characterization. *P and P*, as any other novelistic text, obeys three functions other than characterization: *descriptive, narrative, dramatic*. In each case the Truth-demand can have special effects which I will study briefly.

P and P very rarely offers descriptions except for a few phrases, sentences or paragraphs which are always integrated into a narrative segment or a dramatic scene. Most often it is a topical reference to a precise location: *P and P*'s characters know and say where they are; spatial and temporal indexes are connected with and help to frame narrative summary or conversational development. There is, however, an exemplary exception: the detailed description of Pemberley, Darcy's estate. This description gives more than objective, truthful information about a certain space. It is a necessary part of Darcy's portrait. Even more, it is the double image of the Country and love. It explains for me the famous remarks (including the irony) made by

Elizabeth when she fancies herself mistress of Pemberley and links her love of Darcy to the visit of his estate. The "Truth" of Pemberley is the spatial form for love: paradise for lovers, the only place where love is protected and where it gets its lasting chance. Jane Austen said that pictures of perfection made her sick and wicked. Pemberley is the single exception, and is opposed to the pseudo-perfection of the castles in Gothic and sentimental novels; it is *true* imagination and not nonsensical fancy!

The relation between the truth-demand and imaginary narration raises a crucial problem well known to twentieth-century novelists: what can the truth of a narration be? *P and P* offers the reader a minimum number of events and some probable coincidences. Most of the events are direct confrontations, social gatherings, mainly conversations. Narrative summaries are third-person language; very often they sum up conversation, sometimes within a conversation. They are transitional "constative" statements; their principal function is to lead from one scene to another. The structural intentionality of the narration would require an important and detailed analysis which is beyond the present phenomenological exercise. Let us observe that narration is by essence a very frustrating experience, in spite of the universal human compulsion to narrate everything possible: to narrate is inevitably to sum up—which is a strange mixture (strange for the lover of truth) of superficial and incomplete perspectives with concentration on intense moments. The most striking choice in *P and P* is its actual limitations of narrative processes: and, to use a well-known and maybe worn-out linguistic distinction, it shows an extraordinary preference for "discourse" over "history." I understand this situation as the literary consequence or effect of the Truth-T. I.[6]

I hope that we are now ready to understand the *paradigmatic connection between truth and dramatization*. In most novels, even of our century, with the generalization of the techniques of shifters and mirror-languages, dramatization is an auxiliary to narration or to characterization. It is an efficient way to give information, to introduce variety in narrative summaries, or to emphasize important moments. In *P and P*, the situation is just the reverse. *Narration has become the servant of dramatization*. There is no need to repeat what has already been noticed by Jane Austen's critics since the nineteenth century about the true-to-life language of her characters or the importance of conversation as the highest form of human relations and as knowledge of self or other. *P and P* is not a novel in any traditional or modern sense. It is a sort of *at-home private theater*. The consequence is a deep change in the requirements the author puts on the reader. To the usual involvement that accompanies the reading of an imaginary text must be added the *actual visualization of scenes by the imagination*. Not only has the reader to participate in the events, he has to be present as a spectator. The novel tends to become a *free theatralization*: the narration is replaced by a well-organized succession of pictures or scenes, what the French call *tableaux*.

Thus the Truth-problem changes: it is no longer a question of creating the most probable story. The verisimilitude of a scene is its actuality, and for the reader it should be *immediate vision*. It has been noticed that this technique, especially developed in *P and P*, follows Richardson's techniques and that it anticipates narrative procedure such as Flaubert's free indirect speech (sometimes Jane Austen goes further with the use of free direct speech), Henry James's point of view, interior monologue, focalization of the story around a dominant character who is a sort of substitute for the narrator, even for the author. These similarities are obvious, but it seems to me more important to observe that *P and P's* techniques offer something else: more than a dramatized narration, the novel has been metamorphosed into a *scenic presentation and coordination* (it is no longer an imaginary *re*-presentation). The linear order is based upon the *theatrical logic of events*. Characters are individuals onstage, who speak their own languages, the language of their characters, even when this language has parodic or satiric overtones, as in Collins's letters or Mrs. Bennet's part in conversation. The apparent diversity of points of view in *P and P* simply hides the diversity of characters, the appropriateness of their languages in a succession of conversations which are extensively exposed or, from time to time, concentrated; then the narrator has become a sort of announcer-observer-commentator.[7]

We arrive at the most delicate moment in our T. I. intuitive exploration. If my methodological "application" has been correct up to now, we have understood two capital noetic decisions in the text: *The appropriate intervention of abstract concepts which belonged to the contemporary vocabulary of the social sciences, as they were elaborated in eighteenth-century Europe; and the transformation of narration into dramatic presentation.* There is something more to be understood which deals with stylistic transcendental intentionality. Austen's criticism in general and that on *P and P* in particular has

Edouard Morot-Sir 53

insisted on the function of irony, humor and wit, and on satirical attacks against characters as well as against social behaviours or customs; Jane Austen is recognized as a "comic author," but the epistemological status of these notions, in spite of brilliant interpretations, is not clear. Critics offer their personal definitions. Then, the main weakness is not at the level of definition since everyone has the right to choose his definitions, as long as he sticks to them. The real failure is in the epistemological inter-relation among these concepts of irony, wit, humor, satire, the comic, etc.

Whatever the comic effects in *P and P* may be, are they or are they not connected with the Truth Intentionality? The easiest answer would be: comic conducts were added to the truth-language, but they are not part of it. I reject such a solution. One cannot separate form and content, and think that comic values are just the complement of objective values, as salt to sauce. Furthermore, the coexistence of these two groups of values raises an immediate problem which no Austenian text could avoid: Jane Austen's hostility toward the sentimental novel is well known, as is her correlative taste for parody. The passage from the *Juvenilia* to the novels of the great period, with *Northanger Abbey* as transition, and maybe *P and P* as her highest achievement, has to be understood in relation with the comic concepts.

Is it possible to state that comic language in its variety is the typical *truth-language*? Does it not expose all human weaknesses, moral and social? Do we not speak of the lucid vision of comic writers, be they Cervantes, Molière, Swift, Fielding or Sterne? As a result, the comic aspect of *P and P* would enhance the objective world. The comic spirit would express itself in ironical remarks, satirical portraits, characterial caricatures, parodic mimicries. Such a solution adopted implicitly by many critics is not satisfactory for the phenomenological explorer. The link with the truth-language has to be rigorously described. When the varied comic conducts are used alternately or simultaneously, what is their respective meaning and importance?[8] *P and P* is not *Candide, Tom Jones, Tristam Shandy* or the *Vicar of Wakefield!* If Jane Austen's novel does belong to the vast category of comic literature, such as *Don Quixote*, it cannot be reduced to satire attacking human moral and social customs. The language of *P and P* remains always at the level of objective, detached observation and commentary. It simply tells the truth, it presents human affairs as they are in their daily local acts and setting. The reader is set free from his personal reactions. You can look at *P and P* with tragic or comic glasses. You can cultivate sentimental and/or ironic feelings. You can be amused, moved, satirical, sadistic, etc. As we know too well, reactions to Truth are indefinite in number.

Furthermore, the recent analyses of Jane Austen's irony have psychoanalytic overtones. That is fine if one believes that psychoanalysis is the culmination of literary criticism! There is also a frequent confusion between irony of situation and ironic reaction by verbal devices. I do not pretend to base this exploration of the ironic field on deep definitions or theories of irony. Let us accept simple, empirical distinctions. One of the most frequent is the difference between irony as applied to human conditions—one speaks of ironic destiny, ironic character—and irony as an emotional, intellectual and verbal reaction to any sort of situation, ironic or not. My reaction to Oedipus's catastrophes or to the Trojan war can be tragic or comic, and it can take on various languages. For *P and P*, our earlier identification of its T. I. should help to clarify this delicate matter. If I am correct, Jane Austen's work is dominated by the double intentionality of Love and Truth. It is easy to see that Love, when Truth is applied to its universe, becomes the ironic world *par excellence*, as an indefinite proliferation of ironic situations. Among these possible situations, *P and P* offers a few exemplary ones, each different and typical: irony of child-parent relations, irony of the relations between lovers in their interpsychological attractions and repulsions. Love is the lived contradiction of ideal as romance and of reality made of obstacles due to character, ignorance, stupidity, social prejudice, money, property, etc.

However, *the knowledge of an ironic situation is not itself necessarily ironic*! It has to be proved that Jane Austen's reaction was ironic as some critics suggest; they say that the spinster of Chawton was bitter, pessimistic, maybe sadistic. My present duty is not to guess the secret feelings and thoughts of the author. Whatever they may have been, if we compare *P and P*'s language with the language of well-known ironists, it is difficult to see strict similarities. My strongest argument against Austenian irony derives from the present phenomenological analysis: irony is not compatible with a truth-language; it supposes a moral intentionality which entails and justifies changes in the use of truth-criteria. I do not observe evidence of such ironic distortions in *P and P*.

Am I saying that the first sentence of our novel—to take a well-known passage—is not ironic? Let us read it again: "It is a truth universally acknowledged that a single man in possession of a good fortune, must be in want of a wife." To me, it is not irony, it is pure witticism used to express a sort of universal law, as universal as the Newtonian law of attraction. Here is my hypothesis: *if irony and truth are not in the same intentional field, on the contrary wit and truth are in perfect unison.* Thus in *P and P wit is put to the service of Truth for the exposure of Love.* I call wit, with its ups and downs, its successes and failures, its possible contaminations with irony and its own forms, *the pure pleasure of intellectual Intentionality when it expresses itself in an organized language.* Its most frequent qualities and criteria are liveliness, sprightliness, quickness, paradigmatic surprise, grammatical elegance, word-propriety confronted with uncovered *équivoque*. Wit has also a captivating dimension when it is seen as an intersubjective process, when its target is no longer a regional ontology, but other people, especially the loved one. Then *the art of wit becomes the art of teasing*, which is foreign to the art of irony, even when improper teasing borrows its arms from the ironic arsenal. It is wit, not irony, that makes Elizabeth say that Darcy has to learn to be laughed at. It is a truth-decision which makes of Elizabeth a perfect wit and an obsessive teaser, especially when she is with the person she loves, not knowing it at the beginning: her teasing evolves from aggressive provocation to tender coyness. Compare her language to her father's bitter and ironic statements—the exception being when he talks to her. To me, *P and P* is the *Poem of Wit and Teasing*. Obviously wit is replaced by irony from time to time, but almost always the ironic turn of phrase is required by the language of a character. And wit remains the general form of the novel. To come back to the first sentence I quoted, it is a witty way to uncover a universal and objective truth. And it gives the tone to the book.

Teasing, as a derivative of wit and a tool to explore others' reactions, is also the way to protect truth against the fancies of love. To love and to remain lucid can be a very exacting job, and it is that for Elizabeth, even when her lucidity turns out to be illusory. This deep significance of teasing should be emphasized: is not *tender teasing* a decisive part of the secret charm of *P and P*? The text itself is a teaser, instead of being, for example, as texts too frequently are, pushy, seductive, haughty, nasty, or ironic and sado masochistic.[9]

To sum up, in our text *wit is the Transcendental companion of Truth*: the Truth of Love, in its full mandate, requires the *Truth of*

Language associated with the necessary distance between emotional and intellectual languages, distance which permits avoiding the pitfalls of sentimental literature.

This remark leads to a final problem: how does the parodic tendency of Austen's *Juvenilia* and its remnant traces in the works after *Northanger Abbey* fit with my understanding of the phenomenological relations between truth, wit and teasing? The present search for T. I. of *P and P* would not be complete without the clarification of the intersemantic connection of truth and parody, with the cooperation of wit and teasing. The first sentence of *P and P* can again be our point of departure. It is clear that this universal statement has a parodic tone: *it parodies itself as scientific statement*. Parody is a behavior which belongs to the category of imitative acts, and among them are imitative statements. Formally, parody is the *comic imitation* which goes from impersonation and pastiche to travesty, caricature and burlesque. It is often used as a tool by the ironists; it is present in the imagination of the Grotesque, but its deep intentionality is *imitation with a sense of the comic*. Wit likes to take it as an accessory. Many witticisms are parodic turns of phrase: even the objectivity of the vocabulary appropriate to each character is parodic to some extent. To transpose Sartre's famous statement in *Being and Nothingness*, *P and P's* characters *play at being themselves*; they give, if I may say so, perfect imitations of what they are. Such a parodic play is obvious for Collins, Mrs. Bennet and Lady Catherine, but it exists also for Elizabeth, Darcy or Jane. They are at times more Darcys or Elizabeths than permitted! In this perspective *parody is a means of remaining close to psychological reality*. Except on rare occasions, the text does not give in to the easy temptation of forcing and caricaturing characters. The parodic effect is not obtained by some subtle distortion of objective characterization. Far from it, *the more objective the language is, the more parodic it is*. Thus comes the inevitable consequence: *objective language is parody to perfection*. How is it realized? by a very simple device which is linked to the difference between daily reality and literary significance. In our daily life we are rarely ourselves full-time; or, to risk an academic parody, in the course of our lives we become characters with tenure, but we are only on occasion full characters—I mean, in the full expression of ourselves. Here is the brilliant trick: *P and P's* characters are fully themselves at each moment of their appearance and performance; their idiosyncrasies never relax! This characterial tension is enough to produce the parodic effect and to go beyond flat or round realism.

Let us apply this conclusion to the linguistic process of motivation (in the meaning the word has to the Russian Formalists). The undisputable witty turn of the phrases and sentences with abstract terms gives to these abstractions a subtle parodic touch—the narrator imitating this time Dr. Johnson, Adam Smith or any other philosopher or theologian, or philosophical language in general. The truth-vocabulary is gently mocked or teased: that is no more than a taste of salt to brighten sober scientific statements, and to avoid that worst of sins for literary language, pedantry.

If such a view is correct, the difficult problem of the passage from *Juvenilia* to *P and P*, with the progressive achievements of *Northanger Abbey* and *Sense and Sensibility* could receive a tentative solution thanks to the analysis of their T. I. In the history of Jane Austen's texts, there has been no change at the deep level of T. I. *From the beginning they were already looking for truth.* They were literary protests on behalf of objectivity. Later the same parodic aim was still present though in disguise. *P and P* is still an investigation on "love and friendship;" its characters have a drive toward their own perfection similar to that reflected in Jane Austen's first attempts. If events are less numerous, they remain happily or unhappily accidental. The difference is at the surface-level of technical intentionality. Truth-language organizes the alliance of wit and parody; both are integrated into the new justification of characters, along with the techniques studied above—the abstract psychological vocabulary and the scenic projection.

My phenomenological demonstration requires yet another step: is the relation between truth and parody, as seen in *P and P*, a happy accident due to the genius of the author, or is it a deep literary necessity which emerges in more or less satisfactory surface-achievements? The answer to this crucial question would be prepared by a detailed analysis: I can but initiate it. Imitation is the easiest solution for any truth-performance, but it is the fallacy of the mobile mirror, or "cinéma-vérité," so to speak. It is tragic or comic, with mixtures and confusions. The passage from the scientific organization of truth to literary expression is achieved when, in the confrontation between the universal abstractions and their illustration, illustration takes precedence over abstract language, not only for pedagogical reasons or esthetic enjoyment, but more deeply, for truth-necessity: truth is to be found in concrete languages, not in abstractions. Then comes inevitably the double devaluation of the two aspects of language; parody is immediately implied. It is potentially present in the tragic language which is the parodic sublime of divine language. Comedy is the parody of tragic characters. More generally, *any form of literature is potentially parody of the divine or human in the Theater of language.*

Leaving the phenomenological language which I have tried to speak, I have the choice between two languages: either to return to more human and humane languages, translating my phenomenological exploration into the language of the gentleman, or to add to my Husserlian experiment a hyperlinguistic finale. I favor the second option which will force me to go beyond the optimistic and complacent verbal rationality which inspires any phenomenological research. Thus, the last question applied to *P and P* could be: *What is beyond the logical elegance, the discreet but inflexible coherence of this imaginary linguistic world?* Elizabeth, in her conversations with her aunt, Mrs. Gardiner and with Darcy, comes back, again and again to that question: *Is not incivility the very essence of love?* Love against civility, sociability, rationality,—love against marriage, when marriage is an obstacle to love,—love as obscure and radical decision, constant tension to free oneself from the anonymity of Being and its deterministic order, be it natural or social: *P and P* is the *Comedy of Love* in the sense that human beings' destinies are multiple aspects of the universal fight for love, with rare winners and definite losers.

Furthermore, "un-civility" uncovers a deeper state, where the meaning of love is questioned by the very fact that love is simultaneously feeling and saying, sensibility and knowledge. While human beings, men and women, are clumsily fighting for Love, their language of love is fighting for Truth. Thus, the fatal and ontological oddity: *the truth of love is in contraposition to the love of love.* Truth is the wide-open tear in the secret texture of love. Truth becomes the methodological ordeal of life: knowledge is the formidable and rigorous test of happiness, not only for the characters, but for the text itself. Can we make love and say or write love without initiating its servitude into the civil pattern of marriage and the rationale of psychological theories? This is the ultimate Austenian question. I do not mean that *P and P* is an invitation to free love, as some of the radicals of Jane Austen's time were preaching. Far from it! I mean that for her, marriage is the Unescapable. Even under the best conditions—matching of exceptional characters, almost ideal characters, an estate and a house which are true bodies for love—love has an uncertain future, i.e., a future about which the narrator makes no comment: Elizabeth and Darcy's destiny and future happiness are left open.

Pemberley is the Abode of Love within the novel which is the Abode of Truth. Both Love and Truth are made civil and maybe are in some way saved thanks to the elegant and rigorous architecture of their respective bodies. There is no love without its social destination; there is no language of romance which would not fall into magic: there is no poetry of love: poetry cannot be our enchanted guide into the Palace of Being: there is no poetic truth except for the *poetry of linguistic integrity*. In its impeccable coherence of words, P and P stands against the two chronic pathological states which threaten the Transcendental Intentionality of Love: the Romance of Love, and the Romance of Truth. *Linguistic integrity* is the deepest intentionality and the greatness of its "comic author," or, as Jane Austen also signs herself, of our "obliged and humble servant," and above all, I might add, the "humble servant" of Human Truth. Love can be a failure. Probably human beings are innocent, mere victims of their characters and of the Town, image of human social rulings. But the artist is never blameless: at her own risk, her wit imitates the laughter of the gods, when the longing for Truth is oriented toward the distant Castle of Love.

As a matter of ultimate critical effort, one problem should be honestly faced: Was it possible to find out the tension between Truth and Love in *P and P* and the movement of their languages? The fact that I was led to it through an effort to return to Husserl's basic concepts justifies nothing by my own philosophical temper, or my good or bad luck. However, the Husserlian semantic structure of T. I. offers a few conceptual superiorities over any sort of realist or idealist readings. It invites to confront love and truth within the tension which makes of the language of consciousness a double vection toward the completion of an object as love and the organization of a subject as truth. It implies that there are two simultaneous powers, very active within Austen's writing—the search for love and the search for truth, one calling for the other, one achieved if only the other is achieved, and the rest being misfires and failures. Neither optimistic nor pessimistic, Jane Austen's writing is constantly provoking its readers, and plays for them the role of metaphysical teaser. To write is to tease and to be teased; but there is a gap between the feeling of being teased and the understanding of it. In the present case I am grateful to Husserl for helping me fill in the gaps and illuminate my reading of Jane Austen. It is my guess that Husserl's analytical strictness can make many other readings deeper and richer.

NOTES

1. Such a psychological approach is based upon a vague epistemology. One finds its presence, strong or weak, in almost all critical works since 1947. In current criticism on Jane Austen, it occurs mixed with more modern approaches such as psychoanalysis, structuralism, marxism, etc.
2. Quoted by Gaston Berger: *Le Cogito dans la philosophie de Husserl* (Paris: Auber, 1941) 75. French translation, "La *fiction* est l'élément vital de la phénoménologie comme de toutes les sciences eidétiques."
3. Cf David Hume, *A Treatise of Human Nature*, Book II, *Passions*, First Part, "Pride and Humility," Second Part, "Love and Hatred," Third part, "Will and Passions."
4. It is clear, inevitable even, that in the case of literary works as well as in any species of regional ontology, the dominant transcendental intentionalities which unify regions are common to many regions—for example, to many novels, plays and poems. The diversity of literary works can be explained a) by the diversity between noematic and noetic choices: a great number of combinations are possible if, for example, we consider only the four essences of Love, Happiness, Truth, and Beauty; b) by the choices made for each essence; c) by the unique harmony or tension which results from the coexistence of the preceding choices. Let us repeat once more that the word *choice*, as it is used here, does not belong to the vocabulary of the psychologies of conscious or unconscious intention, but to pure epistemological reflection.
5. This observation deals with the question of *lexical similarities*: it does not pretend to solve the historical problem of Jane Austen's borrowings from the philosophers of the 17th and 18th centuries.
6. One could go further in this direction and wonder if the Truth-T. I., as it appears in the development of modern European thought, is not responsible for the important changes in the esthetics of the novel, and if it has not led to the present ambiguous ontological status of all literary forms, a status between knowledge of and discovery of reality?
7. Jane Austen specialists know well her connection with Richardson's techniques and the important role of theatrical devices in his novels. However, there is a decisive difference between the author of *Clarissa* and the author of *P and P* at the transcen-

dental level. While in Richardson's novels the direct "vision" is justified by literary and moral purposes, in *P and P* it is the best instrument for the pitiless objectivity of truth, and secondarily for literary effects. *The imagination of Truth rigorously disciplines the imagination of love.*

8. See the discussion of the satiric novel in Ronald Paulson, *Satire and the Novel in Eighteenth-Century England* (New Haven: Yale University Press, 1967).

9. The inventory of these secret textual intentional violences exerted on readers has not been established.

POSSIBLE WITNESSES: THE HYPOTHETICAL CHARACTERS IN *LA COMÉDIE HUMAINE*

Maryann Weber, SND

Jean Paris begins his recent study of Balzac (*Balzac*. Paris: Balland, 1986) with a discussion of the "problématique du personnage," in which he challenges the traditional view of Balzac's characters as coherent subjects of a fictive biography. Paris notes that Balzac blurs the distinction between real and fictional persons, muddies biographical chronologies or even contradicts himself, manipulating his characters by retrospective metamorphoses. Despite Balzac's files, his doll models, and documentation, he undermines the identity of his characters and consequently those patiently compiled dictionaries of the "personnages." To these instances of semantic instability, chronological confusion, and shifts of textual status, we can add another example of Balzacian duplicity, the fragmented, quasi-characters whom I have called *postiches* or "possible witnesses."[1]

These *postiches* are fragments of characters, without names or narrative roles, who intervene in *La Comédie humaine* to "see," to make someone else see, or to demonstrate how not to see. They are witnesses to the fictional world whose testimony is scrutinized and not always accepted. As I will argue in this paper, they constitute an important textual device for introducing ideological commentary and function as placeholders for absent actors.

Before analyzing their functions, however, it will be useful to examine these fragmentary characters more closely. There are, for instance, the "Parisien égaré" and the "lover of symbols" from the opening pages of *Le Père Goriot* (2:217-8) and the doctor of social sciences from *La Cousine Bette* who would have discovered Bette's hidden lover had such a witness actually existed (Be. 5:29). Some appear in the novels as a pair of eyes peering through a window or a figure disappearing rapidly down a street. Others are present only in a hypothetical mode. After eliminating all the clear-cut references to the narratee, and all the pronouns of complicity ("nous," vous," and "on,") there are about 1176 of these *postiches* in *La Comédie humaine*.[2] Nearly half that number are purely hypothetical and are accompanied by verbs in the conditional, future, hypothetical imperfect or the imperfect subjunctive, i.e., *le conditionnel passé deuxième forme*, one of Balzac's favorite tenses for the possible witnesses. The rest have a fleeting presence in the text as stereotypes (present tense) or observers (*passé simple* or *plus-que-parfait*).

All the witnesses are anonymous, but a few are characterized by their professions. There are numerous poets, archeologists, historians, philanthropists, physiologists, philosophers and especially painters who, as men of vision, are the observers *par excellence* in the Balzacian world. Others have specialized attributes which qualify them for particular observations, such as editors of the Civil Code (CM 2:423), learned travelers (Pay. 6:86), specialists in heraldry (B 2:11), a sick millionnaire (Do. 6:551), those unhappy souls who are accustomed to looking heavenward (F30 2:213), an attentive connaisseur (AS 1:348) or a woman with a telescope (FL 1:479). Comical *postiches* include Indian theosophists (Sér 7:338–9), alchemists (MC 7:111), a Cannibal (MCP 1:79), property owners with starched collars (BS 1:90), nosey neighbors, rakes, a mediocre painter (RA 6:616) and even "distinguished vagabonds" (S et M 4:279).

Frequently the possible witnesses are tagged with superlatives so that their expertise redounds to the credit of the narrator and strengthens his position by equating his judgment with that of the leading authority in the field. These superlative *postiches* include the most observant Parisian (S et M 4:303) and the best informed historians (S et M 4:319). A variation of the technique is to top the expert: the narrator sees and relates to the narratee what the most perspicacious observer would have overlooked (P 6:80), what the most astute resident of the locale could not interpret, or the most talented artist could not paint (MCP 1:60). The narratee thus becomes a member of the privileged circle of the knowledgeable. Other superlatives seem merely to add dramatic interest: the most thoughtless traveler, the most hurried diplomat, the most jovial grocer, the most fearless man (DL 4:69) or the most brutal (R 3:99), the most skillful rake (Cor. 7:111).

The largest group of *postiches*, however, do not have any civil status and are simply designated as generic "observers," sometimes with flattering or insulting adjectives attached. There are learned observers, profound observers, perspicacious or distinguished observers, and even the unenviable "observateur le plus vulgaire" (Be. 5:29). The *observateurs postiches* are present in each of the major divisions of *La Comédie humaine*: ("Scènes de la vie parisienne," "Scènes de la vie de province," etc.). The device spans the entire career of Balzac: examples can be found from the first text later incorporated into *La Comédie humaine*, *Les Chouans* (1828–9), to the last posthumous volume. Even the fragments and uncompleted novels provide further examples of the *postiche*. The correlation that does become evident, however, is a thematic one: the possible witnesses abound in the novels and short stories which dramatize the espionnage motif (on a personal or political level) such as *La Cousine Bette*, *Le Curé de Tours*, *Ferragus*, *Splendeurs et Misères des courtisans*, and *Sur Catherine de Médicis*, or which contrast the onlooker's vision and the protagonist's blindness, as in *La Duchesse de Langeais* or *La Recherche de l'Absolu*. These quasi-characters are, on the other hand, almost completely excluded from those texts dominated by a strong first person narrator, irrespective of the themes developed, because the narrator himself then views, comments on, and interprets events. No *postiches* populate the fictional world of "L'Auberge rouge," "Z. Marcas," *Mémoires de deux jeunes mariées*, or "Une Passion dans le désert."

While it cannot be said that there are consistent or exclusive patterns of hypothetical characters which dominate any text, distinctive clusters of *postiches* representative of a particular type or profession do occur in certain novels. There are several passersby in *La Maison du chat-qui-pelote*, underscoring and repeating the subterfuge of Sommervieu who pretends to be a mere passerby in the opening scene in order to watch the window of the woman with whom he is beginning to fall in love. "Observers" are more numerous in *La Femme de trente ans*, reinforcing the thematic importance of vision and blindness. Two poets corroborate the idyllic locale of *Le Lys dans la vallée*. Archeologists, artisans, architects and painters are called on to view the Brittany of *Béatrix*, while the viewpoint of strangers, foreigners, and newcomers is contrasted with the insiders' view of the residents of Saumur in *Eugénie Grandet*, and negative models predominate in *La Recherche de l'Absolu* where the protagonist is himself an anti-hero. Although the hypothetical characters of a novel do not collectively trace the thematic development of the work, the semantic traits of these witnesses, particularly those in the opening pages of a text, often highlight the particular stance of the narrator (political, poetic or historical) in relating his tale.

If the possible witnesses were merely a formal device, they would be intriguing but relatively unimportant. The real interest of the *postiches* lies in their ideological and place-holding functions and in their relation to the realist project.

The hypothetical characters are linked to the ideology of the text in several ways. Some observers have semantic traits with sociocultural implications. Certain negative qualities are almost exclusively linked to foreigners ("ignorants") or to women ("chicaneuses," "légères"). A few are loaded stereotypes: the harshest judge, the most sceptical lawyer, the most difficult usuer (EG 2:579), the liberal most full of hatred (Lys 6:310). At times they are grouped into ironic clusters which denigrate political groups: "republicans, mediocre artists, humanitarians and fools" (PMV 7:557), "spies, simpletons and politicians" (S 4:265), "thieves, spies, lovers, diplomats: that is, all slaves" (FE 1:505).

The use of the *postiches* allow the writer simultaneously to make a statement and to evade responsibility for it, since it is never voiced by either the narrator or the implied author. For this reason the possible witnesses constitute an extremely effective screen technique which allows a viewpoint to be introduced without attributing it to an identifiable source. They also act as a supplementary information system. Through their eyes pass stereotyped views and, on the rare occasions when they speak, their discourse is a staccato of clichés and *doxa*, the pseudo-knowledge which a society possesses about itself and transmits in unconscious and self-perpetuating ways.[3] In the Balzacian text the hypothetical witnesses convey popular beliefs or misconceptions about the fictional characters or about larger social issues: all Parisians are more knowledgeable than all provincials, every Frenchwoman knows how to trap a man, etc. The *postiches* thus become *foyers normatifs*, insertion points of the "ideological effect" of the text (Hamon 112–13). While they do not individually or collectively represent the whole or even the major part of the political and social thought contained in *La Comédie humaine*, the judgments they convey do reveal stereotypes and prejudices.

The judgments made by the possible witnesses are cross-examined, and the *postiches* are scrutinized and sometimes dismissed as incompetent. It is interesting to note that although the witnesses never have names, they are always evaluated by the narrator for their competence and performance. This maneuver allows the scriptor to shift the attention of the reader (in certain instances) from the *doxa* and onto the hypothetical observer. Every possible combination of positive and negative evaluation of the competence and performance of the hypothetical witnesses can be found in *La Comédie humaine*. There are competent observers whose performance is adequate: "Un philosophe aurait vu les misères de l'hôpital" (PdC 6:431) or "un peintre aurait... fait de cette figure une belle image: (PdC 6:438). And there are those who are generally competent, but who err this time: "En voyant l'inconnu, l'observateur le plus perspicace n'aurait pu s'empêcher de le prendre pour un homme de talent attiré par quelque intérêt puissant à cette fête de village" (BS 1:91).

Some observers ("l'ignorant," "l'étranger," "le provincial,") despite their personal inadequacies, do correctly perceive a situation, because the facts are so clear. "L'observateur le plus vulgaire se serait dit, en les voyant, que ces deux êtres étaient arrivés à ce funeste moment où la nécessité de vivre fait chercher une friponnerie heureuse" (Be. 5:29). Finally, certain incompetent observers perform as expected. "Cette explication est nécessaire... pour éviter les sottes critiques de ceux qui ne savent rien" (SPC 4:474). Or "à ce mot arrêtons-nous et plaçons ici pour les ignorants une explication" (EF 1:460). Of course, the virtual reader does not identify with "les ignorants": the scriptor creates bonds of complicity with the virtual reader who knows himself superior to those ignorant *postiches*. But the textual game is even more complicated, because this explanation comes from the mouth of another *postiche*, "un étymologiste très distingué qui a désiré garder l'anonyme," and the explanation itself is not merely doubtful but utterly fanciful. So it is up to the reader to decide whether the explanation inserted "for the ignorant" serves to enlighten the ignorant, or perhaps to identify them.

The group of discredited hypotheticals we have just examined is the most interesting because these strawpersons enable the writer to refute the possible objections of sceptical readers or to evade responsibility for an expressed opinion. "Certaines personnes casanières habituées à douter de tout parce qu'elles ne voient rien" might contradict the existence of characters like "Marche-à-terre" but the lack of experience these homebodies betray invalidates their criticism of the narrator (Ch. 5:632). Other inept witnesses who are discredited include flighty women who might challenge the verisimilitude of the novel. "Ici quelques femmes légères essaieront peut-être de chicaner la vraisemblance de ce récit, elles diront qu'il n'existe pas en France de fille assez niaise pour ignorer l'art de pêcher un homme . . . que la plus vertueuse et la plus niaise fille qui veut attraper un goujon trouve encore un appât pour armer sa ligne. Mais ces critiques tombent . . ." (VF 3:301). Instead of defending himself directly, the writer set up a straw opponent whom he can destroy, thus indirectly reaffirming the realism of his tale. In *Modest Mignon* the narrator approves the "spectateur instruit" who thought that his presentation of contrasts was "sublime" (MM 1:195). Through the *postiche* acting as intermediary, the narrator makes this rather immodest evaluation of his talent more palatable to the reader, because a third party, an objective expert, has ostensibly made the claim.

As *postiches* they mark an absence as well as a presence, like the anonymous "quiconque" on the opening page of *Une ténébreuse affaire*: "Quiconque eût pu contempler cette scène, caché dans un buisson, aurait sans doute frémi" (TA 5:492). This hypothetical observer is clearly a ruse, a trick of the scriptor, who invents his characters and scenes and then invents that doubly fictional being who *might* have been hidden in a bush. But no one is there, the textual bush is empty, the characters are not spied on within the diegesis. Do they go unseen then? Or is this hole, this blank, the place where someone could have been hidden in the bushes, the opening offered to the reader and through which he slides into the fictional world? The writer makes the reader see the entire scene that follows precisely from the viewpoint of the one absent from the bush. Other *postiches* collect information for the reader by risking actions that only hypotheticals might dare attempt, like the one who would have slipped his hand under Mme Jules' belt to discover the tell-tale perspiration when she lied (F 4:20).

When the *postiches* convey information and focus vision, they are clearly aiming their interpretations at the reader. A closer analysis of a wider spectrum of examples reveals the pervasiveness of this orientation. Since the *postiches* usually occur only in a single sentence, it is relatively easy to cull the verbs which accompany them and to examine the semantic content of those verbs. The *postiches* from 13 texts fall into the following pattern: they observe and decode (verbs: *remarquer, observer, voir, contempler*) 27%, they understand (*reconnaître, penser, découvrir*) or interpret (*analyser, attribuer, estimer*) 64% and they react (*tressaillir, frémir, admirer, pleurer*) 9%. Observing and decoding, understanding, interpreting and reacting personally are precisely the reading processes as they have been defined and described by research in cognitive psychology. There is, therefore, a complete apprenticeship in how to read the fictional world which is encoded within *La Comédie humaine*.

The *postiches* also function as place holders for the reader by raising hypotheses about the narrative. Generating hypotheses is the key moment in the act of reading, the most dynamic strategy of the reader.[4] Not only do the *postiches* mime hypothesis formation, but they are themselves hypotheses. Inhabitants of a possible world different from that of the characters, they turn the Balzacian text into a "complex world structure" where a "number of possible worlds are linked to the actual-in-the-novel worlds" (Pavel 61). By exploding the surface coherence of the text, they cause us to re-examine any simplistic classification of *La Comédie humaine* as realist fiction.

The *postiche* is basically a romantic technique diverted by Balzac to further the realist project. There were some instances of hypothetical characters in the novels of Sir Walter Scott which Balzac had read and admired, and it is possible that Balzac may have learned the technique from his predecessor, although Scott interjects them very seldom. (There are only four in *Waverly*, for instance). The more obvious and directly identifiable presence of both implied author and narrator in romantic novels in general (and Scott's fiction in particular) links the *postiche* to the narrating voice in those texts, flattening their identity into simple figurations and limiting their functions. They appear as merely playful inventions of the implied author.

In the Balzacian narrative, however, their functions are much more complex. The realist narrative accredits itself through the internal consistency of the narrative world and the credibility of a reliable narrator. As Lilian Furst has observed, "the narrator continues assiduously to foster the self image of expertise" because his role as enunciator and guarantor of truth "is fundamental to realism's entire tactics of self-accreditation" (Furst 18). Bolstering his own position by the testimony of some expert possible witnesses, the Balzacian narrator can even discredit those other witnesses who might have disagreed with him. As representatives of "real" groups (painters, historians, scientists, etc.) the *postiches* have a referential function: they reinforce the verisimilitude of the text and create images which have a counterpart in the extratextual world. Yet, as hypotheticals, representatives of other possible worlds (often contrary to fact-in-the-novel), who are called in only for a one-line observation, they simultaneously undermine the verisimilitude and remind the reader that the text is, after all, only fiction. The use of the *postiches* also partially deconstructs the surface coherence usually considered characteristic of realism because the possible witnesses (at least the metanarrative and metadiscursive ones) have no contacts with the characters but stand in a mediating position between the fictional world and the virtual reader.

Not only is the relationship of the *postiches* to textual coherence and verisimilitude ambiguous and even contradictory, but the hypothetical observers suggest a possible way of conceptualizing realism itself. The older definitions of realism as representational and mimetic art have already been seriously questioned over the past twenty years, and the conventionality theory now has serious opponents as well.[5] The hypothetical observers are perhaps more than an isolated element within the text; they can be viewed as models of the realist project: the creation of an elaborated hypothesis which stands in relation to the "real" world as a fictionally possible interpretation. As an encompassing hypothesis, the realist novel is so pragmatically convincing that the reader participates in the fabrication and elaboration of this hypothesis without questioning the precariousness of the modality underpinning the whole text and may forget that not only the details but even the basic assumptions are vulnerable. The quasi-characters (the little people who really aren't there) are useful in rethinking realism, not as mimesis or shared convention, but as an act of supposition forcefully and imaginatively conceived, as a compelling hypothesis.

NOTES

1. The possible witnesses have received relatively little attention. They are mentioned by Henry and Olrik who call them "tics" of Balzacian language, and by Rousset and van Rossum-Guyon who assimilate all of them with the narratees. See also Paris and Weber.
2. Although some types of *postiches* do strongly resemble the narratee, the possible witnesses can be distinguished in several ways: they usually occur in only one sentence, they do not recur, have a great mobility across the enunciative levels of the text and never serve as the interlocutor of the narrator for a single episode, let alone an entire

story. Furthermore, the *postiches* are very often accompanied by the conditional or other hypothetical verb forms and serve as adequate or as good "bad examples" for the narratee.
3. For a discussion of the term *doxa* see Prendergast 50ff.
4. For the relation between hypothesis formation and the act of reading see Spiro 8, Rumelhart 4. See also Iser on the relation between blanks and hypotheses 169–70, 182, 202.
5. There is an excellent discussion of changing conceptions of realism in Furst.

WORKS CITED

Balzac, Honoré de. *La Comédie humaine.* 7 Vols. Paris: Seuil, "L'Intégral," 1966.

Furst, Lilian. "Realism and its 'Code of Accreditation.'" Unpublished manuscript, 1987.

Hamon, Philippe. "Texte et idéologie." *Poétique* 49 (1982) 105–25.

Henry, Alain and Hilde Olrik. "Le double jeu du récit." *RIDS* 42. Copenhagen: Romansk Institut, 1976.

Iser, Wolfgang. *The Act of Reading: a Theory of Aesthetic Response.* Tr. David Wilson. Baltimore: Johns Hopkins UP, 1978.

Paris, Jean. *Balzac.* Paris: Balland, 1986.

Pavel, Thomas G. *Fictional Worlds.* Cambridge, MA: Harvard UP, 1986.

Prendergast, Christopher. *The Order of Mimesis: Balzac, Stendhal, Nerval, Flaubert.* Cambridge: Cambridge UP, 1986.

van Rossum-Guyon, Françoise. "Aspects et fonctions de la description chez Balzac." *L'Année balzacienne* 1980, 111–29.

———. "Redondance et discordances: métadiscours et autoreprésentation dans les Parents pauvres." *Balzac et les Parents pauvres.* Ed. Françoise van Rossum-Guyon and Michiel van Brederode. Paris: CDU-SEDES, 1981, 147–63.

Rousset, Jean. "L'inscription du lecteur chez Balzac." *Le Statut de la littérature: Mélanges offerts à Paul Bénichou.* Ed. Marc Fumaroli. Geneva: Droz, 1982.

Rumelhart, David E. "Understanding Understanding." *Understanding Reading Comprehension: Cognition, Language and the Structure of Prose.* Ed. James Flood. Newark, DE: IRA, 1984, 1–20.

Spiro, Rand. "Constructive Processes in Prose Comprehension and Recall." *Theoretical Issues in Reading Comprehension.* Ed. Spiro, Bruce and Brewer. Hillsdale, NJ: Erlbaum, 1980, 245–78.

Weber, Sr. Maryann. "Le lecteur virtuel dans trois textes narratifs français du dix-neuvième siècle: structures, stratégies, idéologies." Diss. Middlebury College, 1983.

"PARIS CHANGE!": PERCEPTION AND NARRATION

Lilian R. Furst

Paris Change! mais rien dans sa mélancolie
N'a bougé! palais neufs, échafaudages, blocs
Vieux faubourgs, tout pour moi devient allégorie
Et mes chers souvenirs sont plus lourds que des rocs.

"Paris change!": the opening exclamation to the second part of Baudelaire's *Le Cygne* beckons as an encompassing title and cue for a further consideration of Paris in nineteenth and early twentieth century literature. The physical appearance of the city was indeed being transformed with the gradual accomplishment of Napoleon's design, and so too was its image in literature. That, however, is not my topic; the links between the city's actual face and its literary portrait have been extensively and scrupulously documented by a host of critics, most notably Pierre Citron in his monumental study.[1] But certain other aspects of changing Paris in literature have been given much less attention. Foremost among them is the correlation between the nature of the literary image and the format of presentation. I want to show how the narrational forms offer a figurative reiteration, virtually an "allégorie," to revert to Baudelaire, of the way the city is perceived by the protagonist. To approach Paris in literature from this angle is in effect to invert the customary procedure of enframing the literary portrayal referentially in an existent (or past) actuality. My argument is that the reader's concept derives not from knowledge of an extratextual reality but from the protagonists' perceptions and from the experience of reading the narrational format. What is more, these two are closely and reciprocally interdependent.

This is the proposition I want to explore in three major fictions in each of which Paris forms a central motivational factor as well as the location of the action: Balzac's *Le Père Goriot* (1834), Zola's *L'Assommoir* (1877), and Rilke's *Die Aufzeichnungen des Malte*

Laurids Brigge (1910). Despite their apparent heterogeneity, these works have certain similarities, apart from the setting, that enable the comparison. All three of them, particularly in their opening sections, show the impact of Paris on a young recently arrived newcomer: Eugène de Rastignac has just come from the Angoulême area to study law, Gervaise Macquart has moved some three months previously from Plassans, and the Dane, Malte, has at the outset been in the city a mere three weeks. All three are in their early twenties as they make their initial encounter with Paris, and in their attempts to grasp and order their confusing impressions of the city, they are also trying to construct their lives, assimilating the city in their minds and vice versa. Their *prise de conscience* assumes differing forms, determined by the disparity in their background, situation, and personality. Rastignac is the energetic, ambitious, extroverted young man from the provinces,[2] from an impoverished middle-class family, set on making his career and his fortune through the opportunities for upward mobility afforded by the Paris of 1819–1820. Gervaise, by contrast, is defined, and limited, primarily by her gender; she is a working class woman who has come to Paris not of her own volition, but in the wake of her lover, Lantier, the father of her two illegitimate children. With scant education and a sinister heredity of alcoholism and degeneration, she strives at most to survive in the squalid slums of the midcentury industrializing metropolis. Malte, as the scion of an ancient aristocratic lineage, is wholly devoid of social, worldly aspiration; a highly sensitive, complex, introverted aesthete, he endeavors to come to grips with himself, his past and present beyond the noisy commotion of the turn-of-the-century city. For each of the three the confrontation with Paris marks a major turning point. Rastignac, with his will to power and possession, decodes the city as an object of desire, challenging, exciting, alluring, and full of promise. To Gervaise, the female possessed by both men and by her environment, Paris is a perplexing script; glimpsed longingly as a possible access to security, it becomes increasingly and predominantly a threatening whirlpool of apprehension. For Malte, as he struggles to gain possession of self and universe, it seems the frightening incarnation of his dread. What emerges in each case is less a substantive image of Paris than a subjective interpretation through the psyche of the protagonist. And it is in the narrative strategies that these widely varying visions of Paris find their objectification.

Of the three, Rastignac's is most clearly the story of an initiation. He is surprised, indeed shocked by his first experiences in Paris. His bewildered impressions are shaped into a cohesive picture through the help of two self-appointed mentors, Mme. de Beauséant and Vautrin. Despite the great disparity of their situation and language, they in effect reveal to him the same social structure. Their advice, backed by his own observations, opens Rastignac's eyes to Paris as an established, hierarchical system which rests on the twin pillars of money and class. The *pension* Vauquer, whose successive floors correspond to the tenants' financial standing, represents in microcosm Parisian society, while the fates of the individual inhabitants, as they move up or down stairs, offer Rastignac exemplary case-histories of the vicissitudes of life in the city.

Paris, then, is perceived as a place governed by an order that is discernible, though complicated and apparently contradictory in character. On the one hand it is, as Vautrin assures Rastignac, "comme une fôret du nouveau monde," open ground for any fortune-hunter, who will be well received provided he presents himself "avec sa gibecière bien garnie."[3] Yet at the same time its social intercourse is regulated by an exacting formal ritualism, by "ces lois draconniennes du code parisien" (1031), from which not even love is exempt. It is the duplicity of the city's unwritten code that Rastignac has to learn: that the surface adherence to strict conventions of dress, speech, and deportment only serves the better to mask the underlying law of the jungle. For those like Rastignac bent on *"parvenir"* (935) at almost any cost, Paris is not only a challenge and an object of desire, but also a mechanism to be mastered and manipulated. Though the operative system may be cruel and morally despicable, it can nevertheless be both understood and used by those astute—and ruthless—enough to grasp its workings and its opportunities. The mood prompted by Rastignac's perception of Paris is one of cynical optimism.

Because he believes fervently in the possibility of success, Rastignac devotes himself single-mindedly to learning to play the Parisian game as quickly and as adroitly as he can without allowing himself the luxury of reflection, let alone of ethical judgments. He is still sufficiently tender-hearted to be moved by the despoliation of Goriot, who has remained an ignorant outsider to the rules of Parisian society. But even while giving the old man pity and tendance, Rastignac sees him as a cautionary example of failure in Paris. His early recognition that the city is "un bourbier" (886) doesn't deter his determination to conquer it. The sub-text of warfare is underscored by such recurrent terms as "combat" (917, 936), "abordage" (919), "champ de bataille" (947, 981), "un boulet de canon" (936, 947), and "lutte" (948). It is perhaps in extension of this masculine vocabulary that Paris is cast into a female role as a sexual quarry. In Anastasie, who is identified as "si éminemment Parisienne" (897) and in her sister, Delphine, Rastignac sees all the city's entrancing glamor. That they turn out to be Goriot's daughters, who have attained their glitter parasitically, literally at his expense, makes them the most telling incarnation of the exploitative Parisian formula preached by Vautrin. No less symbolical is the final tableau of *Le Père Goriot*, when Rastignac overlooks the city from the heights of the Père Lachaise cemetery where Goriot has just been buried.

The striving for mastery that animated Rastignac within the fiction is practiced by the narrator over his fiction. And just as inside knowledge is the key that opens up to Rastignac the covert order of Paris, so too it is the source of narratorial authority. Through his ubiquitous presence in *Le Père Goriot* the narrator exercises the kind of control over the fiction that Rastignac longs to acquire over the city. From the outset, in the presentation of the *pension* Vauquer, the speaking voice at once asserts and displays an intimate familiarity with the scene of the drama. He knows Madame Vauquer's past, her maiden name and social standing, he can fix precisely the economic and geographic location of the boardinghouse, he has seen and smelled it from the inside, and he is privy to the life-histories and family background of its various inhabitants. His encompassing hold on the people and the place fosters his self-image as a reliable guide and as the guarantor that indeed "*All is true*" (848). His frequent direct addresses to the reader, as he takes him/her by the hand, as it were, consolidate the narrative contract and affirm his predominance. His later occasional reflections on the story in progress, for example, his designation of Rastignac's tale as "un des sujets les plus dramatiques de notre civilisation moderne" (948), far from being inept breaks in the illusion, are further manifestations of his power over the narrative. As a skilled reader of the Parisian scene, this audible, directing narrator acts as a correlative model for Rastignac, who engages the city with the same robust sense of purpose and the same decisive speed with which the narrator steers his narration.

A similar consonance between the diegetic and the narrational levels is characteristic of *L'Assommoir*, however much it differs from

Le Père Goriot in other ways. Gervaise never has the commanding overview, physically and intellectually, that Rastignac seems to have achieved at the end of *Le Père Goriot*. Significantly, when she surveys the city from the top of the Vendôme Column on her wedding day, her gaze automatically gravitates back to her little *quartier*, recoiling in trepidation from the larger vista.[4] This episode aptly suggests her marginality[5] to the mainstream of Parisian life; she spends her days and years sequestered in a circumscribed area, moving only as far as her limping legs can carry her, excluded by poverty and ignorance from the splendors of Paris, of whose very existence she appears hardly to be aware. In fact, even though technically within the city walls, Gervaise continues to live as if in a province, with the language and culture of a ghetto sub-group. In contrast to the overriding order that becomes apparent to Rastignac, it is the jumble of Paris that strikes Gervaise as she wends her slow way through the maze of streets and the labyrinthine corridors of the tenement house. She lacks the capacity ever to marshal this haphazard agglomeration of people and things into any structured sense. Instead, the prevailing moral as well as physical confusion translates in practical terms into an intuition of the arbitrariness of fate. Gervaise is destined to be the victim of the city, not its master, like Rastignac.

Her perception of the city changes according to her own situation, and it is the outcome of an instinctive response rather than the cognitive understanding that Rastignac has. From the beginning she has an ominous sense of fear that stems from her view of Paris as an insidious oppressor and imminent danger to its inhabitants. In the opening scene, as she sits at the window waiting until daybreak for Lantier's return, she construes the workmen streaming into the city as a "troupeau" of animals going to its death: "la cohue s'engouffrait dans Paris, où elle se noyait, continuellement" (377). The herd moves on, and she sees the men "les joues terreuses, la face tendue vers Paris, qui, un à un, les dévorait, par la rue béante du Faubourg-Poissonière" (378). The menacing undertones of "dévorait" and "béante" make Paris into a monster as voracious as the mine in *Germinal*. In *L'Assommoir* too there is a machine, the still, which appears to Gervaise like a grim and threatening beast:

> L'alambic, avec ses récipients de forme étrange, ses enroulements sans fin de tuyaux, gardait une mine sombre; pas une

> fumée ne s'échappait; à peine entendait-on un souffle intérieur, un ronflement souterrain; c'était comme une besogne de nuit faite en plein jour, par un travailleur morne, puissant et muet. (411)

The image of the crouching, greedy brute recurs a third time in Gervaise's first glimpse of the tenement house, which becomes, like the *pension* Vauquer, a symbolic replica of the city:

> La maison paraissait d'autant plus colossale qu'elle s'élevait entre deux petites constructions basses, chétives, collées contre elle; et, carrée, pareille à un bloc de mortier gâché grossièrement, se pourrissant et s'émiettant sous la pluie, elle profilait sur le ciel clair, au-dessus des toits voisins, son énorme cube brut, ses flancs non crépis, couleur de boue; d'une nudité interminable de murs de prison, où des rangées de pierres d'attente semblaient des mâchoires caduques, bâillant dans le vide. Mais Gervaise regardait surtout la porte, une immense porte ronde, s'élevant jusqu'au deuxième étage, creusant un porche profond, à l'autre bout duquel on voyait le coup de jour blafard d'une grande cour. (414)

Such lurid metaphorization of the city creates a telling vehicle for Gervaise's perceptions.

Her primary response of apprehension is temporarily suspended after her marriage to Coupeau when it is superseded by hope: hope of success, not on Rastignac's grand scale of a whole fortune, but in the modest form of a small laundry business of her own and a comfortable home. The move to Paris thus assumes for her, as for Rastignac, the guise of an opportunity. Unlike him Gervaise can hardly be deemed a social climber, yet for a while at least she looks towards the prospect of a better, more secure life for herself and her children through the economic potential afforded by the city. But the hungry monster is till there, and gets to swallow her too, as if in contempt of all her efforts to survive. As she slides into the abyss that is Paris for the workers in the slums, she is as devoid of insight into what has happened as of power to stop it. While Rastignac's ascent has its climax in his final commanding panorama of the city from above, Gervaise's descent hits bottom in her death in a hole under the stairs in the tenement house. The male middle-class path in Paris towards the end of the second decade of the nineteenth century held the pos-

Lilian R. Furst 79

sibility of *parvenir* in the sense of expansion and possession. By contrast, the female working class route around the middle of the century is inexorably one of restriction, enclosure, and ultimately the self-surrender of *s'abandonner*.

Gervaise's immersion in the city finds its narrational parallel in the reader's immersion in her mind. The narrator's voice is less insistently to the forefront in *L'Assommoir* than in *Le Père Goriot*, tending often to merge with the viewpoint of the protagonists. This is apparent in the episode already mentioned of the wedding party's view from the top of the Vendôme Column, which is registered successively in the third person through the eyes of various participants, then in indirect discourse in their own words ("Non, décidément, ça vous faisait froid dans les boyaux" 419), back to third person narration, and finally, with the phrase "Paris, autour d'eux, étendait son immensité grise" (450), shifts to a poetic description by a narrator far more cultured than the wedding group. His patently literary, visionary metaphor of Paris as an ocean is in startling contrast to the wedding guests' myopically detailed fragmentation.

Such shifts in focalization generally take place more directly between the narrator and Gervaise. The opening chapter, for example, begins with a third person narratorial account of Gervaise sitting at the window ("Elle regardait à droite," "Elle regardait à gauche," "elle levait les yeux," "elle apercevait" 376), glides shortly into a less determinate focalization, which comprises both her angle and the narrator's in the somewhat ambivalent turn of phrase, "il lui semblait" (380), and ends within her consciousness in the transposition of the key reiterated sight of the abattoir and the hospital into indirect discourse:

> C'était sur ce pavé, dans cet air de fournaise, qu'on la jetait toute seule avec les petits; et elle enfila d'un regard les boulevards extérieurs, à droite, à gauche, s'arrêtant aux deux bouts, prise d'une épouvante sourde, comme si sa vie, désormais, allait tenir là, entre un abattoir et un hôpital. (403)

Despite the tenses, which clearly indicate the switch to indirect discourse, the appearance of the traditional literary metaphor of Paris as a "fournaise"[6] suggests the extent of the duality of perception contained in the language. While "fournaise" could emanate from Gervaise, it seems more likely to attribute it to the narrator. His stealthy intratextual presence signals the circumscription of Gervaise's freedom, as if he were insinuating himself into the very core of her being. In her discourse the narrator performs the same coercion as the forces of the city do in her life. The repeated drift from her point of view to his and back, sometimes to the verge of indistinguishability, denotes the lack of self-determination in *L'Assommoir*. Things—success, Lantier, Coupeau, understanding of Paris—escape Gervaise and slip away, as do her thoughts and her discourse under the sway of an extraneous power. The technique is closely reminiscent of that of *Madame Bovary* with its notoriously subtle *glissements* into and out of Emma's consciousness. Perhaps the parallel tells us something about the control of women's minds in the mid-nineteenth century. Certainly the narrator's intrusion into Gervaise's stream of consciousness points to the supplanting of her will. It is the linguistic equivalent of her slump into passivity as well as the embodiment of her impotence. And the reader too, undergoing the frequent transfers from one mentality into the other, is made to share in the precariousness that is at the heart of Gervaise's experience of Paris.

Malte Laurids Brigge seems worlds away from *L'Assommoir* not only in the personality of its protagonist but also in its narrative situation since the experiencing persona and the narrator are one and the same. There is, however, a line of continuity insofar as Gervaise's dominant response is repeated in an intensified version in Malte. Her dumb, chronic, unreflective apprehension is transformed into an acute, highly verbalized, self-conscious dread. The anxiety of his estrangement is already implicit in the striking opening sentence: "so, also hierher kommen die Leute, um zu leben, ich würde eher meinen, es stürbe sich hier."[7] With this terse inversion of the norm, which has the form and impact of a maxim, Malte sets himself apart from his milieu and from average expectations. His dissenting, querying position as an outsider is conveyed by the antithetical structure of the sentence with its sharp contrast between the constative statement of the common assumption in the indicative tense in the first half and the subjunctive in its closing words, "es stürbe sich hier," unusual both in the impersonal formulation and in the rare conjugation. The association between the city and death, a major motif of *Malte Laurids Brigge*, is thus made at the very outset, together with that foregrounding of language that is the hallmark of the poetic use of words. The following three sparser declarations corroborate the initial theme and mood: "Ich bin ausgewesen. Ich habe gesehen: Hospitäler. Ich habe einen Menschen gesehen, welcher schwankte und umsank" (7). These laconic, fractured observations have the same shock effect on the reader as the city has on Malte. The starkness created by the absence of physical designative detail heightens the emotional momentum, which is further reinforced by the unfamiliar plural, "Hospitäler," that suggests their omnipresence, as if the city were filled with places of dying. Another instance of this universal tendency to fall (and, by extension, to die) comes in the person who sways and sinks; his anonymous, generic status as a "Mensch," not particularized even by gender, underscores his paradigmatic and puzzling character. The syncretic notation of random street encounters: the pregnant woman pushing herself heavily along a wall, the "Asile de nuit" in a house personified as "starblind," the gross, greenish child with eczema on his forehead, the smell of iodine and of grease from fried potatoes: all these disjointed perceptions express the nauseating revulsion felt by Malte as he takes stock of Paris. In the word "Angst" (8), which forms the culmination of the opening section near its end, incongruously aligned with "Jodoform, pommes frites," the sensation is finally named and avowed. What makes this evocation of Paris so distinctive is its live narrational enactment—as against mere description—of Malte's response to the city. All the disparate elements coalesce to engender nervous tension: the short, staccato sentences, the abrupt starts and stops, the discord between the frantic rush and distressing noise of the city on the one hand, and on the other the frozen immobility of the individual, the sudden assaults of the unexpected: this amounts to a mimicry of the agonizing existential fear that threatens to silence Malte.

Paris is for Malte the opposite to what it is for Rastignac: the object of dread, not of desire; a place of decline and death, not of rising life; the catalyst to disorientation, dissolution, an erosion of selfhood. It is only by withdrawing from the immediate sense impressions of the city into the geographic and historic otherness of his past that Malte can stem the loss of self and of cultural values. Instead of expanding outwards into the city, like Rastignac, Malte seeks refuge from it by a return to his memories. Only by taking fuller possession of the recesses of his consciousness can he avert the dangers posed by the city. The radical defamiliarization that he experiences in facing "l'épouvante"[8] in and of the modern city can be countered solely by a refamiliarization with his cultural roots and heritage.

This is the context for the central action of *Malte Laurids Brigge*, that of writing. The text represents Malte's *Aufzeichnungen*: his adventures and journeys are of and in his mind. Repeatedly he emphasizes that things become real ("wirklich") through the act of the imagination ("Einbildung"): Bettine, for instance, he notes, "ist wirklicher in mir geworden" (242) through the creative activity of his memory to the point that "ich seh dich ein" (243). It is from within ("von innen"), not from without ("von außen") that true knowledge may be derived. His continued reliance on such inner sources is linked to his idiosyncrasies as a reader:

> So ist mir klar geworden, daß ich nie ein richtiger Leser war. In der Kindheit kam mir das Lesen vor wie ein Beruf, den man auf sich nehmen würde, später einmal, wenn alle die Berufe kamen, einer nach dem andern. Ich hatte, aufrichtig gesagt, keine bestimmte Vorstellung, wann das sein könnte. Ich verließ mich darauf, daß man es merken würde, wenn das Leben gewissermassen umschlug und nur noch von außen kam, so wie früher von innen. (234–35)

Because this anticipated turn to the outer has never occurred for Malte, he goes on maintaining his primary allegiance to the internal realm of his phantasy and memories. The images created by *erinnern*, visionary *sehen*, and *erzählen* are the ones that have validity for him.

So it is through his inner eye that Malte perceives Paris. His approach is the antithesis to that of Rastignac, who is essentially outer oriented because he believes in the existence of an objective reality anterior to and independent of his own mental processes. He therefore scrutinizes the surface appearance of things and people as a means to acquire reliable information. In *Malte Laurids Brigge*, on the contrary, the city is a product of Malte's mind. The image is internalized, phantasmagoric, disturbed and disturbing, as a projection of Malte's consciousness. The metaphorization of the city, apparent in *L'Assommoir* through the moves into Gervaise's mental space, is posited in *Malte Laurids Brigge* as the sole reality. The subjectivity of the first person narrator has annexed and, in a sense, abolished the actual city to substitute for it a place of his own making. And that place becomes the repository and embodiment of his *Angst*. The decay, disease, dissociation of things, dehumanization of people, and death that he sees in Paris are the disintegrating forces he senses and dreads in himself. Paris becomes an allegory (and maybe, scapegoat), just as writing becomes a bulwark against the threats objectified in the city. Writing denotes association, orientation in time and place, recuperation of the past, acceptance of life and death, and ultimately a refinding of oneself. It involves a transcendence of the chaotic turbulence of the present to forge a link with the past in the hope of a future. The radical subjectivity of this perception and the private nature of Malte's spiritual quest find appropriate expression in the first person narration. Himself a "wohnlose Seele" (262), a wanderer whose natural intimate bond to place has been disrupted, Malte tries through the probing and recording of his inner realm to rescue the individual from the reification of the masses in the city. His deliberately distinctive voice consciously sets itself apart through its use of language as potently as through its vision. The searching and tentative quality of this mode of narration has been well described as a "hypothetisches Erzählen," characterized by the constant interruption of the narrative by comments "die darauf hinweisen, daß das Erzählte nur eine Hypothese darstellt."[9] Such hypothetical narration conveys the transitoriness, the vulnerability to contingency of Malte's Paris and of his world, yet not without leaving open at least an aperture of hope for the future.

To compare the perception and narration of Paris in these three novels is to realize once again the range of experience and of format covered by the nineteenth century as well as the scope of the changes it precipitated in both environment and sensibility. Yet there is finally an overarching generic grouping under which these very divergent texts can be subsumed: Bakhtin's category of the "novel of ordeal."[10] It is a significant comment on the nineteenth century that ordeal is not by dragon but by city. The city, as it emerges in its modern shape, is at once the most attractive and the most frightening incarnation of the century's "progress."

NOTES

1. Pierre Citron, *La poésie de Paris dans la littérature française de Rousseau à Baudelaire* (Paris: Editions de minuit, 1961), 2 vols.; cf. also George B. Raser, *Guide to Balzac's Paris* (Choisy-le-Roi: Imp. de France, 1964); Robert Minder, *Paris in der neueren französischen Literatur 1770–1890* (Wiesbaden: Steiner, 1965); Stefan

Max, *Les Métamorphoses de la grande ville dans les "Rougon-Macquart"* (Paris: Nizet, 1966); Nathan Kranowski, *Paris dans les romans de Zola* (Paris; Presses universitaires, 1968); Marie-Claire Bancquart, *Images littéraires de Paris 'fin-de-siècle'* (Paris: aux éditions de la différence, 1979); Hans-Joachim Lotz, "L'image iréelle, bizarre et mythique de Paris chez Balzac et Baudelaire," in *Paris au XIXe siècle* (Lyons: Presses universitaires, 1984) 93–106. For a more general overview see Burton Pike, *The Image of the City in Modern Literature* (Princeton: Princeton Univ. Press, 1981; also Edward Timms & David Kelley (eds.), *Unreal City: Urban Experience in Modern European Literature and Art* (Manchester: Manchester University Press, 1985), specially 24–44, Peter Collier, "Nineteenth Century Paris: Vision and Nightmare."

2. cf. A. K. Chandra, "The Young Man from the Provinces," *Comparative Literature*, 33 (Fall 1981) 321–341.

3. Honoré de Balzac, *La Comédie humaine*, ed. Marcel Bouteron (Paris: Gallimard, 1956) 2: 939. All subsequent references are to this edition.

4. Emile Zola, *Les Rougon-Macquart*, ed. Henri Mitterand (Paris: Gallimard, 1961) 2: 449–50. All subsequent references are to this edition.

5. cf. Bancquart, *Images* 74 ff.

6. Citron, in *La Poésie de Paris*, traces *fournaise* to Vigny's poem, *Paris* (1: 274), and cites its recurrence in Hugo, Lamartine, Alexandre Dumas, Banville, and Michelet, inter alia (2: 422).

7. Rainer Maria Rilke, *Die Aufzeichnungen des Malte Laurids Brigge* (Wiesbaden: Insel Verlag, 1951) 7. All subsequent references are to this edition.

8. Maurice Blanchot, "Rilke et l'exigence de la mort," *L'Espace littéraire* (Paris: Gallimard, 1968) 151.

9. Judith Ryan, "Hypothetisches Erzählen: Zur Funktion von Phantasie und Einbildung in Rilkes *Malte Laurids Brigge*," *Jahrbuch der deutschen Schillergesellschaft* (1971) 341–74; rpt. Hartmut Engelhardt (ed.), *Materialien zu Rainer Maria Rilke, "Die Aufzeichnungen des Malte Laurids Brigge"* (Frankfurt: Suhrkamp, 1974) 244–79. Reference to this reprint, 265.

10. The phrase is used in M. M. Bakhtin, *The Dialogic Imagination*, ed. Michael Holquist (Austin: University of Texas Press, 1981) 106, as equivalent to "*Prüfungsroman*," and developed into a typology in *Speech Genres and Other Late Essays*, ed. Caryl Emerson and Michael Holquist (Austin: University of Texas Press, 1986) 11–16.

FROM STAGE TO PAGE: THE IMPOSSIBLE THEATERS OF FLAUBERT AND MALLARMÉ

Marshall C. Olds

As all temptations entail risk, so does the desire to find a common ground for thinking about Flaubert and Mallarmé. The come-on is in recognizing two of the earliest formulations of the Modernist preoccupation with problems of language and representation. The danger, as Maurice Blanchot has let us infer, is in seeing too rigorous a parallel between esthetics at different stages of historical maturation.[1] A book about nothing is not yet the Book containing nothingness, the crisis of subject matter is not yet the crisis of the subject. Yet there is something suggestive in this pairing that overcomes the distance between narrative realism and poetic symbolism and goes beyond the initial attraction of vocabularies of negation and indeterminacy. If these two writers usher us into the house of modern literature (albeit by different doors!) it is less for purposes of deconstruction than for those of reconstruction. In both the case of Flaubert and that of Mallarmé, the crises frame the reexamination of fundamental Romantic notions. In this discussion, we will be concerned with those of the individual, as they are expressed through representations of character and the lyric self. Access to those selves is no longer channelled through the inner life. Instead, the approach is from the outside through gesture, scenic context and a relationship with things. Where Romanticism isolated in order to stress the unique, this new optic shows the phenomenal in order to universalize. Flaubert's esthetic development along these lines is perceptible in the difference between the predominantly psychological treatment of Emma and the reified depiction some twenty years later of the "femme en bois," Félicité. For Mallarmé, there is an analogous development in the change from the personal voice of "L'Azur" and "Brise marine" to the Orphic Master of the late work.

The aspect of this parallel development that I will outline here concerns the latent theatricality found in the works of both authors.

More than the metaphors of the theater—as important to them as to their entire century—it was the models that writing for the theater provided that contributed to the revitalization of the other, more significant work. Both experimented with writing for the stage and, though serious in their attempts, both failed as playwrights, at least in part because their efforts, while inspired by the stage, fit uneasily with theatrical conventions; as Mallarmé would have it, his early "Faune" required the theater but was impossible in the theater. That this tutorial should have come for both through the theater is coincidental and of no special importance in itself. Yet, these failures had the happy result of offering solutions to problems that the earlier conceptions of narrative and lyric respectively couldn't solve. Briefly put, the problem was how to escape subjectivism, and the solution was to allow representation to acquire a new exteriorizing function.

Several facets of this question with respect to Flaubert's career have been discussed elsewhere, specifically the change in scene construction first developed in *L'Education sentimentale* and, in *La Tentation de saint Antoine*, where the blending of narrative and theatrical codes informs questions of point of view.[2] Referring occasionally to conclusions established in those studies, the Flaubert section of the present essay focuses on where the narrative abstraction of *Bouvard et Pécuchet* is allied to Flaubert's earlier practice of the theater, primarily the experiments of the 1850s and '60s. The Mallarmé section then raises the question of why the poet should have turned to writing for the theater when he did and points out some of the poetic consequences of this shift that have not been studied in this light, especially with respect to the representation of the hero. Along the way, I will briefly summarize the dramaturigical career of each writer.

A passage from *Bouvard et Pécuchet* invites us to our subject. During their study of the formation of the earth, the two copyists are struck by the succession of geological periods during which new formations and life forms spring forth as if from nowhere, finally obliterated by the upheaval separating each epoch from the next. This is one of the rare instances in which they feel compelled to totalize their learning and, referring to each epoch as a *tableau*, they sum up natural history this way: "Toutes les époques avaient été séparées les unes des autres par des cataclysmes, dont le dernier est notre déluge. C'était comme une féerie en plusieurs actes, ayant l'homme pour apothéose."[4] Despite the obvious irony, this may seem an innocent enough mention of a rather stylized genre of popular theater. However, it is one of a handful of references scattered throughout the *oeuvre* that call attention to precisely a type of theater practiced by Flaubert: the *féerie*. The first of these references, early in second *Education* (2: 40), would have been made not long after Flaubert had read dozens of fairy plays and had written his completed *féerie*, *Le Château des coeurs*, along with several others projected.[5]

What was this career and where did the *féerie* fit in? Flaubert's early interest in the theater, his childhood performances and ideas for comedies are well-known. Little discussed is the fact that this interest remained active until nearly the end of his life, the last play dating from 1874. Beyond the juvenilia, the synopsis of Flaubert's writing for the theater is as follows: in the five years between 1847 and 1852, he outlined, made notes for or partially wrote twenty-nine comedies or farces. Around 1855, toward the completion of *Madame Bovary*, he wrote the farcical and elaborately scenic pantomime, *Pierrot au sérail*.[6] Then, in the early sixties, came the series of *ébauches* for fairy plays and *Le Château des coeurs*, followed in 1872 and '74 by the two bourgeois comedies, *Le Sexe faible* and *Le Candidat*. While all but one of the completed or substantial first drafts were begun as collaborations, there is reason to believe that Flaubert was responsible for most of the writing and rewriting.[7] Superimposed on this activity were the repeated efforts to work out *La Tentation*, four of them between 1849 and 1872.

The content of Flaubert's plays is immediately familiar: the ironic depiction of the social, sexual and political mores of the middle class, the bawdy humor of the *garçon*, and the uneasy union of dream and reality. The question of form, however, is quite a different matter. With the exception of the last two plays, which are unabashed attempts at boulevard theater, there is an avoidance of anything resembling the tenets of dramatic *vraisemblance* which, in the context of French theater, are grounded in dialogue. The dialogue of Flaubert's plays usually ironizes theatrical conventions, as in the early spoof, *La Découverte de la vaccine*, a pastiche of Voltairian tragedy about the cure for gonorrhea.

It was not around dialogue or its parody that Flaubert's theater evolved, however. What differentiates the *féeries* of the sixties from the earlier comedies concerns the more detailed directions to the actors and the elaborate increase in the indications for stage setting and décor. The pantomime *Pierrot au sérail* is transitional in this respect. The story is of the type Flaubert found amusing: having finished his studies, Pierrot prepares to set off on the voyage that will complete his education. Unwilling to part from Colombine, he stuffs her into a trunk along with a jar of plums in brandy. The next scene finds the lovers in the desert where each is abducted by marauders, but not before Pierrot has shown his preference for the plums over Colombine. The couple is reunited at the Sultan's harem where Pierrot becomes Grand Turk. Disconsolate, he gives himself over to gluttony and eats until he explodes. In a mock apotheosis, he rises to strains of the *Marseillaise* and is greeted in heaven by Mohammed who is surrounded by women circus performers and beer-swilling *Hércules de nord*.

With all dialogue gone, the burden for signification falls on visual cues. This is accomplished by a network of clichés comprised of gesture, dress, situation and décor. The play borrows from popular farce for its gags and produces puppet-like characters. Causality is subverted by the absence of connecting scenes and by a new element in Flaubert's writing, the closing apotheosis *ex machina* which, because of its implausible nature, ironizes the whole.

We cannot be entirely sure why Flaubert turned to the *féerie* after finishing *Salammbô* in 1862. Diversion, certainly, but perhaps that novel's mythical and racial paradigms were already leading him away from the realism of *Madame Bovary*. What is certain is that his interest was formal. Of the nearly thirty plays he had recently read and of his own *Château* he remarked, "Je veux seulement attirer l'attention du public sur une forme dramatique splendide et large, et qui ne sert jusqu'à présent que de cadre à des choses forts médiocres. Mon oeuvre est loin d'avoir le sérieux qu'il faudrait et . . . j'en suis un peu honteux."[8] The plot conceived by Bouilhet is every bit as shameful as he suggests. In their eternal battle against the Fairies, the Gnomes have stolen all human hearts, but two innocent lovers are destined to recapture the prize. They are separated, and Paul's search for Jeanne takes him through a series of fantastic landscapes controlled by the Gnomes where he continually fails to recognize his beloved who is disguised. Because of their purity, the two are finally reunited and the Gnomes vanquished. There follows a celebration at the home of the banker Kloekher, who has been converted to feelings of love and charity. In Kloekher's garden, a stairway to heaven opens up and the hero climbs to eternal life among the Fairies with his betrothed. His faithful valet, left holding the heart of the last wicked man, is transformed into the playing card, *le valet de coeurs*.

Despite the heaviness of the plot, the conception here, as in the other fairy projects, goes beyond that of *Pierrot*. There is similarity in the disjointed action, scenic artifice and shallow characterization. But the action is now divided into a series of totally discrete tableaus, each separated from the next by a complete scene change *à vue*, eradicating any causal agent other than the fantastic. The plot has gone from a simple line of arbitrary adventures to an overall structure of loss, quest, retrieval and reward. Within this structure there is a sequence of repetitions of the same action (the hero's arrival, failed seduction by the "false" heroine, the hero's resumption of the search) until a conclusion is imposed.

With respect to décor, the exploitation of clichés becomes more concentrated. This is most apparent in the theme suggested by each place name. All props and costumes on the *île de la toilette* pertain to dress, in the *royaume du pot-au-feu* to the middle class, and so forth. As one might guess, décor is suggestive of the values and personalities of that place. Something that Flaubert considered to be an innovation on his part was the external projection of what a character says into the representational foreground. Maxime Du Camp cites an instance of this found in the unfinished play *Le rêve et la vie*: "Ainsi un père cherche son fils, le trouve dans un café, buvant et fumant; il s'irrite et lui dit: 'Tu n'es qu'un pilier d'estaminet,' à l'instant le jeune homme devient un pilier et un des linteaux de la porte." [9]

A step beyond this is the use of clichés in the formation of puns. All popular theater uses them, and Flaubert—who never could resist—puns in the *féerie* in the form of verbal-visual gags. As in the case just mentioned and that of the valet's transformation, the pun may take the form of a trite metaphor, calling forth its literal signified. Or more interestingly, it may be just the reverse, where a signified silently evokes its hackneyed signifier. A typical example comes from *Le Dictionnaire* under the entry, *Montre*: "Dans les Féeries, quand un personnage tire la sienne, ce doit être un oignon—cette plaisanterie est infaillible" (2: 312), "oignon" being a popular term for a pocket watch. *Le Château des coeurs* frequently uses such metonymic transfer. In the stage directions for the tableau, *L'île de la toilette*, tenor and vehicle are reversed for the figures *champignon* (coat rack) and *mouche* (artificial beauty spot). The playful result is confusion between the literal and figurative axes: "des costumes bariolés pendent à de grands champignons. Des mouches voltigeant dans l'air iront se coller d'elles-mêmes sur le visage des femmes: la mouche assassine, la capricieuse, la provocante, etc." (2: 340). Later, the bourgeois *littérateurs* have mirliton flutes hanging from their belts, playing on the derogatory term *poésie de mirliton*. Décor begins to rival dialogue in its semantic possibilities.

Space permits nothing more than an enumeration of the principal changes in the final *Tentation* that reflect Flaubert's work with the *féerie*: better definition of the action into tableaus, more consistent use of hallucination to separate them, rewriting the conclusion to conform to the retrieval and reward motif, significant expansion of the stage directions and the subtle addition to them of narrative codes that in turn have derived from earlier theatrical practice. An example of this last point is found in the opening scene description: "des nuages disposés comme les flocons d'une crinière gigantesque" (1: 523). Such indications work on two distinct levels: first as a cliché and then, retrospectively, as a diegetic image prefiguring the text's hallucinatory transformations of the inanimate into the animate. This is the narrational equivalent of the semantically charged verbal-visual gag.

In *Bouvard et Pécuchet* there is certainly theater in the air. Bouvard sets the tone by divulging his life-long wish to be an actor (2: 203), his dinner banter provoking the question to Mme Bourdin "si elle aimait les farces?—ça dépend de quelle espèce, répondit-elle" (2: 216), and his projection *en beau* of humanity's future which reads like a *féerie* by Jules Verne: "On ira dans les astres—et quand la Terre sera usée, l'Humanité déménagera vers les étoiles" (2: 301). There is even a self-parodic wink at the *theatrum mundi* theme in *Madame Bovary*: "[Bouvard] alla au Théâtre des Arts, et il souriait à ses voisins, disant qu'il était retiré du négoce et nouvellement acquéreur d'un domaine aux alentours" (2: 207). The theater is in Rouen, precisely where Emma, playing a similar role, "se cambra la taille avec une désinvolture de duchesse" (1: 649). Other examples come to mind: the vaudevillesque first meeting of the two copyists, the presentation of the garden, and the theater readings.

Based on the outline of the *féerie* given earlier, it should be clear that a number of the novel's well-known features are variants of that form, most obviously the adaptation to chapters of the linear tableau structure. As in the plays, this syntagma is loosely held together by the quest motif and is governed by the same overall structure of loss, quest, retrieval and reward, this last being the return to copying and what is variously described in the scenarios as "joie finale et éternelle" and the completion of the *monument*.[10] Each episode follows the same pattern as those of the *féerie* and the *Tentation*, and there is again the sense that acausality or arbitrariness is at work. It is chance now that propels the action, rather than the fantastic or the divine: a glimpse of Mélie at the pump affords the transition from political science to love, that of the villagers on their way to mass from metaphysics to religion.

Since narrative is more flexible with point of view than didascalia, setting in the novel need not carry as heavy a burden as in the plays. It is far from silent, however. We have seen how, in *La Tentation*, Flaubert modified the verbal-visual gag by using cliché to create a diegetic image and establish point of view. Such intrusions also occur in *Bouvard*, as in the opening sentences: "Comme il faisait une chaleur de trente-trois degrès, le boulevard Bourdon se trouvait absolument désert. Plus bas, le canal Saint-Martin étalait en ligne droite son eau *couleur d'encre*" (emphasis added). Again, we have innocent metaphor and trivial cliché. Retrospectively, though, the image takes on an added meaning in its comical hinting at the comic encounter between the scriveners, the same two whose bridge forms a circumflex accent over the bean patch and who will never be able to leave their copies.

The episodic tableau structure also intensifies questions of setting, and there is often such a concentration of diegetic paraphernalia that one has the impression of a chain of *au pays de*. Indeed, the house at Chavignolles is variously a laboratory, museum, gymnasium, storehouse for religious bric-à-brac and school. As in the plays, there is nothing like development or growth of awareness in the characters, and their movement across these settings is artificially imitative, like that of the ostrich crossing the stage in *Pierrot*, "une patte en l'air, et glissant très vite, sur des roulettes" (2: 419). What development there is results from the sheer accumulation of the different themes and their associated settings.

Most important in all of this is that the *féerie*, as an *exercice de style*, seemed to allow Flaubert to solve a double-edged narrative problem that narrative could not solve: how to externalize representation of character in order to liberate it from a psychologically based understanding, and how to develop a form adequate for this? One sees

Flaubert experimenting relatively early on with this question, most notably with the projected summerhouse sequence where Emma looks through a series of different colored window panes that project changing emotional hues on the landscape. This scene foreshadows the tableau structure of later work, though does not disassociate description from Emma's states of mind. A comparative example from *Bouvard* is the copyists' outline for their biography of the Duc d'Angoulême. Like the summary of natural history, these pages are an internal reduplication of the novel in parodic form, where the emphasis is again on representation. The disarticulated moments of the Duke's life show what results from characterization when approached from the outside perspective of events and deeds. Coherence is achieved, imposed, only by recognizing the accumulation of external signs—objects and places—that is, through the signifying décor. The biographers are brought to a comic awareness of this fact as they breathlessly grasp at straws: "On doit y relever l'importance qu'eurent les ponts. D'abord il s'expose inutilement sur le pont de l'Inn, il enlève le Pont-Saint-Esprit et le pont de Lauriol; à Lyon, les deux ponts lui sont funestes—et sa fortune expire devant le pont de Sèvres" (2: 241).

The topic of the *féerie* and narrative by no means exhausts discussion of Flaubert's evolving practice of characterization. Neither does it suggest that all writing in this last decade made use of these structures. The two boulevard plays are very conventionally grounded in dialogue, and *Hérodias*, while extremely "theatrical" in the sense of spectacle, is in altogether a different mode. But *Saint Julien* and *Un Coeur simple* most certainly do make use of these structures and, along with the last novel, draw attention to the *féerie* as a provocative metaphor for representation and as a significant model as well.

Unlike Flaubert, Mallarmé's interest in the theater did not originate in childhood. It wasn't until 1864, when he was in his early twenties, that he began to experiment with the possibilities of dramatic verse. Both "Hérodiade" and "L'Après-midi d'un faune" began as theater projects, though neither was finished as such. "Hérodiade" was in fact never completed, Mallarmé returning to it at various points throughout his life for elaboration or reworking. The text's sections are in different poetic forms but of them, the dramatic dialogue and monologues date from this period. The "Faune," originally "Monologue d'un faune," was first written as a one-act dramatic monologue, with non-speaking parts for the two nymphs who flee from the faun's embrace as he awakens. Mallarmé went so far as to submit the manuscript to the Théâtre Français, where it was decided that the text did not contain "l'anecdote nécessaire . . . [et] que cela n'intéresserait que les poètes."[11] These poems were conceived at the outset of the Tournon crisis years, the period during which Mallarmé revolutionized his poetic thought and practice, and when he first began to formulate the project of *Le Livre*. Walter Strauss and Leo Bersani have written authoritatively about the metaphysical and psychological dimensions of this crisis,[12] but the question that has yet to be asked is: What is the significance of the fact that Mallarmé should, at this juncture, turn to the language of the theater to help him write his way out of the trap where Baudelaire's lyricism had lured him? The pitfall was to see poetry as the mediating vehicle by which to go beyond both experience and the language of experience. With his new poems, he instantly became committed to what was to be a liberating form of expression (1440).

Mallarmé's turning to the theater was encouraged by his fascination with Shakespeare's *Hamlet* and its eponymous hero, references to which began at about this time and continued throughout Mallarmé's life. Hamlet's brooding nature clearly doubles Mallarmé's own obsessions with being and seeming and, through Hamlet, he came to see the actor-hero as one of the principal metaphors for the poet. Not surprisingly, the dramatic aspect of the play that held Mallarmé's attention was the soliloquies, scenes devoid of the "necessary anecdote." *Hamlet* was important in this respect: "La pièce, un point culminant du théâtre, est, dans l'oeuvre de Shakespeare transitoire entre la vieille action multiple et le Monologue ou drame avec Soi, futur" (1564). The concept underlying this was one of a dramatic work where space and character were the most general and stylized kind: "Une salle, [le verbe] se célèbre, anonyme, dans le héros" (371). "Hérodiade" is such a celebration and is strikingly different from the earlier poems in several key respects. The first concerns the heroine herself whose purity is in opposition to the unauthentic, fallen state of the earlier lyric hero. Hérodiade's nudity is the reflection and object of reflection in her isolated room, and the "blancheur vierge" of her body, a *lieu nul*, is the blank page on which the drama of her marriage with the saint is to be written. In this coincidence between heroine and décor, Mallarmé has begun to explore a new conception of spatialization, going well beyond the earlier motifs of fallen hero, spiritual barrier and exile. A new set of metaphors is engaged whereby drama becomes a function of space and place and where the hero, both metaphor (of the place) and metonym (of the space), is the *lieu* in which the anonymous celebration of the text occurs.

That theater externalizes internal drama was a prevalent notion in the dramatic theory of nineteenth-century France. Quite aside from questions of voice, such a conception gave an especially important role to décor and allowed a further elaboration of the Romantic idea that material reality may be invested with a capacity for signification. In the work undertaken in the mid 1860s, Mallarmé seemed aware of this potential. As dramatic incident, "l'anecdote," came to be replaced by the wait for some future incident (or confirmation of a past one), décor emerged as the principal index of the absent event. It in fact sets the stage for the event, creates the space that it will occupy and so becomes the primary agent of causality and meaning. As in the famous sonnet in *yx*, also conceived at this time, everything happens "selon le décor."

In all of its incarnations, the "Faune" is the text that most actively engages the décor. As in "Hérodiade," the externalizing projection of inner drama on outer reality is not complete and metonymic identification is established between the faun and his surroundings—"Mon doute, amas de nuit ancienne, s'achève / En maint rameau subtil"—which serve as an interlocutor, the faun addressing himself directly to the landscape and impatiently stamping his foot (hoof) when he doesn't get the answer he wants. As in "Hérodiade," incident is suppressed and the hero is projected in terms of the landscape, which in turn exists as a function of the hero: "Chaque grenade éclate et d'abeilles murmure, / Et notre sang, épris de qui le va saisir, / Coule par tout l'essaim éternel du désir." Here, too, this identification generates the central metaphor of the poem: that the landscape and the virgin hero are together the stage and the page on which "l'anecdote nécessaire" will, or did, take place. The production of meaning is the business of both: "O bords siciliens d'un calme marécage... CONTEZ / Que je coupais ici de creux roseaux...." Mallarmé characteristically enfolds the identity of the hero and that of the *lieu*: *conter* merges with *couper* in the former's Latin root (*puto*, to trim a bush or tree and, figuratively, to render an account). The mind is the internalization of space and space the externalized image of the mind.

In the years following the Tournon crisis, references to the theater abound in Mallarmé's essays, as he outlined the ritualistic and increasingly public character of art. During the two decades beyond the mid sixties, his conception of the ultimate work, *Le Livre*, evolved from being a lyric to a dramatic work. The notes for this unfinished project evoke a conception of the theater as microcosm of the world and as sort of macrocosm for the mind: "le théâtre inhérent à l'esprit."[13] In an essay from the 1880s, Mallarmé finds in the inside of a theater the image of a hierarchical cosmos, beginning in the lowly *parterre* and rising through the higher orders of the boxes and various balconies, finally to the divinities presiding over the *culte* from the painted vault of the ceiling (367). Elsewhere, he writes of the typically huge chandelier hanging in most theaters high above the stage. For him, it duplicates the night sky and represents the constellar figuration of some primitive drama which is in the process of being reenacted below.[14]

With this elaborate metaphor, Mallarmé was able to open up further his relationship to language beyond viewing it as an obstacle that had to be broken through and transcended, to one where language was the space in which the action of thought would take place. Indeed, the major poems begun in the early 1870s—"Toast funèbre" and "Prose pour des Esseintes"—with their luxurious word gardens, offer variations of these spatial motifs. Mallarmé incorporated the metaphors of the *theatrum mundi* and the *theatrum mentis* and then went beyond them to see in the language of the theater a model that could be adapted, this time to lyric poetry. This model was one of new space. Mallarmé appears to have struck upon it during work on the dialogue scene between Hérodiade and her Nurse and on the faun's monologue. It concerned the *vers partagé*, the single alexandrine shared by two characters, so prevalent in Corneille and Racine. Mallarmé always sought new rhythms, and the change in voice accompanied by the visual dislocation encouraged unusual patterns—as in the 3–5–4,

H: "Oh! tais-toi!
N: Viendra-t-il parfois?
H: Etoiles pures"

—and also great freedom with internal rhyme. Mallarmé must have been attentive to the spatial arrangement of such lines because he began to use a line that broke with no change in voice. In the original faun's monologue of 1865, the breaks allow mainly for stage directions and, with no necessary change in meter, are rather like the *vers partagé*:

Les mains jointes en l'aire:
Si...
Comme parant de des mains disjointes une foule imaginaire;
Mais ne suis-je pas foudroyé?
Se laissant choir:
Non, ces closes

In the revisions, the work becomes a lyrical piece from which the stage directions have been eliminated but where the breaks remain untouched:

Je tiens la reine!
O sûr châtiment...
Non, mais l'âme

It is impossible to tell what time element should be accorded these blanks. Their principal effect is *visual*, Mallarmé having insisted on the spatial dimension of the physical page.

There are many well-known statements and social *boutades* focusing on the logocentricity of poetry: "Mon cher Degas, la poésie ne se fait pas avec des idées mais avec les mots," "Il faut vaincre le hasard, mot par mot," and so forth. As important as they are, they do not prepare us for the radical restructuring of the poem that will occur finally in "Un coup de dés."[15] At that famous moment of seeing the poem for the first time, Valéry was exactly right not to insist on the fragmentation and discontinuity of thought, but on its spatialization: "Il me sembla de voir la figure d'une pensée, pour la première fois placée dans notre espace."[16] Our space, that of the Master's drama, is the universe, the mind and the page, all reflecting each other, all perceptible as traces of Mallarmé's virtual theater in the observation (itself defining a space) that "Rien n'aura eu lieu que le lieu, excepté peut-être une constellation."

To conclude, what brings Flaubert and Mallarmé together here is a general pull towards a new formulation of the individual, fueled by a shared distrust of Romantic subjectivism. The two sets of correspondence amply document the laborious and painful efforts of both writers to overcome the immediate self (inspiration, the Muse, chance) in favor of a highly controlled mode of composition where all expression tends toward the impersonal and (self)characterization toward the universal. Likewise, there is little concern with the "type casting" that is such a part of nineteenth-century literature: the identity that comes from the social context of the city. Both writers are a-Parisian—Flaubert's only "Parisian" novel refuses that (Balzacian) context to its protagonist, and for Mallarmé the Baudelairean preoccupation with the city becomes detached urbanity[17]—and both deride the official languages associated with urban life. The important question of context is not suppressed but finds a new orientation thanks in part, I would suggest, to the close interaction between character and setting that dramatic writing forced both writers, in separate ways, to confront. The notion of milieu becomes at once broader and more intimate, as the objects surrounding us form constellations of meaning. We are what we contemplate. This material necessity replaces the Romantic vision of Nature (later the City) and in the best of cases, the identity between self and décor may carry its universalizing impulse toward a recognition of the sacred, at least momentarily. Mallarmé's swan fails to redeem itself in life, though is sacralized in art by its universal, stellar counterpart. Likewise in "Un coup de dés," the Master's thought will attain its final point: the constellation of the poem's space. For Flaubert, the best case scenario is probably not in his unfinished novel, itself too heavily ironized along with all other epistemological and social uses of language. A higher game is played out by Félicité, whose life is figured by the objects that accumulate in her room. The same process occurs at Chavignolles, but in the short story the result is not a refuse heap but a sort of *chapelle ardente*. The culminating beatific hallucination must not be read, as it often is, as an ironic comment on mere psychological fetishism. If there is fetishism, it is in the sense of things as religious icons, having the power to put us in touch with the eternal through immanence. I will close with reference to a passage that lays the high ground for Flaubert, points the way to Proust and so invites us to reassess in part Blanchot's chronology. As Félicité is waiting during Virginie's catechism class and listening to the stories of the Old and New Testaments, she is gripped by the universalizing power of art and myth to elevate our lives by investing the randomness of the things in it with a new order of meaning, and her sorrow is dispersed:

> Puis, elle pleura en écoutant la Passion. Pourquoi l'avaient-ils crucifié, lui qui chérissait les enfants, nourrissait les foules, guérissait les aveugles, et avait voulu par douceur, naître au milieu des pauvres, sur le fumier d'une étable? Les semailles, les moissons, les pressoirs, toutes ces choses familières dont parle l'Evangile, se trouvaient dans sa vie; le passage de Dieu les avait sanctifiées . . ." (2: 170).

NOTES

1. "Flaubert, ce n'est pas encore Mallarmé." Maurice Blanchot, *L'Entretien infini* (Paris: Gallimard) 488.
2. "Flaubert's Dis/Enclosures," *FF*, 13 (1988) 57–68. "Hallucination and Point of View in Flaubert's *La Tentation de saint Antoine*," *NCFS*, 17 (1988–89) 170–85.
4. Gustave Flaubert, *Oeuvres complètes*, ed. Bernard Masson (Paris: Seuil, 1967) 2: 227. Volume and page number references in parentheses are to this edition.
5. The vast majority of the scenarios and notes for play projects are only to be found in, Gustave Flaubert, *Oeuvres complètes*, 7 (Paris: Club de l'Honnête Homme, 1971).
6. A date for this play has yet to be established with certainty.
7. See Flaubert, *Oeuvres*, Club de l'Honnête Homme, 7: 12–35.
8. *Oeuvres complètes*, Club de l'Honnête Homme, 20.
9. Katherine Singer Kovacs, Le Rêve et la Vie: *A Theatrical Experiment by Gustave Flaubert*, HSRL 38 ([Cambridge]: Department of Romance Languages and Literatures of Harvard U., 1981) 66.
10. *Oeuvres complètes*, Club de l'Honnête Homme, 607, 631.
11. Stéphane Mallarmé, *Oeuvres complètes*, ed. Henri Mondor and G. Jean-Aubry (Paris: Gallimard, 1945) 1450. Parenthetical references are to this edition.
12. Walter A. Strauss, *Descent and Return: The Orphic Theme in Modern Literature* (Cambridge: Harvard University Press, 1971) 81–139. Leo Bersani, *The Death of Stéphane Mallarmé*, (Cambridge: Cambridge University Press, 1982).
13. See Jacques Scherer, *Le "Livre" de Mallarmé*, 2nd ed. (Paris: Gallimard, 1977).
14. Scherer 62–66.
15. For an interesting study of the use of space in "Un coup de dés," see Virginia A. La Charité, *The Dynamics of Space* (Lexington: French Forum Monographs, 1897).
16. Paul Valéry, ed. Jean Hytier (Paris: Gallimard, 1957) 1: 624.
17. The expression is Robert Greer Cohn's.

FROM CHATEAUBRIAND TO PROUST OR: ARE DIEGETIC IMAGES METONYMIC?*

Marcel Muller

This paper deals with the cultural and aesthetic dimensions of diegetic metaphors. More precisely I will be concerned with the cultural and aesthetic dimensions of the *use* of this figure on one hand, and with the cultural and intellectual dimensions of its *theory* on the other hand. The term "metaphor" will be taken in its broad meaning, encompassing the simile. As for the qualifier "diegetic," I can do no better than refer for its definition to the article by Gérard Genette which put it into circulation.[1] This text has enjoyed a wide readership, as a result of which the concept and the label "diegetic metaphor" have become very popular with commentators of Proust but also with critics in general. Beside defining the rhetorical category, Genette advances a number of theses, three of which will be discussed here:
1) That Proust displays a pronounced tendency to the use of diegetic images.
2) That this represents an innovation on his part.[2]
3) That the role of contiguity in *A la recherche* should be re-evaluated in view of the importance of diegetic images in the text of the novel. Contrary to the fictional Narrator's statements (behind whom we recognize Proust himself) and also to most readers' endorsement of these, metaphor is not, according to Genette, the only commanding trope in Proust's text. Diegetic metaphors deserve to be recognized as "metonymic metaphors," or even, with a reversal of the hierarchy between the noun and the adjective, "metaphoric metonymies."[3]

No one could find fault with the first of these theses. It is indeed

*This article is a result of the rewriting of two papers, read respectively at the Workshop on "History of Rhetoric" organized by Prof. Luisa Lopez-Grigera at the University of Michigan on November 14–17, 1985 and at the Colloquium in Nineteenth-Century French Studies held at the University of Nebraska in October, 1986.

the great merit of Genette's article to have put in the forefront of our reflection a kind of image which, to be sure, had been noticed by other readers, but never analyzed with so much attention. The importance of these tropes in *A la recherche du temps perdu* is great. It is not only a matter of numbers; what is to be underlined is the centrality of the device, witness the elaborate and enthusiastic description of Elstir's canvasses in *A l'ombre des jeunes filles en fleurs*, through which the novelist is telling us something about his own aesthetics. The ekphrasis[4] is relevant to the present discussion, because the essential point of these pages is the art with which the impressionist tends to erase the borderline between seascape and landscape, thus achieving what the Narrator revealingly calls "metaphors."

But if Proust makes a frequent and very personal use of diegetic images, it is historically incorrect to see these as an innovation on his part, for we find this device not only in a number of writers of his time, but before him, all the way back to the Romantics with whom in fact it originates. To start with Proust's contemporaries, Paul Claudel in the successive versions of *L'Annonce faite à Marie* modifies the text so that an increasing proportion of vehicles of images are chosen in the referential context of the objects denoted by the tenor. Georges Rodenbach, in *Bruges-la-Morte*, an underrated novel of 1892, builds his whole narrative on a system of analogies between the liturgical city from which the sea has withdrawn and the widower who worships the hair of his late wife like a relic.[5] We find many diegetic images in Zola: clouds will be said to have the color of rust if the novel is set in an industrial setting, for example.[6] I have collected scores of examples from the poetry of Tristan Corbière. Diegetic images are not absent from the prose of Paul Bourget and Hippolyte Taine. *Madame Bovary* is a rewarding mine, while—interestingly enough, and for reasons which I have been unable to determine—*Salammbô* is very disappointing in this regard. Baudelaire's work provides many interesting illustrations, the most memorable one being perhaps in both versions of "L'Invitation au voyage":

> Mon enfant, ma soeur
> Songe à la douceur
> D'aller là-bas vivre ensemble!
> Aimer à loisir,
> Aimer et mourir
> Au pays qui te ressemble!

and: "Il est une contrée qui te ressemble... Fleur incomparable, tulipe retrouvée, allégorique dahlia... ne serais-tu pas encadrée dans ton analogie...?"[7]

But just as Proust, in spite of all that differentiates him from Rodenbach, Corbière, Bourget, Taine, Flaubert and Baudelaire, in fact adopts and adapts a special kind of metaphor used widely before him by these and many other writers, so do they all owe a great deal to the technique of their predecessors. It is with these, and namely with the Romantics, that the diegetic image originates. Balzac, for example, likes to have his characters use images borrowed from their personal experience. In *Le Colonel Chabert* a former officer of Napoleon's armies compares a man's face with a cannon; another character, who is also a retired soldier, speaks of his modest dwelling as "un bivouac." The Balzacian Narrator, contrary to Hamon's remark quoted in note 7, is no less prone to describe an object or an individual in terms of what surrounds this object or individual: the coast of Norway is said to have the same profile as that of a huge fish, and the Norwegians are attached to their rocks in a way which makes them comparable to lichen.[8] As Gérard Genette, who quotes "Booz endormi" recognizes, Victor Hugo is a consummate master of the art of showing similarities between contiguous referents, as when he describes the ocean in *Les Châtiments* as an "hydre aux écailles vertes"[9] or when he compares an ogival window with a bishop's miter, as in these lines which highlight the diegetic character of the comparison:

> Pendant que l'enfant rit, une fleur à la main,
> Dans le vaste palais catholique romain
> Dont chaque ogive semble au soleil une mitre...

The same poem provides a particularly interesting example of the Elstirian confusion between two contiguous referents:

> Quand l'enfant, allongeant ses lèvres de carmin,
> Fronce, en la respirant, sa riante narine,
> La magnifique fleur, royale et purpurine,
> Cache plus qu'à demi ce visage charmant,
> Si bien que l'oeil hésite, et qu'on ne sait comment
> Distinguer de la fleur ce bel enfant qui joue,
> Et si l'on voit la rose ou si l'on voit la joue.[10]

All these examples will have shown how frequent the use of diegetic images is all through the century. But the animating spirit of this figure does not become obvious until we have moved further upstream and reached Chateaubriand. It is the use of "metonymic metaphors" in his prose which I shall now examine, not simply because he is a great (and in fact practically the first) practitioner of this figure, but on account of the fact that, of all the writers examined, he alone provides a kind of justification for the use of this trope. In the eyes of the author of *Le Génie du christianisme*, the world is not what it had been for Newton, and even less for Voltaire. One of the truths which Chateaubriand purports to demonstrate is that the order which governs the universe is not that of a machine, but of a living organism. Harmony reigns between things, and this harmony expresses itself by different means, one of which being the resemblance between contiguous referents. If we organize Chateaubriand's statements and illustrations so as to present them as would a theoretician of rhetoric, we can say that this contiguity may be observed in space, or in time, or both in space and time, or again in the symbolical space such as the one in which we situate the agent of an action, its object and the relationship between the two (that is: the cause, the effect and the causal connection). In Chateaubriand's view, there is a law relative to the cries of animals according to which each species utters a cry (or in the case of birds, a song) in consonance with its habitat (he claims to recognize affinities between the lion's roar and the desert, for example) or in consonance with the time at which one hears the animal:

> La nuit, tour à tour charmante ou sinistre, a le ros-signol et le hibou: l'un chante pour le zéphyr, les bocages, la lune, les amants; l'autre pour les vents, les vieilles forêts, les ténèbres et les morts.[11]

Or again, (the harmony at times assuming unexpected forms), if the animal is a predator, there is a consonance with the victim of its accustomed aggression: the hawk utters a cry similar to the rabbit's. The same felicitous integration can be observed in the realm of shapes and colors. The eggs of the birds look like what surrounds them:

> Dans les classes aquatiques et forestières, qui font leurs nids, les unes sur les mers, les autres dans la cime des arbres, l'oeuf est

communément d'un vert bleuâtre, et pour ainsi dire teint des éléments dont il est environné. (570)

If the shape and appearance of some animals seem bizarre, this, according to Chateaubriand, is so to the extent that we fail to take into account the fauna and the flora, the mountains, the sky which surround or dominate them, as is the case of the elephant whose trunk, ears, skin and feet perfectly fit in the context of the proboscidian's native India.[12] It is not a question of mimicry which protects a given species by making it invisible to the eyes of its enemies. "Dieu nous donna dans ce petit tableau une idée des grâces dont il a paré la nature;" this is how Chateaubriand expresses himself about the harmony between the slate-grey eggs of the bullfinch and the cope of its back, between the bird comparable to "a flower of purple and azure" and the "wet rose" hanging over its nest, the whole picture being reflected (in rather Proustian fashion) in the water of a pond (570). Everything revolves around the idea of a providential God intent upon providing sources of aesthetic pleasure, or again, around the idea of nature as opposed to culture, called "civilization" (an opposition sometimes confused with that of animal vs. man). A particularly instructive example is the passage in which Chateaubriand contrasts the way mankind and the animals print their respective histories, the former on perishable objects, the latter on life. The illustration he gives for human beings is that of the pharaohs: "Le temps a rongé les fastes des rois de Memphis sur leurs pyramides funèbres." The contrasted element will be a bird, but not one taken at random: the bird chosen is as close as possible to the tombs of the Egyptian sovereigns. It is the ibis which is entrusted with the task of representing nature: "Le temps . . . n'a pu effacer une seule lettre de l'histoire que l'ibis égyptien porte gravée sur la coquille de son oeuf" (570–71).

Let us note (although Chateaubriand does not make the point) that the kinship of this harmonious relationship with metaphor is obvious, if we remember how bizarre many images seem once they are taken out of their contexts, and on the contrary how unobtrusive they become, to the point of escaping our attention at times (whether they happen to be diegetic or not) if they are seen in what can be called their natural surroundings, that is, in the movement of the syntagma. This would lead us to state that an image is in fact always diegetic in a certain sense if it fits in its context; and conversely that the properly called diegetic image, far from being metonymized metaphor, can be seen as the image *par excellence*, since it aims at endowing the referential world with the same coherence that characterizes the metaphorical text (or tissue). Since I have surreptitiously shifted my attention from the world to discourse, that is from referents to signs, I may seize this occasion to remark that, just as Chateaubriand the traveler claims to notice resemblances of color, shape and sound between a creature of God and its natural milieu, Chateaubriand the creator of his own private universe will take pains to select the vehicles of his comparisons from the surroundings of the object or person to be described when he relies on metaphors. The *Mémoires d'outre-tombe* bristle with such images, as when the narrator sees a resemblance between Mme. de Récamier visiting Rome and a beautiful statue, but not a statue by any artist: the sculptor mentioned happens to be the Italian Canova, a contemporary of the model. Or again (and this will bring us back to Proust) when he writes:

> La vie que nous menions à Combourg, ma soeur et moi, augmentait l'exaltation de notre âge et de notre caractère. Notre principal désennui consistait à nous promener côte à côte dans le grand Mail, au printemps sur un tapis de primevères, en automne sur un lit de feuilles séchées, en hiver sur une nappe de neige que bordait la trace des oiseaux, des écureuils et des hermines. Jeunes comme les primevères, tristes comme les feuilles séchées, purs comme la neige nouvelle, il y avait harmonie entre nos récréations et nous.[13]

Combourg is not very far from Combray: the fact that the Narrator of *Le Temps retrouvé* invokes Chateaubriand's autobiography as one of his inspirations should be a sufficient reason for us to give his style a privileged place among the writers who point the way for Proust.

But not only does Chateaubriand use the trope; his remarks in *Le Génie du christianisme* also provide a kind of justification of the device. Now it is certainly not one applicable indifferently to all of the nineteenth-century writers I have mentioned. My claim concerning the validity of this quasi-theoretical justification is a more limited one: to take Proust's statements on nature seen by Elstir (whom he calls "le créateur" with a small "c") and Chateaubriand's teleological statements on nature willed by "le Créateur" (with upper case "c") as views globally applicable to the two writers at either end of the chronological sequence. Each sheds light not only on his own practice while speaking about a creator other than himself (respectively Elstir and God) but also on the practice of the other writer. Proust's use of the word "metaphor" in the pages on "Le Port de Carquethuit" is an unmistakable invitation to establish a relationship between the fictional painter's technique (or "vision") and Proust's own style. It is a short step from here to recognizing Chateaubriand's text on the harmony of nature as a statement on his own art of writing.

Let me ask at this point what the cultural dimensions (as distinct from aesthetic) of the use of the Elstirian image were. While it seemed legitimate to merge Chateaubriand's and Proust's respective pronouncements into a unified statement as long as we remained on the level of stylistics, prudence dictates that, as we shift from this level to an examination of the intellectual context which can help us understand why a writer would attach such importance to a depiction of the world as constituting an organic whole, we recognize the distance which separates a writer born before the French Revolution from one embarking on his masterpiece on the eve of the First World War. To start with Chateaubriand, the emergence of Elstirian images (which could also be called "ecological images")[14] seems easy to understand if we see them as the rhetorical translation of tenets drawn from the new science called "biology" as it developed toward the end of the eighteenth century, and associated with the names of Jussieu, Lamarck and Vicq d'Azir. Particularly relevant to our concern is Lamarck's *Philosophie zoologique*, which makes much of "les circonstances," that is the habitat of each species as a factor accounting for the organization and structure of the living being.[15] Proust may seem far afield from the conflict in intellectual history which sees the recognition of life as a specific phenomenon. Yet if we keep in mind the vigorous renewal of mechanistic thinking in the 1860s and Bergson's subsequent obsessions with the difference between "le mécanique" and "le vivant," we will find it less difficult to accept the idea of a convergence between the author of *La Recherche* and Chateaubriand on this very question. In spite of the scruples that guard against too facile a lumping together of both writers, it is possible to read Proust through Chateaubriand, not only as has been done at the Narrator's explicit suggestion apropos of involuntary memory, but also of his tropes, and to see these informed, as Chateaubriand's had been, by the belief in the superiority of life over the machine, and more precisely in the necessity of situating each living organism in its milieu. In the view proposed here, far in the background of Proust's rhetorical practice is the view of nature as it appears in the "episteme" defined by Foucault and admirably described the same year by Jacob in *La Logique du vivant*.[16] What follows from this is that the function of diegetic (or ecological, or circumstantial) metaphors is to palliate the relationship of contiguity (perceived as the expression of sheer contingence) by *adding* a recognition of the affinities between referents otherwise threatened by the cadaverization of mutually indifferent, not to say estranged, beings. "Adding" is the key word here, for the extreme structuralist interpretation (endorsed by post-structuralist commentators) is motivated by an irresistible urge to *subtract* from resemblance what can be ascribed to vicinity: metaphors are deemed guilty until proven otherwise ("cette image n'est pas innocente..."), more precisely, they are suspected of being disguised metonymies.

What started as an examination of Proust's alleged innovativeness has made us move backward in time as far as Chateaubriand, and broaden the discussion so as to involve the cultural postulates of diegetic metaphor. This in turn has led to a questioning of the view of this species of image as more aptly labelled "metonymy." By so doing, I have of course jumped ahead and already proposed an answer to the question concerning the third of the theses submitted for discussion. But if, as I hope, I have done justice to the writers concerned, I have not even tried to deal with the critics and theoreticians. What about their cultural postulates?

It does not seem that any attention was paid to the "ecological" image until Stephen Ullmann in 1955, followed by Michel Butor in 1964 and Gérard Genette in 1970, made observations about metaphors involving contiguous referents. It is only with the recent renewal of interest in the theory of tropes that these images have attracted the attention of the critics. But this involves an irony of history. For, when professors reopen the half-forgotten treatises of rhetoric, it is not to rediscover metaphor (which had never known an eclipse as a concept) but the tropes, and essentially metonymy. And this is accompanied by the emergence of contiguity as the criterion for a figure of speech which had been previously defined in a number of awkward ways: as based upon a "real" relationship for example, or on "correspondences." What circumstances account for the fact that a principle of mental association long known to psychologists (Aristotle being the first to mention it) had to wait until our century to play a role in tropology? This is very difficult to understand. What is easy to understand, though, if one takes a close look at theoretical texts written shortly after 1900 is why contiguity plays a paramount role in thinking about rhetoric at that time. As far as I can determine, it is in an article dated 1919 and entitled "Futurism" that Jakobson uses the word "contiguity" for the first time.[17] It may even be the very first occurrence of this word from the pen of any of the Russian Formalists. To us this term evokes the psychologist's triad, in which it is flanked by "resemblance" and "contrast." And with this in mind we find it most natural that anyone interested in tropes would classify them according to these categories. How do I go from "king" to "crown"? from "woman" to "flower"? from "ice" to "fire"? These questions, which are (or should be) part and parcel of the rhetorician's enquiry, quite obviously find their answers in the laws of mental association. One must naturally assume therefore that Jakobson's initial insight consisted in matching the oppositional terms resemblance / contiguity with metaphor / metonymy (and paradigm / syntax). And, to be sure, the neatness and apparently self-evident character of these pairings (combined with the fact that metaphor received thus a purely linguistic definition, even if metonymy was still defined in terms of relationship between the referents) were essential reasons for the success of Jakobsonian rhetoric in the sixties. However natural, obvious or self-evident as these pairings may seem, a consultation of the article of 1919 shows that it was not by such a direct route that the linguist arrived at these definitions. As a matter of fact, he was not at this time particularly interested in tropes, although contiguity was already in the forefront of his thinking: the words "metaphor" and "metonymy" do not occur once in this text (which will not prevent him from claiming later: "J'ai esquissé quelques remarques sur les tournures métonymiques ... en peinture" and giving this article as reference).[18] Is he at least conscious of the possibility of applying the triad "resemblance, contiguity, contrast" to something else? Not even. The model with which he operates is "contrastive contiguity *vs.* fusion of shapes" (which is not the same thing as "contiguity *vs.* resemblance"). These terms are applied to the relationship between constituent parts of a canvas. But even this way of presenting Jakobson's article is misleading, or at least it fails to tell the whole story. It would be more correct to say the he *reads* the concepts *out of* the canvasses. How is it that Jakobson "reads" contrastive contiguity so easily out of the paintings? Contiguity need not imply clash.

But of course, Jakobson is not interested in the art of painting in general: he is writing on the avant-garde, as the title of the article indicates. At this time, he is attuned to the work of artists such as Picasso and Braque, who treat space in a revolutionary way, and he will remain attuned to these as is related by Victor Erlich and Nicolas Ruwet.[19] Now contiguity in Picasso and Braque does not involve harmony (as is so often the case in paintings of the past) but clash. Contrast, not fusion, is the dominant impression produced by these compositions, and it is this aspect which Jakobson highlights with enthusiasm. The impact of Saussure's *Cours de linguistique générale* (with its emphasis on difference as the constitutional character of the linguistic sign) would not have been as great had it not been for Jakobson's fascination with the successors of Cézanne.[20] The association between contiguity and contrast will accompany him all his life. It is also visible even today in the writings of many other people dealing with the art of that period.[21]

The return to rhetoric with its attendant rediscovery of the neglected terms and concepts of metonymy, synecdoche, antonomasia, litotes, hyperbole, irony and periphrasis (but first and foremost metonymy) and the attempt to give strict linguistic definitions of trope will occur later in a climate previously defined by the experiments of the analytical cubists or Kandinksy and the practitioners of collage. This fact is very important for the development of structuralism and the application of structuralist principles to Proust. Nothing could be more remote from Elstir ("On ne savait pas où finissait la terre, où commençait la mer") and nothing could more different either from nature as described in *Philosophie zoologique* than Jakobson's predilection for works of art in which shapes hardly touch each other. The following statement on the relationship between head and torso is particularly eloquent: "Ce lien nécessaire [between color and shape as defined by the psychologist Stumpf and recognized by cubists and futurists] s'oppose au lien empirique entre deux parties qui n'est pas de nature obligatoire: ainsi pour la tête et le tronc. On peut s'imaginer de telles parties séparément."[22] This example of the head severed from the trunk (a separation which goes without saying for Jakobson, but would have seemed inconceivable for Lamarck) epitomizes a whole range of esthetic, linguistic and critical positions in which Saussurian linguistics and the work of Cubo-Futurists will interact in such a way as to give metonymy its well-known definition, but also as to put the emphasis on this trope. And what will follow in the history of criticism will owe a great deal to the fact that the author of the "Closing statements" was an admirer and a contemporary of the avant-garde.

As French critics pick up the lead of the Russian Formalists in the sixties and accept as their Bible Jakobson's propositions on the coupling of the two main tropes with paradigm and syntagma respectively, they will remain faithful to the Picasso-connection.[23] But a new element comes into play which will reinforce the effect exerted upon rhetoric by the fascination with the avant-garde. This element is a very strong hostility toward the alleged idealism of metaphor on the part of intellectuals very much influenced by Marxism. This mistrust of analogy will entail as a consequence an even greater attention to metonymy than had been the case in the criticism of the Russians. Posing the equation: metonymy = contiguity = materialism = antibourgeois values, the French structuralists will claim to recognize as metonymic (or at least as involving a metonymic component) tropes which no one before them would have seen as other but metaphoric. A kind of imperialism, or if one prefers, Irredentism of metonymy develops ranging from the stimulating essay in *Poétique* to less original studies in which almost any kind of relationship will be labelled "metonymic" (including the relationship between words in a text, whether that relationship is that of neighboring words, or, on the contrary, words separated by a great distance). Contiguity thus becomes what Genette himself called somewhere "a password." The disciples of structuralists and even more so the epigones of the disciples will think that identifying some form, however farfetched, of metonymic relationship is to give oneself a certificate of critical awareness.

I have alluded above to an irony of history. There is none if indeed diegetic metaphor is a form of metonymy. There is irony on the other hand if diegetic metaphor must be defined as promoting a figure based upon sheer contiguity to the level of analogical trope. The irony, if there is one, takes the acute form of a coincidence, amusing like any coincidence (although not necessarily significant) and worth being pointed out even if the definition which I propose of diegetic metaphor is questionable. The very same year, the very same summer which sees the publication of Jakobson's article in *Iskusstvo* is also the year and the summer of the publication of *A l'ombre des jeunes filles en fleurs*. From June 23, 1919 (when Proust's novel reaches the bookstores) to August 2, 1919 (date of the issue of the Russian journal) barely five weeks elapsed. Now it happens that it is in the *Jeunes filles en fleurs* that the novelist makes the most ostentatious use of diegetic images, giving at the same time the apotheosis of the device, its swan song and its first developed theory since Chateaubriand. It is in these pages that the Narrator describes "Le Port de Carquethuit" as characterized by the disappearance of the borderline between the sea and the land, a fact for which Proust uses the word "metaphor." It is intriguing to note that, at both ends of Europe, two men who do not know about each other's concerns are similarly impelled to think about the relationships of forms on canvas in tropological terms (or at least, in the case of Jakobson, in terms which will soon lead him to original conceptions in tropology.) But what unites Jakobson and Proust also separates them. If the Russian linguist has the new creators of the beginning of the century in mind, Marcel Proust's gods are certainly not Picasso, Braque or Kandinsky. Their names are Monet, Whistler or Turner (who is a contemporary of Chateaubriand). The convergence between Proust and Jakobson (which is in fact a movement toward divergence) in itself proves nothing. It has simply given me a pretext to juxtapose the novelist's ekphrasis and the theoretician's statement, and thus highlight the contrast between two ways of looking at the same figure of speech. It would be presumptuous on my part to call one of these ways simply wrong and the other (mine) right. I only hope to have shown that there is room for argument about some propositions advanced in "Métonymie ou naissance du récit" and the theoretical postulates of that article, and that such a discussion might lead to a reexamination of the all-encompassing use of the label "metonymy."

NOTES

1. "Métonymie chez Proust ou la naissance du Récit," *Poétique*, n. 2 (1970) 156–173, resumed in *Figures III* (Paris: Seuil, 1972) 41–63. A metaphor is said to be diegetic if its vehicle belongs to the spatio-temporal continuum of its tenor, more exactly if the respective referents of the vehicle and the tenor are situated in relative proximity to each other. Genette refers to observations made by previous commentators of Proust, mainly Stephen Ullmann in *Style in the French Novel* (Cambridge University Press, 1957). He does not mention Michel Butor, *Les Oeuvres d'art imagiares chez Proust* (London: University of London, Athlone Press, 1964),

who focuses much more neatly than Ullmann on the type of comparison which interests us here.

2. In fact Genette is less affirmative on this point than I make him sound to be. The innovative character of Proust's rhetorical practice is not emphasized in his text; one could even claim that whatever implicit pronouncement to that effect one can ascribe to him is undermined by references to Poe (159), Racine (Brûlé de plus de feux que je n'en allumai"), Saint-Amant and Hugo with the famous "faucille d'or dans le champ des étoiles" of "Booz endormi" (161, n. 16). One could further adduce an oral statement made by Genette to the effect that Proust "comme les écrivains classiques" did not want to "prendre ses images de trop loin." But he is definitely ambivalent on this point, for the very same remark was prefaced by "ce qui est nouveau chez Proust." (Colloquium held at New York University on January 20, 1984). Be that as it may, "Métonymie ou naissance du récit" has certainly been interpreted as it is presented here.

3. "[On] est tout naturellement conduit; comme il l'a été lui-même, à en surestimer l'action [namely: of the metaphoric relationship, based upon analogy] au détriment d'autres relations sémantiques" (*Poétique* 157).

4. I take this term in the meaning in which it is used in the article "Ut pictura poesis" of Philip Wiener's invaluable *Dictionary of the History of Ideas*: "rhetorical process by which an object already formed in one medium becomes an object in another medium (description of a poet of a painting or conversely use by a painter of the subject of a poem). The term is absent from Henri Morier's *Dictionnaire de Poétique et de Rhétorique* (Paris: Presses Universitaires de France, 2nd. ed, 1975), while Heinrich Lausberg's *Handbuch der literarischen Rhetorik. Eine Grundlegung der Literaturwissenschaft* (Munich: Max Hueber, 1973) knows it only as meaning "detaillierte Beschreibung einer Person oder eines Gegenstandes."

5. *Bruges-la-Morte* (Paris: Flammarion, n.d.). This title was republished in 1977 by the Editions Jacques Antoine in Brussels.

6. See Josette Féral, "La sémiotique des couleurs dans *Germinal*," *Cahiers naturalistes*, 49 (1975) 136–48.

7. Baudelaire, *Oeuvres complètes*. Claude Pichois, ed. (Paris: Gallimard, 1975) 1: 53–54 and 301–303. For a subtle commentary of these images, see Barbara Johnson, "Poetry and its double: Two 'Invitations au voyage'" in *The Critical Difference. Essays on the Contemporary Rhetoric of Reading* (Baltimore and London: Johns Hopkins University Press, 1980) 31. It is unclear from her commentary if she considers this as being original with Baudelaire. Her remarks are interesting to the extent that the device is indeed original, however references are made to "a conception of metaphor which was in fact an artistic commonplace in Baudelaire's day" and she refers to Swedenborg, Staël, Schelling and the abbé Constant. In the same spirit,

Philippe Hamon commented as follows on a sentence by Flaubert: "le fleuve arrondissait sa courbe au pied des collines vertes, et les îles, de forme oblongue, semblaient sur l'eau de grands poissons noirs arrêtés." *Madame Bovary* (Paris: Le Livre de Poche, 1961) 312. "Après 'les îles semblaient' on s'attend à n'importe quoi, et que lit-on? '. . . comme des poissons': nous retombons du métaphorique dans la contiguïté." (Lecture delivered in Ann Arbor on November 6, 1985). Like Genette, Hamon construes diegetic images as metaphors undermined by contiguity, but this is for him characteristic of realist discourse, as distinct from Balzac's "écriture." The example given by Hamon is that of the "accroc" in Mme. Vauquer's gown, which is said by the narrator to imply and announce what surrounds her in space and time. I fail to see why this involves contiguity any less than the comparison between the islands and fish.

8. Here are the quotes and their references: "la bouche de Boutin se fendit comme un mortier qu'on crève" (II: 105); "nous ne brillons pas ici par le luxe. C'est un bivouac tempéré par l' amitié" (II: 1114). "Ne dirait-on pas que la Nature s'est plu à dessiner par d'ineffaçables hiéroglyphes le symbole de la vie norwégienne, en donnant à ces côtes la configuration des arêtes d'un immense poisson? Car la pêche forme le principal commerce et fournit presque toute la nourriture de quelques hommes attachés comme une touffe de lichen à ces arides rochers" (*Seraphita*, X: 458). Here are a few other examples: "Je suis usé comme un canon de rebut" (II: 1139). "Il y eut entre la comtesse Ferraud et le colonel Chabert un combat de générosité dont le soldat sortit vainqeur" (II: 1139). In *Louis Lambert*, Mlle de Villenoix, who is Jewish, is said to have a skin with "la blancheur mate des robes du lévite" (X: 422). In *Séraphita*, "deux eiders volant du même vol, le son dans l'écho, la pensée dans la parole, sont peut-être des images imparfaites de cette union" [namely of the Swedish count Séraphitus and his wife] (X: 514). All references are to *La Comédie humaine*. Marcel Bouteron ed. (Paris: Gallimard, 1962–1964).

9. "Oh! je sais qu'ils feront des mensonges sans nombre", *Les Châtiments*, Livre I, pièce XI, *Poésie* (Paris: Le Seuil, Coll. L'Intégrale, 1972) 1: 509.

10. "La rose de l'infante," *La Légende des siècles* 2: 102–103. This tendency manifests itself very early in Hugo's work, for example in *Les Orientales*, where the desire to remain within the range defined by the title of the collection often dictates the choice of the metaphorical vehicle. In "Le château-fort" the flanks of a rock are said to shine "comme une armure" and the fort which dominates the rock is "roulé comme un turban autour de son front noir" (XIV 1: 232). In "Les adieux de l'hôtesse arabe," seen from a distance, the black hill seems to be a camel's back. The concern for local color plays an obvious role in this.

11. *Essai sur les révolutions. Génie du christianisme.* Maurice Regard, ed. (Paris: Gallimard, 1978) 568. References to this title will henceforth be given in the text.

12. It is interesting to note that the paragraph which contains the description of the

elephant opens with a classical metonymy ("plume" for "writer"), which is a paradox if one endorses the thesis developed in this article. However this should not disconcert us for when Chateaubriand is writing, digital tropes are not yet downgraded and metaphors have not yet ousted metonymies. At this stage, their status is not as clearly defined as will be the case later, in Flaubert for example, where non-metaphorical tropes are used but negatively connoted, as when the old servant is called "un demi-siècle de servitude" (*Madame Bovary* 184) or the kind of mistresses that Rodolphe has known are designated by the phrase "lèvres libertines ou vénales" (231).

Let us note in passing that the harmony between contiguous referents can be translated in terms other than rhetorical ones, for example in Part II, Book III ch. vii of *Le Génie du christianisme*, where Chateaubriand quotes Bernardin de Saint-Pierre: "Quand viendrez-vous nous voir? lui [to Virginie] disaient quelques amies du voisinage.—Aux cannes de sucre, répondait Virginie.—Votre visite nous sera encore plus douce et plus agréable, reprenaient ces jeunes filles" (704). The "Tu me demandes pourquoi tu m'aimes. Mais tout ce qui a été élevé ensemble s'aime" of Bernardin de Saint-Pierre (equally quoted by Chateaubriand [705]) announces the "Qui se ressemble s'assemble," which, according to Genette, summarizes the spirit of diegetic metaphors (159). The fact that these quotes come from Bernardin de Saint-Pierre should make us recognize in him the real inventor of the diegetic image. Unless of course, still guided by the *Génie du christianisme*, we remember Theocritus and conclude that diegetic metaphor has always already been in existence: "Charmante Galatée, pourquoi repousser les soins d'un amant, toi dont le visage est blanc comme le lait pressé dans mes corbeilles de jonc . . . ?" (*Idyl*, XI, 1. 19 and ss. reproduced p. 701 of Chateaubriand).

13. *Mémoires d'Outre-Tombe* (Paris: Le Livre de Poche, 1973), 1: 129 (in "Premier souffle de la Muse").

14. It is not a coincidence if the same century produced this neologism (the word was proposed by Haeckel) and the widespread use of the trope. For a view of ecology as applied to style, see Annette Smith, *Gobineau et l'histoire naturelle* (Geneva: Droz, 1984), chapter VII.

15. Jean-Baptiste de Lamarck, *Philosophie zoologique ou Exposition des considérations relatives à l'histoire naturelle des animaux*. Nouvelle edition (Paris: Ballière, 1830). I must express my gratitude to Michel Serres, who pointed out the interest of this text for my research.

16. Michel Foucault, *Les Mots et les Choses. Une archéologie des sciences humaines* (Paris: Gallimard, 1966) and François Jacob, *La Logique du vivant. Une histoire de l'hérédité* (Paris: Gallimard, 1970).

17. Roman Jakobson, *Questions de poétique* (Paris: Editions du Seuil, Collection "Poétique", 1973) 25–30. Translated out of the Russian "Futurizm," *Iskusstvo*, 7 (August 2, 1919).

18. *Essais de linguistique générale.* Traduits de l'anglais et préfacés par Nicolas Ruwet (Paris: Editions de Minuit, 1963) 63 n. 1.
19. Nicolas Ruwet, Preface to his translation of Jakobson, *Essais de linguistique générale* 7 and 8. He refers to the "Portrait" of the Russian linguist published by Victor Erlich in *Orbis. Bulletin international de documentation linguistique*, VII, 1 (Louvain, 1958) and quotes a statement by Braque endorsed by Jakobson in his *Selected Writings*: "Je ne crois pas aux choses, mais aux relations entre les choses."
20. While the model provided by music goes a long way toward explaining the recognition of the autotelic character of the work of art (see Tzvetan Todorov, "Roman Jakobson poéticien," *Poétique* 7 [1971] 276 and John Neubauer, *The Emancipation of Music from Language. Departure from Mimesis in Eighteenth Century Aesthetics* [New Haven and London: Yale University Press, 1986]), it could be argued that the revolution which occurred in the plastic arts between 1880 and 1907 played an equally determinant role. As for the influence of philosophers, while Kant's name must inevitably be pronounced in this context, one should not forget that of Husserl (read with great interest by the young Jakobson) and go so far as to point out that behind the phenomenologist stands a thinker who happens to be a great inspiration of Paul Valéry. The denunciation of mimetic art in Valéry's poetics finds its equivalent and its precedent in the cogito's *Einklammerung*. In this reading the Cartesian *epoche* would be the very first gesture leading to the triumph of both Russian and French formalism.
21. Witness the use of "juxtaposed" as a synonym of "contrasted with" in Christina Lodder, *Russian Constructivism* (London and New Haven: Yale University Press, 1983). The *Times Literary Supplement*'s reviewer of the book even complains about this tacit equation (January 13, 1984) 41.
22. "Futurisme" (26). See also "décomposé" (25), "désunir," "on découpe librement l'objet," "on découpe consciemment la nature" (26). In the same spirit, Boris Eichenbaum in 1923 will contrast Akhmatova's poetry and the Symbolists' in the following terms: "Les symbolistes mettent l'accent précisément sur la métaphore ... comme une manière de rapprocher des séries sémantiques éloignées. Akhmatova rejette le principe de l'extension, qui repose sur la puissance associative du mot. Les mots ne se fondent pas les uns dans les autres mais se touchent, pareils aux morceaux d'une mosaïque.... A la place des métaphores apparaissent dans toute leur variété, les nuances littérales des mots, fondées sur des périphrases et des métonymies." (Quotes and translated by Tzvetan Todorov, "Roman Jakobson poéticien" 280).
23. The eponymic quality of this painter will still be alive when Genette publishes "Discours du récit," for this study invokes the chronological parallelism between the cubist's experiments after 1907 and those of Marcel Proust as he starts writing his masterpiece. See *Figures* III, 223, n.3.

PROUST: *MISE EN QUESTION* OF THE MYTH OF ORPHEUS

Germaine Brée

"For a long time I used to go to bed early." By its awkwardness, the opening sentence of Proust's book, the first encountered by the anglophone reader, blunts the impact of the French: "For many years, I went to bed early." Although it sacrifices the "longtemps", that opening clearly posits a period now closed. The "I" so introduced is thus from the start positioned outside the context of those years. The reader, even the most sophisticated "archi-reader," will never know, even after journeying through the 3000 pages of the book where that initial-initiating "I" is situated in regard to the narrative which it originates yet within which it does not seem to be placed.

After the first pages—recollections of the sleeping-waking rhythms of the persona within that enclosure (i.e., the "overture" to the book), the narrative seems to be taken in charge by that persona himself. It is situated within a historical time-span between the mid-nineteenth century and the years following World War I, though not entirely chronologically. The narrative often breaks away from the frame, turning back on itself to some past time which may or may not coincide with the persona's life-time; or it introduces tantalizing new versions of stories previously told. At other times it makes a jump into a future which could be known only to the "I" who for so long "went to bed early;" but who inversely at the end of the tale presumably works all night and sleeps only during the day. It may too carry the "I" and with it the characters that "I" mentions beyond the boundaries of those specific printed pages. For instance, we read of Albertine that "her continued society was painful to me in another way which I cannot explain in this narrative."

It took some years of intense readings of Proust's book and a mind as subtle as the late Paul de Man's before this "retrospective-prospective" movement of *A la recherche du temps perdu* became clear, complicating the reader's sense of the text itself, and of the unsettling literary patterns the shifting focus of the "I" or "I's" inject into the flow of the text. Here the introduction by the translation of a line from a familiar Shakespeare sonnet further confused the issue, "Remembrance of Things Past": "When to the sessions of sweet silent thought I summon up remembrance of things past".

Proust had given no such orientation to the reader's approach to the text. *In Search of Time Lost*, the literal and easy translation of his title must have seemed disconcerting to his translator, Scott-Moncrieff, a more than usually sophisticated man of letters though he was. The two titles could hardly be more antithetical. "Remembrance" associated with "sweet silent thought" suggests the peace of recollection in tranquil distraction, a mood that has little in common with the anxiety of a "quest," a search for something "lost." From the start, nonetheless, Proust had signalled to the reader that there would be an outcome: *Le Temps retrouvé (Time Regained)*;[1] this the translation optimistically suggests. But the famous last lines of *Le Temps retrouvé* are hardly reassuring:

> I understood now why it was that the duc de Guermantes... when he rose to his feet and tried to stand upon them, swayed backwards and forwards upon legs as tottery as those of some old archbishop to whose support there rushes a mob of sturdy young seminarists and had advanced with difficulty trembling like a leaf, upon the almost unmanageable summit of his 83 years, as though men spend their lives perched upon living stilts which never cease to grow until sometimes they become taller than church steeples, making it in the end both difficult and perilous for them to walk and raising them to an eminence from which suddenly they fall. And I was terrified by the thought that the stilts beneath my own feet might already have reached that height.

The image is curiously burlesque, not at all comfortable nor grandiose: a brief eminence perhaps, then a quick awkward downfall. Is Proust throwing his characters away to the wolves as they finally confront the Time-Death conditioning of human life? The qualifier "retrouvé" might then simply point to the re-absorption in time of all human individuals in the uninterrupted flow of the species.

If I have chosen to begin with a brief and elementary excursion into semiotics it is merely to recall how easily Proust's text invites interpretation and eludes it. Even now, two teams of scholars are working on critical editions of the work, complete with innumerable variants, yielding to the reader a text dismembered. This in a sense has put into new relief an overlooked theme within the narrative: the always "still-to-be-written" book vaguely announced in Combray, still not written at the end though projected, whose emergence may be related to the "spectral figure" of the inaugural "I." In her excellent essay on Proust, *Thresholds*, Gerda Blumenthal underscores Proust's use of the Orphic legend as a structuring figure, an affinity touched upon by Walter Strauss in his *Descent and Return: The Orphic Theme in Modern Literature*. In the last ten years or so literary scholars, historians, anthropologists have studied the life of the Orphic legend in both classical and modern culture with its origins and its metamorphoses through the centuries.[2] Except for Blumenthal, they do not refer specifically to *A la recherche du temps perdu*. But, for instance, Elizabeth Sewall's *The Orphic Voice* among others like Walter Strauss's *Descent and Return*, traces the series of "metamorphoses", the transmutations of the Orphic myth over the last one hundred and fifty years of Western literature. There is a certain consensus as to the source of the myth's appeal to the modern psyche. I quote Elizabeth Sewall here. The pervasive desire "to conquer a metaphysical dualism in the name of Orpheus, reconciliator of opposites, and harmonizer of man and nature, poetry and the cosmos." This function was assigned to "poetry" in a world increasingly fragmented, and the Orphic legend in Sewall's view furnished design, a form, themes and figurations which could be detached from "poetry" understood as verse. A vast prose edifice like *A la recherche du temps perdu* could then be included as part of the vast corpus of "Orphic" inspired works.

Three main inter-related aspects of the Orphic myth centering on Orpheus himself, let me briefly recall, dominate the modern interpretations of the myth: Orpheus the singer, whose magic song seduces the wildest forces of nature and the gods and, overcoming separateness, fuses them into a harmonious whole, transcending separation and change. More appealing to the human imagination, Orpheus, the ill-starred lover-singer-hero who having lost his beloved wife Eurydice through no fault of his own undertakes the grim journey to the underworld and by his singing wins the right to bring her back to light on condition he should not look back at her until she has crossed the threshold separating the dead from the living, who then looks back and loses her again. Out of this grief comes the third Orpheus, withdrawing to Thrace where he is the "revealer of mysteries," founder of an esoteric cult to whom an aggregate of fragmentary writings, *The Orphic Hymns* are attributed. He is torn to pieces by the Maenads and his severed head floats down-river to Lesbos chanting the name "Eurydice." This Orpheus, Walter Strauss has noted, is a kind of quintessential Orpheus, "the quester after the unattainable," a goal which by definition he cannot reach; and whose "only duty" Mallarmé asserts, is to seek the "Orphic explanation of the world." How then does Proust's book relate to these Orphic themes?

There is no doubt at all in my mind that *A la recherche* can indeed be seen as an Orphic quest, but a quest in which the three aspects of the figure fail to harmonize. In fact they are revealed as essentially conflictual, frustrating the searcher's aspiration to its totality and unity of vision he has sought. When he was a child, the narrator tells us, reading the books of Bergotte, he was enchanted by the "voice" from within the text which he ascribes to a "gentle singer," releasing "a hidden stream of harmony," like the song of a "harp arising from an unknown world." This suggests the simple, traditional Orphic model he aspires to emulate. But the end of the quest, when finally the nature of the book to be written is glimpsed, yields something quite different: "At every moment the metaphor uppermost in my mind changed as I began to represent to myself more clearly and in a more material shape the task upon which I was about to embark." The metaphor chosen was Françoise's dressmaking: "I should construct my book like a dress," made of "pieces sewn together;" or again her famous "boeuf à la mode": "I should be making my book in the same way that Françoise made (her) boeuf à la mode. . . ."

It would be tedious to summarize here the stages of what has been diversely described as the Proustian writer's "long night's journey into day" and as his "long day's journey into night," a neat reversal that stresses the text's ambiguities. But, as Kerenyi writes, "Orpheus was connected with darkness, both in his journey to the underworld and also later when he communicates his initiatings at night" (282). After the opening sentence of *A la recherche*, the narrative begins in a restricted space, a room—a bed—a recumbent figure—darkness. It is that darkness which is animated, as the bed becomes ship or flying carpet. The darkness is broken by a fitful play of light: outer lights—a candle, a ray of light under the door—and a vacillating inner light. The sleeper discerns brief shadowy scenes within circumscribed disconnected, discontinuous stage-sets. They are always centered on a figure, which is designated as "I" but the different "I's" remain cut off from each other and are all without knowledge of the present identity of the sleeper. All the "thresholds" as Blumenthal notes can open out into episodes of the sleeper's past. The initial plunge into darkness thus leads to brief "returns" to various past fragments of a life. The first "threshold" to which the narrative returns is, of course, the world of Combray reached by the two separate routes—the dark route of night, of loss and separation; and the brilliant sunlight of the Easter vacation. As Jean Ricardou noted, this resurgence occurs in a dreary winter's afternoon in Paris, telescoping two moments remote from each other in space and time, welding them one to another so that space and time are volatilized. As Ricardou points out, the account of the experience introduces rather disquieting gaps in the attentive reader's perceived notions of reality.[3] Human beings do not occupy two spaces remote in time and place simultaneously. This Proustian strategy challenges the accepted "representational order" of the narrative and the integrity of the "I" who may at any moment "reclaim" an unaccountable "other" who replaces him. It is with these unaccountable "I's" that the reader sets out on the long trek which three thousand pages later comes to a halt with the curious image of human beings teetering on stilts. Within the narrative, the short vertical plunges of the first pages are followed by ever longer horizontal developments, separated by gaps. They then combine and lead to the fiction writer's plan for his future work. At one moment the "I" withdraws from society for several years—a kind of descent—then returns, and in a brief "ascent" simultaneously grasps the design of his book-to-be and of his own identity as the "bearer of a book," itself the bearer of a world "entirely to be redesigned"—a truly Mallarméan Orphic project. But he now confronts his imminent death: the plaint of "Eurydice twice lost" echoes in our minds. We are left with a technical puzzle. Whether as "pretext" or not, Proust wrote a mighty narrative which in the interest of my theme I have described in Orphic terms: "descent into darkness," "ascent" to light and revelation. The pattern is general enough to be all-encompassing.

But are there signs within the text of a more specific *mise en question* of the Orphic myth? Orpheus was after all a familiar denizen of the French literary world at the turn of the century, popular among small coteries of poets who made the myth of Orpheus a programmatic theme presiding over movements such as "Orphicism" in painting and "Orphism" in poetry. These do not seem to have inspired Proust in the least; he was heir to an older trend: the Hellenism discovered by the Parisian poets in the mid-nineteenth century. A casual glance at the name index in the third volume of the Pléiade edition of *La recherche* reveals an astounding wealth of reference to Greek and Roman antiquity: gods, demi-gods, heroes of mythology, writers, philosophers, sculptors, historical characters mingle freely with the inhabitants of the book where "real" and "fictional" characters also mix. But the Greeks and Romans are not alone. Names and figures come thronging in from everywhere: from the Arabian nights, the Bible, medieval and modern art, literature, history. Proust's classical figures, pervasive though they be, constitute one strand only in a complex cultural whole upon which he draws freely, seemingly confident his readers will not be dismayed.

Like other displays of learning or taste, classical allusions in Proust's novel are often used for the light they throw on a speaker's personality most often for comic effect; for example, Dr. Cottard's "What do I know? Socrates said," or "After all my dear fellow, life, as Anaxagoras has said, is a journey." More or less dormant, the "classics" live on in the fabric of language of an "elite" educated in a class society, and familiar with the Offenbach Olympians.

But more revealing patterns lurk beneath the surface of Proust's text. The descriptions of nature in *La Recherche* are intensely animated, though not Romantic. Each flower—lilac, poppy, hawthorn—each wave in the sea lives its own individual life, as nymph, fairy, peri, Nereide, mysterious, charming, familiar, beautiful especially in the child's eyes. A tree can be a benevolent young giant, a flowering bush is a nymph, while a place in the garden is the mysterious abode of the sun and his team of horses.

This transformation is stylistic and the metamorphosing passages from one realm to another are constant: the hawthorns will turn into young girls; and the young girls into hawthorn bushes in a glow of light and color and happiness that is sensed as music. These playful metamorphoses lead to something deeper. Borrowing from Leconte de Lisle's translation of fragments of the Orphic hymns, Proust introduces into his text almost verbatim a rhapsody on perfume—poppy, myrtle, sandal-wood and with it a poetic-erudite development on erotic desire: "Such desires are only the desire of a certain being; vague as perfumes, as styrax was the desire of Prothyriaia; aromats, the desire of Hera, manna, the desire of Nike."

But, the text notes, the perfumes sung by the Orphic hymns are far less numerous than the divinities they cherish. The suggestion is simple: there are many more beings than there are forms of desire. The parallel set up between evanescent enveloping perfumes and erotic desire coupled with the incantatory alignment of fabulous names gives a mysterious aura to the theme of desire itself, leading to the Orphic poetic process of destroying demarcations and so fusing nature and persons, objects and feelings. In this context, the fragrance of a cup of tea is the desire of Combray, and that of the hawthorns the desire of Gilberte. Desire is the force that gives impetus to a mythological creation, born of a feeling of harmony, thence akin to music. At one point the text evokes the murmur of the Oceanides bringing peace to Prometheus bound to his rock and compares them to those sensations wafted from outside which awaken in him a feeling of wholeness of participating in a total mysterious life. But this Orphic theme leads to no further truth, no "intimations of immortality." Nature follows its own strict path providing what Blumenthal calls the "Book of hours," the Orphic sundial, and the passing moments of mythic awareness, as when the painter Elstir regally effaces in his painting the elemental division of land and sea thereby inscribing on the canvas not reality but his own invisible aspiration.

In counterpoint, as it were, the recurrent patterns of human love and loss are clearly linked to the archetypal Orpheus-Eurydice patterns. The paradigm is established at the outset of *La Recherche* when Odette's absence from the Verdurin salon triggers Swann's wild search in the darkened Champs Elysées among the "phantoms" there. This well-known episode activates the structures of the myth: "Anxiously he brushed past those dim forms as though among the phantoms of the dead, in the realms of darkness, he had been searching for a lost Eurydice." At first the allusion seems hardly more than a metaphor; but the themes of loss, pursuit in darkness, the attempt to recapture the beloved, followed by a final and total loss sets a pattern that haunts the many "romances" in the book. The two volumes—*Captive* and *Fugitive*—developing the last cycle of the narrative within the total cycle before the young man's withdrawal to his equivalent of Thrace, have been thoroughly and persuasively explored by Gerda Blumenthal within the optic of the myth. But the recurrent motif of the long drawn-out last Eurydice cycle of *Prisoner* and *Captive* lead to no greater wisdom, only to the recognition of the impossibility of imposing any fixed form on the fleeting quotidian reality of human living. The narrator's utopian pursuit of harmony ends here too, in frustration. Swann at least had once glimpsed the possibility of an initiation to the world of the third Orpheus, the "revealer of mysteries." This occurs in the salon of Madame de Sainte-Euverte in the "magic presence" of the "petite phrase" which transforms the mundane concert into an initiatory rite of which the two performers are the "hierophants." This often discussed scene is, I think, the only one in which the force of an Orphic desire for an Orphic, harmonized world seems for an instant to have been fulfilled.

Proust's book, I think, incorporates the Orphic myth but questions and rejects current interpretations of the myth in terms of art, of the artist's function and the transcendental value of works of art. "Combray" indeed offers to the reader a world "redesigned" but only temporarily, a world whose dark underlying menace is at work even as it is in the making. At the end of the book, the "real" Combray has been destroyed; the "beautiful" or loved people it harbored are dead or on the threshold of death. The Orphic model has been questioned. One of the least reputable characters in the novel, a liar and a cheat, is the singer Morel whose uniform as a member of his regimental band, bears an emblematic lyre on his lapels. I should not wish to overinterpret the Proustian text but I think a statement has been made: the "singer" is not necessarily a sacred figure. So much for one of the myths dear to the nineteenth century.

In the end there remains that inaugural "I", the consciousness perhaps that saved Proust from confusing the worlds of his imaginings and his fantastic technical ability with the structures of reality and kept his book poised on the threshold between the chaos of experience and the urge to "impose" upon it some form of rhetorical unity. The last vision of "the book always as yet unwritten" of which the written book is one avatar brings a singularly contemporary view. The passage from the idea of a work of art as a harmonious, complete whole to the idea of a book made up of fragments always "to be continued" is perhaps one of the factors that have made *La Recherche* "Orphic", perhaps in another way, as a work that has awakened its readers' awareness to certain new vistas in their sense of the complex evolving reality of which they along with everything else, are but a small part and the artist's work, like that of Françoise, is a tentative patterning, and in no way an "explanation" of the world.

NOTES

1. It is not my intention to criticize the translation: merely to point to the obvious fact that any translation affects one's reading of the text.
2. Studies of the myth and its interpretations are too numerous to list. They are sometimes controversial. Among others, besides those mentioned in this essay, see Walter Burkett *The Heroes of the Greeks* translated by John Raffan (Cambridge: Harvard University Press, 1985). Karl Kerenyi *The Heroes of the Greeks*. (1951); Kushner Eva, *Le Mythe d' Orphée* (Paris: Nizet, 1961).3. Jean Ricardou *Pour une théorie du nouveau roman* (Paris: Seuil, 1971).

VALÉRY'S DEGAS AND RILKE'S CÉZANNE

Ursula Franklin

The Austro-German poet's veneration for Valéry and the fact that, years before his decisive encounter with the "Cimetière marin" in 1921, France had become "the capital influence in Rilke's artistic evolution,"[1] have become commonplaces of Franco-German comparative literature.[2] Like most of their fellow poets, both Valéry and Rilke repeatedly expressed their interest in painters.[3] Thus Valéry wrote on Degas, Manet, Morisot, Renoir, Corot, Daumier and Veronese;[4] and he wrote most extensively on Leonardo da Vinci who, even more than Degas, became one of his intellectual heroes, occasoning his most significant reflections on aesthetics and poetics.[5] Rilke documented his involvement with Heinrich Vogeler and his group in the early (1902) monograph "Worpswede;"[6] and a monograph on Rodin of the same year, as well as an extensive essay written in 1907 evince his admiration for the sculptor.[7] Rodin, and a few years later Cézanne, became Rile's artistic—rather than intellectual—heroes. In those early years Rilke also planned to write on Leonardo da Vinci, a project never realized.[8] Rilke's last work, dictated from his deathbed, was a translation of Valéry's Morisot essay, "Tante Berthe."[9] I propose here to examine Valéry's fascination with Degas and the manner of its expression in "Degas Danse Dessin," and Rilke's celebration of his favorite painter in his letters about Cézanne.[10]

I

Valéry's interest in Degas predated his meeting him in the house of Henri Rouart in February of 1896; the poet recalls: "je m'étais fait de lui une idée que j'avais formée de quelques-unes de ses oeuvres que j'avais vues, et de quelques-uns de ses *mots* que l'on colportait," adding that he was always greatly interested in comparing a thing or a person with the idea he had formed of them before meeting them, for such comparisons can give one a certain measure of one's ability to imagine anything on the basis of fragmentary data (1167). Valéry's "Idea" of Degas had, in fact, helped inspire one of his most famous figures, the hero of "La Soirée avec Monsieur Teste," which he had begun writing in April 1894. "Je m'étais fait de Degas l'idée d'un personnage réduit à la rigueur d'un dur dessin, un spartiate, un stoïcien, un janséniste artiste. Une sorte de brutalité intellectuelle en était le trait essentiel. J'avais écrit peu de temps auparavant la 'Soirée avec Monsieur Teste', et ce petit essai d'un portrait imaginaire, quoique fait de remarques et de relations vérifiables, aussi précises que possible, n'est pas sans avoir été plus ou moins *influencé*, (comme l'on dit), par *un certain Degas que je me figurais*" (1168). That figure's verifiability is, of course, grounded in the fact that most profoundly Teste reflects Valéry himself, whence his authenticity. This manner of constructing an illustrious protagonist from an idealized self-image, an *auto-portrait imaginaire*, recalls that other intellectual hero, created less than a year later, Leonardo, also incidentally a painter. We remember Valéry's "confession" at the end of the "Introduction à la Méthode de Léonard de Vinci": "Enfin, je le confesse, je ne trouve pas mieux que d'attribuer à l'infortuné Léonard mes propres agitations . . . Je lui infligea tous mes désirs à titre de choses possédées. . . . Quant au vrai Léonard, il fut ce qu'il fut."[11] And I wonder whether Valéry would have wanted to dedicate the "Introduction" to Leonardo, had it been possible, as he tried to dedicate "La Soirée avec Monsieur Teste" to Degas, who declined to accept.[12]

"Réduit à la rigueur d'un dur dessin," Valéry's Degas has undergone a reduction to the angelic, i.e. the purely intellectual—"brutalité intellectuelle." Both Teste and Léonard are angelic heroes in this Valéryan sense.[13] And it was, after all, Degas who had called Valéry "L'Ange," the poet's favorite sobriquet.[14] The ideal of "un dur dessin," moreover, haunted both the painter, who preferred black and white to color,[15] and the writer who celebrated him in "Degas Danse Dessin," conceived shortly after he had met him.[16]

Like Teste—"un personnage obtenu par le fractionnement d'un être réel dont on extrairait les moments les plus intellectuels pour en composer un personnage imaginaire"[17]—"Degas Danse Dessin" is composed of fragments. The titles of its thirty-two textual fragments indicate their heterogeneity and also point to a rhetorical strategy which aims at creating a refractive—rather than a smoothly reflecting—textual surface of the whole.

Conceived in 1898, our text was delivered in 1936, by a most distinguished team of specialists, in a luxury edition; "chez Ambroise Vollard... avec une fonte neuve de caractères Garamot, sur les presses du maître imprimeur A. Jourde, à Paris... L'édition était illustrée en hors-texte de vingt-six gravures de reproductions sur cuivre,... d'après les compositions originales en noir et en couleurs d'Edgar Degas" (1563). But, before its glorious birth, "la quasi-totalité de ce livre a été connue par fragments, soit avant sa publication en édition de luxe, soit entre cette dernière et l'édition courante."[18]

We need not visualize those "compositions originales en noir et en couleurs d'Edgar Degas" here, however, because, according to Valéry himself, the connection between them and the text is "of the loosest and least immediate kind." He is not at all writing about, but, at best, around them: "Comme il arrive qu'un lecteur à demi distrait crayonne aux marges d'un ouvrage et produise, au gré de l'absence et de la pointe, de petits êtres ou de vagues ramures, en regard des masses lisibles, ainsi ferai-je, selon le caprice de l'esprit, aux environs de ces quelques études d'Edgar Degas" (1163). Valéry's image of doodles in the margins of a text, moreover, inverts the present relationship in that he will—dare we say?—"doodle" texts around pictures! Thus, Degas' pictures become altogether negligible; they have not inspired the text, which is "une manière de monologue, où reviendront comme ils voudront mes souvenirs et les diverses idées que je me suis faites d'un personnage singulier, grand et sévère artiste... d'intelligence rare" (1163).

The first of the thirty-two fragments, entitled "Degas," is itself made up of five fragments and a "Réflexion" about the inanity of histories of art and literature. From all the foregoing it is clear that Valéry does not propose to write critically on Degas' work, nor on aesthetics in the traditional manner. In most of his texts on painters, moreover, he adopts an ironic *deminutio,* or *Demutsformel,* as, for example, in the "Triomphe de Manet," in which he assures us that he neither intends, nor has the capacity, to seek out the essence of Manet's art; "l'esthétique n'est pas mon fort; et puis, *comment parler des couleurs*" (1332)? In "Berthe Morisot," he again insists: "je ne me risquerai dans la critique d'art dont je n'ai nulle expérience" (1302); and in the opening sentence of "Autour de Corot," he warns: "On doit toujours s'excuser de parler peinture: (1307). This ironic *dissimulatio* by a famous author who has written brilliantly on aesthetics ("L'Infini esthétique," "Discours sur l'esthétique," "L'Invention esthétique" and many other well-known texts) confers a titillating Socratic quality on texts like ours, which intends to "turn off" the superficial reader and provoke the faithful.[19]

In the opening fragment of the first piece, after stressing Degas' rigorous refusal of facility—shades of Teste, Léonard and Valéry himself—Valéry breaks off with "je reviendrai sur tout ceci, sans doute... Après tout, je ne sais trop ce que je dirai tout à l'heure. Il est possible que je m'égare un peu, à propos de *Degas*, vers la *Danse,* et vers le *Dessin*," thus indicating the three principal textual blocks rather capriciously—"selon le caprice de l'esprit." Further, while he will not deal with Degas' painting(s)—"enfin point d'esthétique; point de *critique,* ou le moins du monde"—but with his "traits" instead, some of these are not even his own observations: "bien des traits de Degas que je rapporte ici ne sont point de mon souvenir. Je les dois à Ernest Rouart" (1164). As the latter had been "nourished" by the master's aphorisms and injunctions, we are being prepared for second-hand fragments.

The second section of the opening piece is principally devoted to Ernest Rouart's father, Henri, in whose house Valéry had met Degas, which brings us back to the beginning, and Valéry's "préfigurations de Degas" in which "tout n'était pas fantastique" (1168).

The theme of dance, so profoundly associated with Degas' art,[20] and announced in the title as well as in the opening fragments, makes up merely a little over 5% of the entire text. It is restricted to the second essay, "De la Danse." And most surprisingly in our context, it has absolutely nothing to do with Degas, who is never even mentioned, except indirectly in the opening sentence: "Pourquoi ne pas parler un peu de la Danse, à propos du peintre des Danseuses" (1169)? We recall Valéry's accomplished Socratic dialogue, "L'Ame et la Danse" of 1921, in which he paid tribute to Mallarmé's profound reflections on dance, as he does again in the present text (1173).[21]

But Valéry also wrote another essay on dance, contemporary with ours, a "Philosophie de la Danse," published in 1936;[22] and it appears most likely that this text, rather than Degas, occasioned ours. For in the "Philosophie de la Danse," before "entering into his own thoughts on dance," Valéry remarks on the performance of Mme Argentina, "cette grande artiste... de la danse espagnole."[23] Our text closes with a vignette of a dancer who does not in the least resemble the "rats de l'Opéra *au tutu* à la Degas," but rather a

Spanish dancer, probably inspired by Mme Argentina: "grande Méduse, qui, par saccades ondulatoires de son flot de jupes festonnées, qu'elle trousse et retrousse avec une étrange et impudique insistance, se transforme en songe d'Eros" (1173). "De la Danse" also echoes some of the poet's well-known notions on dance frequently expressed elsewhere, such as the analogy of dance and poetry, as opposed to the walking steps of prose.

For a Degas dancer—the most famous one—we must turn to the following essay, "37 rue Victor Massé," and a visit to the master's studio. There, in the general disorder of the third-floor atelier, with its dust, dried paints and the famous zinc bathtub, we find here, "la danseuse de cire au tutu de vraie gaze, dans sa cage de verre" (1174)! This fragment, first published under the title "Chez Degas," almost exlusively descriptive and anecdotal, projects Degas' proverbially "difficult" personality, "il avait et affectait le plus mauvais caractère du monde, avec des jours charmants qu'on ne savait prévoir" (1174). The image of the famous, quarrelsome old man, "vieillard nerveux, sombre presque toujours, parfois sinistre et noirement distrait, avec des reprises brusques de fureur ou d'esprit . . . des caprices" (1172), the aged painter frustrated by his progressive blindness and isolation, emerges from all the books written about him; in fact, today articles are being written in defense of his personality which, ironically, appears to interest posterity, as it did Valéry, almost as much as his art.[24]

But interspersed among the anecdotes, like the resurrection of Zoe—Degas' old housekeeper had fainted in her kitchen, when Valéry resuscitated her to his host's great amazement and gratitude—, or a "Degas mis à nu" (1177), are more significant memories. There was, for example, "une certaine étude de danseuse qui excitait chaque fois mon envie. Il l'avait non tant dessinée que véritablement construite et articulée en pantin: un bras et un jambe coudés net, le corps raide, une volonté implacable dans le dessin, quelques rehauts de rouge par-ci par-là" (1175). The sketch reminds Valéry of a Holbein drawing of a hand, like a hand made of wood, like one at the end of an artificial arm, with fingers put on and bent but not yet planed down. It other words, a piece of work in progress, a fragment *toward* a completion that never interested Valéry as much as its genesis.[25] Thus also Degas' interest in photography, and how it might be used by the painter, but Valéry also perceived brilliantly some of the shortcomings—not of his idol, or Idea of Degas, but of the artist's *oeuvre*: "son oeuvre a peut-être souffert du nombre et de la diversité remarquables de ses appétits artistiques, comme de l'intensité de son attention sur les points les plus hauts, mais les plus opposés de son métier" (1178).[26]

Degas, for years faithfully copying the old masters,[27] and all his life distrustful of the new painting "en plein air," torn between Ingres' conservatism and linear emphasis (Degas' teacher Lamothe, as well as most of his professors at the Ecole des Beaux-Arts had been Ingres' students)[28] and an emerging new art destined to put to rest a style that dated from the Renaissance, was divided by conflicting tendencies—as was Valéry: "Degas se trouve pris entre les commandements de Monsieur Ingres, et les charmes étranges de Delacroix; tandis qu'il hésite, l'art de son temps se résout à exploiter le spectacle de la vie moderne" (1179). Valéry deplores the change of modern taste with which "the grand manner" and subject painting went out of date, for "landscape came and demolished the problem of *subject*, and in a few years reduced the whole intellectual side of art to a few questions about *materials* and the coloring of shadows." Thus the friend of Manet and Morisot here clearly sides with the "intellectual" and "linear" Degas against the "painterly" Impressionists. Yet, later in the same fragment, he concedes that Manet has "une puissance décisive," and that in his best pictures "il arrive à la *poésie*, c'est-à-dire au suprême de l'art." But, he closes, "comment parler peinture?" (1179), echoing the "comment parler des couleurs?" of his Manet essay. And, therefore, in what immediately follows, he will not.

"Degas et la Révolution" is composed of no less than six anecdotes about the painter and his Italian background—to which Valéry attributes his difficult temperament—, about his picturesque grandfather, who had been engaged to one of the "Virgins of Verdun," condemned to death by one of Mallarmé's magistrate ancestors during the Revulution,—anecdotes related by most of Degas' biographers.[29] The following fragment, entitled "Propos," consists of two anecdotal asides about Ingres; and in the next, "22 octobre 1905," Valéry tells us more anecdotes about Ingres, which he learned from Degas.[30] Further purely anecdotal fragments are "Politique de Degas" in which Valéry does not hesitate to entertain the reader with the artist's uncompromising attitude in the Dreyfus affair, painfully reminding us of his own position in the matter.[31] "Mimique" deals, by means of an amusing anecdote, with the painter's gift for mimicry and his "*manière mimique de voir*" which Valéry attributes to his

Napolitan ancestry. "Degas et le sonnet" retells the famous story how Mallarmé—whose presence, not surprisingly, haunts quite a few of these fragments—came to give Degas advice on poetry: "Mais, Degas, ce n'est point avec des idées que l'on fait des vers..." (1208). To make *pictures* with ideas, or to let ideas stand in the way of their execution, had, in fact. been one of Degas' much more serious temptations.[32] Both "Quelques 'mots' et divers traits" and the following fragment, "Autres 'mots'," continue in the anecdotal vein. "Le Dessin n'est pas la forme," itself one of Degas' oft-repeated *mots*, occasions other anecdotes about his intransigence; and in the next piece, "Souvenirs de Berthe Morisot sur Degas," Valéry presents several of these, verbatim from one of her notebooks. The longest of the thirty-two fragments, moreover, "Souvenirs de Monsieur Ernest Rouart," consists of "some very precious reminiscences passed on" to Valéry by that friend, also reproduced verbatim from the source.

This prominence of the descriptive and anecdotal, which confers on the book an entertaining, frequently amusing, even facile allure, might surprise, especially as in the very text Valéry tells us that he is not interested in biography and that "il faut prendre garde à l'*amusant*" (1164). In a later fragment, in which he says that the development of landscape in modern painting has diminished "la partie intellectuelle de l'art," he points to a parallel development in modern literature: "l'invasion de la Littérature par la *description* fut parallèle à celle de la Peinture par le paysage; de même sens que celle-ci et de même conséquence" (1219). And in "Degas Danse Dessin" the descriptive certainly does diminish "la partie intellectuelle." The anecdote, moreover, the *an-ekdoton*, as Valéry was well aware, originally meant "the un-published," that which for reasons of discretion was transmitted only orally. But as Valéry also knew, the anecdote had evolved into a refined textual genre during the Italian Renaissance. Our text, however, is not a typical collection or *recueil* of anecdotes, as these anecdotal fragments are interspersed with others, in which Valéry—despite his inital "point d'esthétique"—sets forth not Degas' but his own ideas on aesthetics. Yet, this is not the text of an aesthetician, but of a poet who, at another occasion, had said: "la pensée doit être cachée dans le vers comme la vertu nutritive dans un fruit. Il est nourriture, mais il ne paraît que délice. On ne perçoit que du plaisir, mais on reçoit une substance."[33]

For the substance of Valéry's thoughts on art and painting, we must turn to those pieces which are constructed around the notion of

"Dessin," the last, but not least important, of the three thematic blocks fragmented throughout the text.

A brief "Digression"—from the anecdotal—reveals why Valéry esteems "le dessin" so highly, i.e. because he knows "of no art which calls for the use of more *intelligence* than that of drawing. Whether it be a question of extracting from the vast complexity of things seen the one pencil stroke that is right, or of summarizing a structure . . . all mental faculties find their function in that work." And, he continues, "who can measure the intellect and will of a Leonardo or a Rembrandt after examining their drawings" (1204–5)! In the following "Autre Digression," Valéry judges modern art harshly: "there hovers a suspicion of ignorance or impotence" over it, "which even the strangest *experiments* intensify, rather than diminish" (1205). Clearly, modern painting is painterly, rejecting traditional drawing, perspective and studio approaches. In "Voir et tracer," Valéry again admires and brilliantly explains the intellectual efforts involved in drawing, "je ne puis préciser ma perception d'une chose sans la dessiner *virtuellement*, et je ne puis dessiner cette chose sans une attention volontaire *qui transforme remarquablement ce que d'abord j'avais cru percevoir* . . . Il y a quelque analogie entre ceci et ce qui a lieu quand nous voulons préciser notre *pensée* par une expression plus voulue. Ce n'est plus la même pensée" (1188). But, is it with thoughts that pictures, or poems, are made?

In "Travail et méfiance," Valéry remarks about the seriousness of Degas' work. Again comparing drawing to writing, he says that "like a writer striving to attain the utmost precision of form, Degas endlessly revises his drawing." And though he may add colors, so that the tutus may be yellow on one, violet on another dancer, "la ligne, les actes, la prose, sont là-dessous; essentiels et séparables" (1190). This is precisely why some critics claim that Degas is not a painter.[34] It was Manet, and not Degas, we recall, who sometimes "arrived at poetry." A piece entitled "Degas, fou de dessin" pictures him as "an anxious figure in the tragicomedy of modern art, divided against himself . . . eager for all the new and more or less felicitous developments in seeing the world and methods of painting it; on the other hand possessed by a rigorous classicism whose conventions of elegance, simplicity and style he spent a lifetime analyzing." For Valéry, "Degas offrait tous les traits de l'artiste pur" (1209). As with Mallarmé, his work had become his passion, and his passion surpassed his works: "le désir de créer quelque ouvrage où paraisse plus de puissance ou de perfection que nous n'en trouvons en nous-mêmes, éloigne indéfiniment de nous cet objet qui échappe et s'oppose à chacun de nos instants" (1210). In "Suite du précédent," Valéry—victim of his own temptations in his time—says that "il se peut que le Dessin soit la plus obsédante tentation de l'esprit" (1211).

I have already pointed to Valéry's stance against modern art in his "Réflexion sur le paysage et bien d'autres choses" as concerns the development of landscape painting. He aims his remarks, of course, against the Impressionists: "peu à peu ils s'engagent le corps à corps avec la *nature telle quelle*. Ils travaillent de moins en moins dans l'atelier . . . Ils luttent contre la solidité ou la fluidité même des choses; certains s'en prennent à la lumière, veulent saisir l'heure, l'instant . . . Puis, l'impression l'emporte: *Matière* ou *Lumière* dominent" (1218). As Valéry made no effort to appreciate this painting, he erroneously believed that "le paysage donne de grandes *facilités*. Tout le monde se mit à peindre" (1219). In "Art moderne et grand art," a title clearly pointing to the dichotomy, he regrets that in tending to "exploit almost exclusively *sensory* sensibility," modern painters do so "at the expense of . . . our capacity for construction" (1220). They are, moreover, driven by a new demon, *"le Démon du changement pour le changement,"* who drives them from fad to fad. Thus, "à peine la lumière laborieusement reconstituée sur les toiles," that Demon "se plaint aussitôt qu'elle mange toutes les formes . . . Alors, de je ne sais quelle réserve . . . il tire une *sphère*, un *cône*, et un *cylindre*; et finalement un *cube*, qu'il gardait pour la bonne bouche" (1222). Valéry is having a good time at the expense of Cézanne, and those inspired by him, like the Cubists, with all of whom he always resolutely refused to come to terms.

As this stance reverberates throughout "Degas Danse Dessin," grounded in that controversial artist, so much the more remarkable and paradoxical is the text's manner, its modernity. For neither Valéry's aesthetics, nor its occasion, his Idea of Degas, are sharply outlined or "reduced to the strict lines of a hard drawing." Nor are they placed into traditional perspective, as it were; rather, the perspective of the whole is—as in an Impressionist painting—established by a multitude of individually trivial anecdotal and colorful pen strokes. And we must take in the entire text to see these little apparently insignificant *taches colorées* "fall into line." Like

Monet's water, Valéry's textual surface is no longer a simple mirror reflecting objects and objectives, but has, as I observed at the outset, a refractive texture.

At first glance, then, the text appears formless in its multiple fragmentations. Here we recall Valéry's fascination with "l'informe," especially in connection with his texts on Leonardo da Vinci.[35] And in one of the *Notebooks*, he writes: "l'informe est plus vrai—moins appris—la forme conquiert l'informe et en sort comme résultat après un temps,"[36]—which pretty nearly describes the strategy and indicates the lesson of our text. Elsewhere in the *Cahiers*, Valéry writes: "j'opère sur *taches colorées* intérieures," and I agree with one of his recent critics, Jeannine Jallat, that: "l'énoncé répétitif de la 'tache colorée' révèle ce qu'une telle manière de voir doit à l'impressionnisme. Sa leçon," she continues, "est reçue tôt et elle commande les formulations de la poétique. Elle s'étend très tard jusque dans les derniers *Cahiers*. C'est là une conviction d'autant plus forte qu'elle parle chez un amateur d'art classique qui, ici et là"—and most notably in "Degas Danse Dessin"—"regrette les grandes machines historiques et la peinture à sujets et prend soin de sauver Degas du péché . . . d'"impressionnisme'."[37]

We have seen this "lesson of Impressionism" inform and form our entire text; and in one of its fragments, entitled "The Ground and the Formless," Valéry gives us a lesson in reading—both modern pictures *and* texts: "to say that they are formless does not mean that they have no *form*, but that there is nothing in their form enabling us to duplicate them by any simple act of recognition or copying. . . . The question, then, is to render *intelligible* . . . an object which has no determined structure, no cliché or remembered form to guide us . . . And as the thinker tries to defend himself against set phrases"—forms—"which protect the mind from surprises . . . so the artist can, in studying the formless, that is the *singularity* of form, rediscover his own singularity" (1194–95). For us, the apparent formlessness of "Degas Danse Dessin" with its *taches colorées* reveals both its singularity and its sources, which never ceased to haunt the poet.[38] And also a certain Irony, of which Valéry—creator of Leonardo and Teste, of *his* Degas and *Mon Faust*—was surely well aware.

II

Rilke never met Cézanne, but discovered his work a year after the painter's death, by chance, during a visit to the "Salon d'Automne" on October 6, 1907. The impact of this chance encounter, one of the most decisive events of Rilke's artistic life—and he had no other—, is documented in a group of seventeen letters addressed to his wife, the sculptress Clara Rilke-Westhoff, from October 6 to 24. In these letters the poet records his impressions and reflections after his daily visits to the Salon's two Cézanne rooms. Just as Rilke's private life became progressively devoured by his artistic existence, so his personal correspondence became part of the *oeuvre*, or at the very least stood entirely in its service, somewhat like Valéry's *Cahiers* in the corpus of his work. Thus, although Rilke never published these letters, from which he subsequently incorporated sections into *Die Aufzeichnungen des Malte Laurids Brigge,* they have become known to his readers as *Die Briefe über Cézanne.*[39]

In the first of these, Rilke remarks that it is "scarcely credible" that his stroll through the elegant and aristocratic Faubourg Saint-Germain should have taken him to the "Salon d'Automne" and its surprises, to Cézanne who would not have been understood by the bygone age symbolized by that part of Paris; "aber für uns gilt er und ist rührend und wichtig" (184). Thus, from the outset, Rilke identifies with modern art; he will later become one of the first to draw on Picasso.[40] The following day, Rilke writes that, as usual, in this Salon, too, the spectators seem more interesting to him than the paintings, except in the Cézanne rooms. Because "da ist alle Wirklichkeit auf seiner Seite: bei diesem dichten sattierten Blau, das er hat, bei seinem Rot und seinem schattenlosen Grün und dem rötlichen Schwarz seiner Weinflaschen" (184–85). And this Cézannean truth and reality, Rilke immediately perceives, is essentially one of color. He conveys to us Cézanne's Blue, his Red, his Green and his Black, before showing us any objects, like the typical wine bottles of his still lifes.

The impact of Cézanne's colors lead Rilke back to the Louvre, as he relates in the following letter, to the Venetians, Cézanne's masters: "Als ob diese Meister im Louvre nicht gewusst hätten, dass es die Farbe ist, die die Malerei ausmacht" (185).[41] Rilke is particularly fascinated by a certain Blue which became "jenes bestimmte Blau des 18. Jahrhunderts," celebrated by LaTour, Peronnet, Chardin. And he muses about a monograph one could write about that Blue, from Chardin to Cézanne, for Cézanne's very own Blue, "Cézannes sehr eigenes Blau hat diese Abstammung, kommt von dem Blau des 18. Jahrhunderts her" (186). Chardin was the great intermediary: "schon seine Früchte denken nicht mehr an die Tafel, liegen auf Küchentischen herum und geben nichts darauf, schön gegessen zu sein." And if Chardin's fruits care nothing for being nicely eaten, "bei Cézanne hört die Essbarkeit überhaupt auf, so sehr dinghaft werden sie, so einfach und unvertilgbar in ihrer eigensinnigen Vorhandenheit" (187). This obstinate existing, the "Dinghaftigkeit" of those Cézannean apples and onions objectified in color, this faithful and simple thingness of the humblest objects became one of Rilke's ideals as the poet became the disciple of the painter.

Rilke opens his letter of October 9 by announcing: "heute wollte ich Dir ein wenig von Cézanne erzählen;" this anecdotal epistle is based on Emile Bernard's "Souvenirs sur Cézanne" which were currently appearing in the *Mercure de France*.[42] As Bernard had been one of the few young painters relatively close to the master during his last years, had been permitted to paint by his side, and had received letters from Cézanne after Bernard left Aix,[43] most subsequent Cézanne biographers draw from this source. Thus the facts Rilke relates are commonly known: the turning point in Cézanne's fortieth year due to his encounter with Pissaro who instilled in him the passion for work, his father's turning banker from hat-maker and amassing sufficient wealth to allow his son to devote his life to painting, his painful break with Zola over his portrayal of Cézanne in *L'Oeuvre*, his identification, on the other hand, with Frenhofer in Balzac's *Le Chef-d'oeuvre inconnu*, Cézanne's faithful practice of his religion in his later years, his fear of the world and his growing loneliness and voluntary isolation for the sake of his work, which even prevented him from attending his beloved mother's funeral. But in Rilke's text all these well-known facts are transformed by the poet's vision, a vision colored, in turn, by the master's paintings.

Rilke draws a portrait not dissimilar to Valéry's Degas, of a difficult and frustrated old man for whom his work had become a consuming passion, and for whom this passion always surpassed his works. Thus Cézanne worked "ohne Freude eigentlich ... in fortwährender Wut, im Zwiespalt mit jeder einzelnen seiner Arbeiten, deren keine ihm das zu erreichen schien, was er für das Unentbehrlichste hielt. La réalisation nannter er es" (187). Rilke defines this realization as "das Uberzeugende, die Dingwerdung," the convincing nature, the becoming thing "which through his own experience of the object elevated its reality into the indestructible;" this was "die Absicht seiner innersten Arbeit," the aim for which the old painter worked himself daily "to the point of exhaustion." Then Rilke explains, somewhat distrustful here of his source, it appears,[44] Cézanne's method of starting his landscapes and still lifes with the darkest coloring, "covering its depth with a layer of color which he extended a little beyond the first and so on, extending color upon color until he gradually arrived at another contrasting pictorial element, a new center from which he then proceeded in similar fashion." The two procedures, that of taking over from the observed and the appropriation and personal use of what he took over, "des sicheren Übernehmens und des Sichaneignens und persöhnlichen Gebrauchens des Übernommenen" (188), must have warred within him, reflects the poet, probably recalling his own experience, the struggle of his own originality coming to terms with the intertext. "Und der Alte ertrug den Unfrieden" (189), suffered this inner dissension like all the other sacrifices to his unique calling, and all the misunderstandings, of which his falling-out with Zola must have been one of the most painful. Rilke closes his letter telling his wife that tomorrow he will write about himself, adding: "Du wirst wissen, wie sehr ichs auch heute getan habe . . ." (192), thus the poet's profound identification with the painter.

A few days later, Rilke tells Clara that he had asked the painter Mathilde Vollmoeller to accompany him to the Cézannes in order to compare his own, perhaps somewhat literary, impressions with those of the painter. But the friend's remarks, as recorded by Rilke, contain nothing that he had not perceived himself.

As Rilke five years earlier found direction for his own work with Rodin, he now finds it in Cézanne. In a letter of October 13, he writes that before now he would not have been ready to learn from the painter, but "daran wieviel Cézanne mir jetzt zu tun gibt, merk ich, wie sehr ich anders geworden bin. Ich bin auf dem Weg ein Arbeiter zu werden." And though he may well just be on the first milestone on the road to becoming a worker, he can now comprehend ("begreifen") that old man "der irgendwo weit vorne gegangen ist, allein, nur mit Kindern hinter sich, die Steine werfen (wie ich es einmal in dem Fragment von den Einsamen beschrieben habe)." This detail of Cézanne's last years, of the children in Aix ridiculing him and throwing stones after him, recurs in the letters and must have deeply impressed Rilke, perhaps as a metaphor for artistic isolation. Rilke later incorporated the "fragment of the Lonely" in *Die Aufzeichnungen des Malte Laurids Brigge*, a book in gestation during the Cézanne encounter.[45] But from the anecdotal, Rilke returns to the essential: Cézanne's colors. Unlike Valéry—"comment parler des couleurs?"—Rilke cannot help speaking about them, again and again: "Als ob diese Farben einem die Unentschlossenheit abnähmen ein für allemal". These colors, then, in taking away his own irresolution, are profoundly educative for the poet: "the good conscience of these Reds, these Blues, their simple truthfulness educates one," and "if one submits to them as readily as one can, they appear to do something for one" (199). The good conscience and truthfulness of Cézanne's Reds and Blues, even more so than the painter's life, are a lesson in artistic integrity for the young poet, his disciple. Thus Cézanne must also have gone beyond his love for the things he depicted, reached a point where love is consumed in creation: "Dieses Aufbrauchen der Liebe in anonymer Arbeit, woraus so reine Dinge entstehen, ist vielleicht keinem so völlig gelungen wie dem Alten." Was this not Rilke's own path—through and beyond love toward the pure realization of the humblest of things? Cézanne "knew how to repress his love for each single apple and to store it in the painted apple forever" (200).[46]

In another letter, Rilke again stresses his identification with Cézanne, as he tells his wife that it is "garnicht die Malerei, die ich studiere ... Es ist die Wendung in dieser Malerei, die ich erkannte, weil ich sie selbst eben in meiner Arbeit erreicht hatte"—we think here of poems like "Die Gazelle." The poet's readers will recall the profound meaning of those decisive "turning points" in his poetic development.[47] It is, continues Rilke, because of this deep kinship with Cézanne that he hesitates writing about him formally: "therefore I must be cautious with the attempt to write about Cézanne, which of course tempts me very much ... One ... who comprehends his pictures from so private a perspective has no right to write about them" (205–6). He is too close; but write about them he must, namely in these letters to Clara—which are ours as much as hers.[48]

The following day, Rilke relates a deeply significant discovery: his own favorite Baudelaire poem, "Une Charogne," appears also to have been Cézanne's. For Rilke, it made "die ganze Entwicklung zum sachlichen Sagen, die wir jetzt in Cézanne zu erkennen glauben" possible. The beautiful and accomplished poem about a repulsive and rotting carcass taught modern artists—poets as well as painters—"to master artistic observation to the point of seeing, even in the horrible and apparently repulsive, that which is, and which, with all else that is, counts [das Seiende zu sehen, das, mit allem anderen Seienden, gilt]" (207). "You can imagine," he exclaims, "how moved I am to read that Cézanne still knew this very poem—Baudelaire's 'Charogne'— entirely by heart in his last years and would recite it word for word."[49] The real work of the artist begins "only after this enduring"—of the horrible and most repulsive—"and he who has not got that far will get to see in heaven possibly the Virgin Mary and some saints and prophets—but of Hokusai and Leonardo, of Li-Tai-Pe and Villon, of Verhaeren, Rodin and Cézanne,—and of God himself they will even there only be able to tell him." Finally Rilke shows how Cézanne helps him understand his own creation, his Malte: "And suddenly (and for the first time) I understand the destiny of Malte Laurids. Is it not this, that this test surpassed him" (208)? Thus, one of Rilke's major works, his only novel, could not have come into being as we know it, without Cézanne.[50]

In another letter, again discussing colors, Rilke says that before Cézanne no one had ever demonstrated "wie sehr das Malen unter den Farben vor sich geht. . . . Ihr Verkehr untereinander: das ist die ganze Malerei." The artist must, in fact, let the colors interact without interfering, for "whoever interrupts, whoever arranges . . . already disturbs their interactions." The poet here obviously attributes his own creative process—his patient waiting for and obedient response to inspiration—to the painter. For Rilke, the artist—painter and poet—must be the docile instrument and servant of his Muse; small wonder, then, that Valéry's "Palme" was one of his favorite poems.[51] And it is from this perspective that we can understand that for him "the painter (as any artist whatever) should not become conscious of his insights; without taking the detour through his reflections, his advances, enigmatic to himself, must enter so swiftly into his work that he cannot recognize them himself at the moment of their transition" (214). But in the very writing of this paradoxical statement, the writer becomes aware of the difficulty of verbalizing the complex process. Thus also Cézanne's own difficulties in writing about his work to Bernard who is, according to Rilke, "ein schreibender Maler, einer also, der keiner war."[52]

In the following letter, of October 22, the closing day of the

"Salon d'Automne," Rilke attempts a minute (albeit verbal) reproduction of one of Cézanne's great paintings. And unlike Valéry, where the connection between Degas' pictures and the text was "of the loosest and least immediate kind," Rilke would indeed have us visualize the painting which he describes with infinite care stroke by stroke: the portrait of Mme Cézanne in the red easychair of c. 1877.[53] He has literally tried to learn the picture's color correlations by heart, "like a many-digited number." He can feel this "Farbenzusammenhang" in his sleep; "my blood describes it in me, but the Saying somehow remains outside [geht irgendwo draussen vorbei und wird nicht hereingerufen]" (216). *Aporia*—for Write—*Sagen*—the poet must, obediently.

He proceeds from the "earth-green" wall and even draws one of its "cobalt blue" ornamental crosses with vacant center, "-¦-" in the text. From this background he moves to the red easychair, the "cinnabar" tassel on one of its armrests "having no longer the wall behind it, but a broad lower border of a green Blue against which its contradiction rings loudly." And on this easychair, "which is a personality," is placed a woman whose description begins with the dress and its stripes of "green Yellows" and "yellow Greens," up to the edge of her "blue-gray" jacket, fastened in front with "a blue silk bow playing with green reflections." Finally he comes to the face of the portrait, in whose "brightness the proximity of all of these colors is utilized for a simple modeling [Modellierung]; even the Brown of the hair posed round over the crown and the smooth Brown of the eyes must respond [muss sich äussern gegen] to its surroundings. It is as if each spot were aware of all the others, so much does it participate, with adaptation and rejection taking place in it, so that each one in its own way provides for and helps create the balance; as the entire picture ultimately holds reality in equilibrium" (217). Rilke concludes that "everything has become, as I have already written, a matter of the colors among one another, of one of them bracing itself against another, accentuating itself against it, reflecting upon itself." And what Rilke here says about Cézanne's colors is reminiscent of what Mallarmé once said about words: "Les mots, d'eux-mêmes, s'exaltent à mainte facette reconnue la plus rare ou valant pour l'esprit, centre de suspens vibratoire; . . . prompts tous, avant extinction, à une réciprocité de feux distante ou présentée de biais comme contingence."[54] Though Rilke exclaims "how difficult it becomes when one wants to get really close to the facts" (218), we must concede that no poet has ever come closer to those painterly facts. Yet, the following day, he again deplores that "more than ever words seemed impossible, and still, the possibility to use them compellingly should exist, if one could only behold such a painting"—Cézanne's portrait—"like nature; then as an existing thing [ein Seiendes] it should also somehow be expressible" (219). And he will attempt it again, to express this new *Seiende*, of one of Cézanne's self-portraits and, in one of the last letters, of the still life with the black clock.[55]

***

Rilke left Paris almost immediately after the closing of the "Salon d'Automne," but Cézanne never left him,[56] —just as Valéry was haunted by the figure of Degas all his life. On the other hand, while Valéry projected into his Degas the traits of his ideal intellectual hero, and Rilke recognized in his Cézanne his artistic "Vorbild" and ideal, the two painters have found in Valéry and Rilke their ideal poets. For as Valéry's keen comprehension of Degas' struggle to come to terms with an artistic tradition and the art of the future is reflected, as we have seen, in the very form of his own text(s) about the controversial artist, so Rilke's awareness of Cézanne's quest for an entirely new and modern way of painting is mirrored in his own persistent efforts to express, to realize the *Sagen* of, this newly created *Seiende* in his Letters about the first and foremost modern painter.

NOTES

1. Renée Lang, "Rilke and His French Contemporaries, "*Comparative Literature*, Spring 1958, 136. Cf. also by the same author, "Ein fruchtbringendes Missverständnis: Rilke und Valéry," *Symposium*, 13 (1959) 51–62.
2. Maurice Betz, *Rainer Maria Rilke in Frankreich* (Wien, 1938); by the same author, *Rilke in Paris* (Zürich, 1948). Charles Dédéyan, *Rilke et la France* (Paris, 1964). Maja Goth, *Rilke und Valéry: Aspekte ihrer Poetik* (Bern und München, 1981).
3. I recall Heinrich Heine's "Salon of 1831," Baudelaire's consummate art criticism, Laforgue's brilliant new aesthetics of Impressionism, and the valiant—if less brilliant—defense of Cubism by Apollinaire, to name but a few.
4. Paul Valéry, *Oeuvres* II (Pléiade Gallimard, Paris: 1960) "Degas Danse Dessin," 1163–1240; all my quotations from the text will be from this edition, unless otherwise

indicated, and marked by page number. Valéry's other essays on painters, in the same volume, are: "Berthe Morisot," 1302–6; "Autour de Corot," 1307–25; "Triomphe de Manet," 1326–33; "Les Fresques de Paul Véronèse," 1294–97. The twelfth volume of *The Collected Works of Paul Valéry*, Bollingen Series XLV (Panthéon, New York: 1960) contains English translations of the above, as well as of "Honoré Daumier," text for a volume of reproductions of Daumier's paintings, *Les Trésors de la peinture française* (Paris: Skira, 1938), and "Souvenirs sur Renoir," in *La Revue hebdomadaire*, January 3, 1920.

5. Paul Valéry, *Oeuvres* I (Paris: Gallimard, 1957), "Introduction à la Méthode de Léonard de Vinci," "Note et digression," and "Léonard et les Philosophes (Lettre à Ferrero)," 1153–1259. Further references are to this edition.

6. Rainer Maria Rilke, *Sämtliche Werke* 9 (Frankfurt: Insel Verlag, 1976) 7–134.

7. Rainer Maria Rilke, *Sämtliche Werke* 9: 135–278. For a critical discussion of Rilke's "Worpswede" and his Rodin, cf. Karl Eugene Webb, *Rainer Maria Rilke and Jugendstil* (Chapel Hill: Univ. of North Carolina Press, 1978) esp. pp.21–45, "Rilke as an Art Critic."

8. *Rainer Maria Rilke Lou Andreas-Salome Briefwechsel* (Frankfurt: Insel Verlag, 1975) 164, where he writes to Lou, in a letter of May 13, 1904: "Nach der Rodin-Monographie dachte ich an eine Carpaccio's, später an eine Leonardo's; was mir dazu fehlt, ist nicht Kunsthistorikerwissen (das ich gerade vermeiden möchte) wohl aber das einfach Handwerkliche des Forschers."

9. Karin Wais, *Studien zu Rilkes Valéry-Übertragungen* (Tübingen: Max Niemeyer Verlag, 1967) 110, 156.

10. Rainer Maria Rilke, *Briefe* I (1897–1914) (Wiesbaden: Insel Verlag, 1950). I shall quote from this edition, unless otherwise indicated, and mark the passages by page number.

11. *Oeuvres* 1: 1232–34.

12. Cf. *André Gide-Paul Valéry Correspondance 1890–1942* (Paris: Gallimard, 1955) 277–78.

13. Cf. "Teste, Agathe, and 'L'Ange Lionardo'," in my *The Broken Angel: Myth and Method in Valéry* (Chapel Hill: NCSRLL, 1984) 40–52. Also my "The Angel in Valéry and Rilke," *Comparative Literature*, XXXV, 3 (Summer 1983) 215–46.

14. For one of the numerous reflections about it in the Notebooks, Paul Valéry, *Cahiers* I (Paris: Gallimard, 1973) 131: " 'L'Ange'—m'appelait Degas. Il avait plus raison qu'il ne pouvait croire. Ange=Etrange, Estrange=étranger . . ." Cf. also our text, 1213.

15. Degas' friend, Ambroise Vollard—whose *Souvenirs About Cézanne* was to inspire Rilke—relates in "*Degas: An Intimate Portrait*," transl. R. T. Weaver (New York: Crown Pubishers, 1937) that "Degas was never greatly preoccupied with color as such . . . He tells us himself that he should probably have stuck to black and white if

the world had not clamored for more and yet more of those vivid pastels, wherein he used patches of red, green and yellow to such superb decorative effect" (14). Or, "Degas used to say that if he had let himself follow his own taste in the matter, he would never have done anything but black and white" (69).

16. In March of 1898, Valéry wrote to Gide: "J'écrirai (sur Degas non désigné plus clairement): Monsieur D. ou la Peinture." *Gide-Valéry Correspondance* 316. The subsequent shift in the title from "peinture" to "dessin" is significant.

17. *Oeuvres* 2: 1381.

18. Thus the editorial commentary of the Pléiade-Gallimard editors; for this textual history, cf. pp. 1562–63.

19. For Valéry's relationship with his reader, cf. my "Valéry's Reader: 'L'Amateur de poémes', *"The Centennial Review*, 22 (1978) 389–99.

20. We recall here the magnificent exhibition "Degas the Dancers" at the National Gallery of Art (November through March 1984–85), celebrating the sesquicentennial of the artist's birth. Cf. the exhibition catalogue *Degas the Dancers*, George T. M. Shackelford (Washington: National Gallery of Art, 1984).

21. Cf. my "Mallarmé's Living Metaphor: Valéry's Athikté and Rilke's Spanish Dancer" in *Pre-Text Text Context*, ed. Robert L. Mitchell (Columbus: Ohio State University Press, 1980) 217–27.

22. *Oeuvres* 1: 1390–1403.

23. *Oeuvres* 1: 1403.

24. Cf. the Editorial, "Degas as a Human Being," *The Burlington Magazine*, 105 (June 1963) 238–41.

25. This stance has become proverbial for Valéry; for one of many examples: "Je confesse une fois de plus que le travail m'intéresse infiniment plus que le produit du travail" (*Oeuvres* 1: 1455).

26. For some critics, this results in a most dangerous eclecticism in Degas' work. For example, André Lhote, in "Degas et Valéry," 133–42, *La Nouvelle Revue Française*, 52 (1939), condemns Degas' lack of commitment and resulting eclecticism: "Chez Degas, au contraire, les tentations les plus contradictoires sont subies simultanément.... C'est justement parce qu'il *compose* éternellement avec ce qu'il eût dû rejeter en bloc, qu'il peut... 'achever' ses ouvrages ... Moins sollicité par cette *finition* prématurée, il eût pu se poser des problèmes plus urgents, imposés par la féroce actualité" (135).

27. Cf. Theodore Reff, "Degas's Copies of Older Art," *The Burlington Magazine*, 105 (June, 1963) 241.

28. Roy McMullen, *Degas His Life, Times, and Work* (Boston: Houghton Mifflin, 1984) 31–36.

29. McMullen, *Degas His Life, Times, and Work* 2–5, 18 *et passim*.

30. Slightly differing versions of the meeting of Degas with Ingres are retold by

McMullen (36–7); cf. also D. Halévy, *Degas parle* (Paris: La Palatine, 1960) 57–59; A. Alexandre, "Degas, nouveaux aperçus" in *L'Art et les artistes*, 29, (1935) 147; J. Fevre, *Mon oncle Degas* (Geneva: Pierre Cailler, 1949) 70.

31. Cf. Valéry's letter to Gide of February 14, 1898, *Gide-Valéry Correspondance* 312: "On m'embête encore beaucoup avec l'affaire D. Dieu sait quand cela finira. Je répands autant que je puis la bonne parole, c'est-à-dire: qu'importent ces dévorations d'insectes? Cherchons la véritable liberté, celle à fournir à un homme chargé de l'Etat." We recall here that Cézanne, too, was against Dreyfus, and how Zola's valiant public defense of justice contributed to the inevitable rupture between the painter and the novelist who had been the closest of friends since childhood.

32. McMullen, *Degas His Life, Times and Work* 106–8.

33. *Oeuvres* 1: 1452.

34. André Lhote, in "Degas et Valéry," (140): "on s'aperçoit que Degas n'était pas un peintre, mais un dessinateur; ce n'est qu'à l'aide du pastel qu'il a pu réaliser des oeuvres échappant à son éternelle indécision".

35. Cf. Jeannine Jallat's intelligent discussion of "l'informe et la figure" in her *Introduction aux figures valéryennes* (Pisa: Pacini Editore, 1982) 19–47.

36. *Cahiers* II (1974) 802.

37. Jallat, *Introduction aux figures valéryennes* 23ff.

38. Cf. Jacques Derrida's discussion of the "sources" of Valéry, even those "écartées," in "Qual Quelle: les sources de Valéry" in *Marges de la philosophie* (Paris: Editions de Minuit, 1972) 325–63.

39. Maurice Betz translated and published the letters separately: Rainer-Maria Rilke *Lettres sur Cézanne* (Paris: Editions Corrêa, 1944), with an excellent Introduction.

40. I recall here the impact of Picasso's *Saltimbanque Family* on the fifth *Duino Elegy*, as well as the many comments in Rilke's correspondence on the paintings of Picasso's blue and rose periods.

41. For Cézanne's admiration for the Venetian masters, cf. Maurice Raynal, *Cézanne* (Lausanne: Skira, 1954) 17: "Even at this stage he banked on color as the form of expression that best sorted with his temperament. Thus it was only natural that his admiration should go to the Venetians...."

42. Emile Bernard, "Souvenirs sur Paul Cézanne et lettres inédites," *Mercure de France*, 1 and 15 October, 1907. Cf. also by the same author, "Paul Cézanne," *L'Occident*, July 1904. Ambroise Vollard, *Paul Cézanne* (New York, 1926), Rilke also read.

43. Cf. John Rewald, *Paul Cézanne* (London: Spring Books, 1950) 153–4, 161, 167, 171–77.

44. Rilke feels something of Cézanne and Bernard's ultimate estrangement when he remarks "wenn man dem Berichterstatter aller dieser Tatsachen, einem nicht sehr

sympathischen Maler, . . . glauben darf" (188). For Cézanne's disillusionment with Bernard, cf. Rewald, *Paul Cézanne* 173.

45. Rilke, *Sämtliche Werke*, 11: 879–80, "Wenn man von den Einsamen spricht, . . . Die Kinder verbanden sich wieder ihn, . . . und warfen ihm Steine nach, damit er sich rascher entfernte. . . ."

46. Rilke had reached this "pure realization" in one of his most famous poems, "Die Gazelle," with which he closes this letter: "Ich hab die ersten Korrekturen von der Insel. In den Gedichten sind instinktive Ansätze zu ähnlicher Sachlichkeit. Die 'Gazelle' lasse ich auch stehen: sie ist gut" (200).

47. Seven years later (Paris, June 1914), Rilke entitles one of his most significant poems "Wendung," *Sämtliche Werke* 3: 82–4. At this moment in the poet's development, the turning point will be from the pure beholding back to the heart: "Denn des Anschauns, siehe, ist eine Grenze./ . . . Werk des Gesichts ist getan,/ tue nun Herz-Werk."

48. In March of 1908, Rilke is still thinking of writing a Cézanne monograph, as he writes to Anton Kippenberg, his editor: "Zwischendurch soll, im kommenden Sommer noch, eine Arbeit über Cézanne abgeschlossen werden, deren Wiederaufnahme auch von meiner Rückkehr nach Paris abhängig ist" (235). But he never wrote the work, perhaps, also, because the writing of the *Malte* absorbed all other projects during these years.

49. In the same letter, Rilke reminds Clara of the passage on "Une Charogne" in the *Malte*, whose drafts he sent her regularly: *Du* erinnerst sicher . . . aus den *Aufzeichnungen des Malte Laurids*, die Stelle, die von Baudelaire handelt un von seinem Gedichte: 'Das Aas' " (207). The definitive passage in the *Malte*, published in 1910, seems to echo our letter: "Erinnerst Du Dich an Baudelaires unglaubliches Gedicht 'Une Charogne'? Es kann sein, dass ich es jetzt verstehe. . . . Es war seine Aufgabe, in diesem Schrecklichen, scheinbar nur Widerwärtigen das Seiende zu sehen, das unter allem Seienden gilt. Auswahl und Ablehnung gibt es nicht" (*Sämtliche Werke* 11: 75).

50. The vital link between Rilke's Cézanne encounter and his writing of the *Malte* surfaces again in a letter, written to Clara over a year later (September, 1908): "I actually ought to have written it [the *Malte* book] last year, I feel it now. After the Cézanne-Letters, which touched it so closely and severeley, I had arrived at the limits of this figure: for Cézanne is none other than the first, primitive and barren succeeding of that which in M. L. did not yet succeed. Brigge's death: that was Cézanne's life, the life of his last thirty years" (252–3).

51. He celebrated it in an accomplished translation, or rather *Umdichtung*, in the last years of his life. Cf. Rilke, *Übertragungen* (Frankfurt: Insel Verlag, 1975) 281–83.

52. Rilke keenly perceived Cézanne's growing impatience with Bernard, who was

preparing to write a work about him. Thus the painter wrote him in 1904: "Talks on art are almost useless. The work which produces progress in one's own profession is sufficient compensation for not being understood by imbeciles." "Do not be an art critic, but paint; therein lies salvation" (Rewald, *Cézanne* 161).

53. For a reproduction of the famous painting, cf. Raynal, *Cézanne* 49.
54. Mallarmé, *Oeuvres complètes* (Paris: Gallimard, 1945) 386.
55. The self-portrait may be one painted toward 1879; for a reproduction of the still life, "The Black Clock," 1869–70, cf. Raynal, *Cézanne* 33.
56. Thus, in a rare letter discussing his "influences," Rilke writes in 1924, two years before his death: "—und als das stärkste Vorbild stand, seit 1906, das Werk eines Malers vor mir, Paul Cézannes, dem ich dann, nach dem Tode des Meisters, auf allen Spuren nachging" (*Briefe*, II [1914–1926] 440).

PIRANDELLO'S ANTI-ARISTOTELIAN MOVE: CHARACTER AS TEXT

Alice N. Benston

Aristotle's conviction that plot, rather than character, is primary in drama is based on the premise that action is efficacious: not only does it matter what we do, but, in fact we become what we are in the way we choose or refuse to act and by the manner in which we respond to events. There is no construct such as personality or character prior to or outside of an individual's involvement within the nexus of human interaction, all of which are placed within a stable metaphysical structure. A dramatist chooses events so as to create a world in which character happens. Thus the selection and ordering of events, Aristotle maintains, is the essential act of the playwright, and from this major premise, he constructs the formal principles of his *Poetics*.

Modern drama's "war to the death with the past," as Ibsen called it, questions some or all of Aristotle's tightly constructed argument and the heritage it gave Western dramatists. Brecht most explicitly declares war on Aristotle in order to create the possibility of meaningful social action in a world without metaphysical systems. Sensing the implied metaphysics of limitation, stasis and determinism in the form of the classics, he argues against closed structures in order to suggest the possibility of different choices, different actions. It has been insufficiently noticed that Pirandello's drama is also devastatingly anti-Aristotelian, perhaps because Brecht took the role of anti-Aristotelian theorist and others made more obvious assaults on inherited formal principles. For, in Pirandello's works, character is destroyed rather than revealed, reversing the fundamental dramaturgical rule of classical drama.

Very early in his career Pirandello defined modernism as a radical lack of belief in external systems, which, when held, lend significance to our actions. Aware of this absence we each, in our private subjectivities, fabricate constructs in order to authenticate or authorize our actions. Further, Pirandello held that this change in world view does not mean that fundamental human desires have altered. Rather, the source of modern tensions is the need to express passions in a world that has lost a stable referentiality. In an early novel, *The Late Mattia Pascal* (*Il fu Mattia Pascal*), he presents a character who has come to perceive a metaphysical absence and has taken a Pascalian leap of faith into theosophy. At one point he bursts into Mattia's room announcing, excitedly, that the tragedy of Orestes is to be played at a marionette theater that evening:

> Automatic marionettes, the very latest invention . . . Now listen to the curious idea that's occurred to me: if at the climax of the play, just when the marionette who is playing Orestes is about to avenge his father's death and kill his mother and Aegisthus, suppose there were a little hole torn in the paper sky of the scenery. What would happen? . . . Orestes would be terribly upset by the hole in the sky . . . Orestes would still feel his desire for revenge, he would still want passionately to achieve it, but his eyes, at that point, would go straight to that hole, from which every kind of evil influence would then crowd the stage, and Orestes would feel suddenly helpless. In other words, Orestes would become Hamlet. There's the whole difference between ancient tragedy and modern . . . a hole torn in a paper sky. (145)

This manipulation of the-world-as-stage metaphor is the key to Pirandello's modernity. Here the stage is the world. Along with Nietzsche and many subsequent commentators, Pirandello regards *Hamlet* as the great precursor of modern sensibility. Presented in this little drama, Hamlet is a character without an author, an Orestes who no longer can count on the validity of his actions, since there is no higher authority even watching, let alone directing, his actions. This, however, is Pirandello's Hamlet with a Pirandellan theatrical sense of his being. Shakespeare, after all, has his Hamlet come to the conclusion that "His eye is on the sparrow," and, however ironized or painful, the Renaissance world-as-stage metaphor continues to be enabling, even if only in Macbeth's weary acknowledgement of the meaninglessness of the actions of the "poor players."

Macbeth's "tale of fury, signifying nothing" is also echoed in Pirandello's novel. Mattia Pascal is introduced as a librarian at the beginning of the story. Only he and an elderly colleague, along with a host of rats, inhabit the place. No one else ever comes to the library.

Alice N. Benston 149

Dusting the chronicles, Pascal one day exclaims to his solitary companion: "Copernicus has ruined humanity forever. We have all gradually become used to the idea of our infinite smallness, and we even consider ourselves less than nothing in the universe, despite all our fine discoveries and inventions. What value can information about our private troubles have, when even mass disasters count for nothing? Our stories are like the biographies of worms" (5). Copernicus, then, has pulled the linchpin of individual importance from the Aristotelian metaphysical structure, and with it goes the protective paper ceiling that allowed us to believe in the importance of our play, an importance that not only justifies but glorifies the deeds of the protagonists in classical tragedy.

Other modern playwrights defy the implications of this diminished view of humanity by claiming the significance of "worms." Synge's *Rider to the Sea* is an example of a successful attempt to replace the tragedy of heroes by exploring basic tragic rhythms in the lives of the most unnoticed. Ibsen replaces the gods with biology and sociology to create a modern tragedy, and Miller argues explicitly for the "tragedy of the little man." But Pirandello dismisses this possibility in his remarkable reading of *Don Quixote* in *On Humor* (*L'Umorismo*). Don Quixote is Cervantes. Sitting in prison, Cervantes realizes that the ideals he had embodied as a soldier, veteran of Lepanto and Terceira, were fictions. He had believed the enemy, who were but windmills, to be real giants. Enchanted by those ideals, he had not realized that his helmet was a barber's basin. Pirandello pictures Cervantes coming to this view of a sudden and bursting out in laughter. From this laughter the epic, whose hero is of one piece, dies, and the modern comic novel, with its report of fractured consciousness, is born. A new comic vision, rather than the recasting of tragedy, is required.

Pirandello's conviction is that, robbed of the comforting belief in external systems, perceiving them to be but fictions, each person has to construct a covering lie, a fiction, in order to live. For, it will be remembered, Orestes may be stripped of external justification for matricide, but not of the emotions. He still desires revenge. Sharing Hamlet's awareness of the rent in the sky, we lack authority and, hence, are all characters in search of an author. Indeed, we cannot return to Wittenberg, once its comforting old truths are disrupted. All the more, then, we crave justice and seek to make a truth out of our desires, loves and hatreds. To the degree that we perceive the discrepancies between our need to express and control our desires and the conflicting desires that are the demands of others we either invite madness, as Hamlet, or yield to self-laughter, as did Cervantes. To demonstrate his perception of the modern world, Pirandello took Cervantes' comic disposition and combined it with an inversion of Hamlet's idea of a theater to create his own dramaturgy. Thus while Hamlet can instruct the players to hold up a mirror to nature, Pirandello places the mirror off stage as well as on, dramatizing the way in which life itself is theatricalized in the modern world. It is artifice that creates the sense of self which, once defined purpose is removed, is but a construct, a "mask," in order that we may "make pretend" that we have a purpose and that others can know it. If the stage is a mirror held up to reality, in the absence of a certainty as to the nature of reality, everything is a mirror game and there is a stage in every mirror.

To shatter the comfortable assumptions of those who have yet to perceive the rent in the sky, Pirandello employs a basically realistic theater. Even in the theater trilogy, the play-within-the-play is carefully contained within the proscenium arch, obeying the fourth-wall conventions. The ruptures, when they come, are all the more astonishing. The wall is breached only three times, and on each occasion, it is realistically justified. For example, the sudden appearance of Madam Pace, in *Six Characters in Search of an Author* (*Sei personaggi*) in a sense is "realistic" because the subject is playmaking and her character is required for the play that is being created. Hence she is "willed" into being by the would-be dramatists. Only early in his career, in *It is So! If You Think So* (*Cosi è, se vi pare!*), does he use an overt raisonneur who is not amalgamated into the action. It is precisely because Pirandello does not believe that there is another, "truer" reality to be discovered behind the world of flesh and blood that he must preserve the conventions of realism.

The illusion is not that we take the material world as real, while a mystery to be uncovered resides beyond. The problem lies in our need for interpretation, which is based on some sense of self. What he would disabuse us of is the conviction that we all read reality the same way. Since, in order to live in the world of flux, we need to create fictions, those covering lies that make it possible for us to act, conflict comes in Pirandello's theater when one construct contradicts another. Hence character, itself a covering fiction, precedes action. This

Alice N. Benston 151

proposition is parsed over and over again in Pirandello's plays. As one of his characters says, Pirandello is "always harping on this illusion and reality string" (*Each in His Own Way*). But even this remark is ironic, since it is the illusion of reality that he is revealing, as the title of his collected works, *Naked Masks* (*Maschere nude*) makes eminently clear. What is exposed is the way his characters create masks and the passions covered by these constructs.

Pirandello seeks to uncover what he considers to be the primary illusion, the conviction that there is some system external to ourselves which provides a sense of stability, a truth or reality providing a justification for our personal fictions. In *It is So!* Laudisi, the spokesman for perspectivism says: "You're the people who are looking for records to be able to affirm or deny something. Personally, I don't give a rap for the documents: for the truth in my view is not in them but in the mind" (A 97). In this play a whole town has been set in turmoil by the confusing relationships among the members of the Ponza family—husband, wife and mother-in-law, new-comers to the town. Why is it that the mother is never allowed to visit her daughter? Is the husband right and the mother-in-law mad, or does she live a lie to protect him from his own madness? It is not sufficient to call these inquirers "busybodies," as Eric Bentley does and oppose them to the Ponzas, implying that their snooping is a cause of the family's suffering (150). Their pain, the cause of which we never come to know, necessitated the masking that bewilders the investigators. The inquisitive, on their part, have a need for certainty as much as the family has a need for its strange arrangement. If the riddle cannot be solved, it is the townsfolk's sense of reality that will be undermined.

In a sense *It is So!* is a parody of *Oedipus Rex*: the bringing of witness and the searching for documents charts a plot that echoes the rhythm of the play that was Aristotle's model. Oedipus' victory is that, in the course of the play, he enacts and maintains his status as the solver of riddles. It is he who takes the action that reveals the full story. In Pirandello's play, the plot will not yield a story, and the mystery solvers will not gain knowledge. All is reversed from the Aristotelian heritage as, comically, the very purpose of Western drama is thwarted. The documents sought and found turn out to be inconclusive, and the explanations given by the mother-in-law and the husband are equally compelling. When, at the end of the play, the daughter is called upon to break the tie, she refuses to unveil, both literally and figuratively. She will only confirm both versions, insisting that she, herself, has no identity beyond that which the other two require.

The function and nature of irony itself is also reversed from its Sophoclean purpose. Those who believed that there was one truth are disabused, and the audience who are led to laugh at the "busybodies" has to face the nature of its own curiosities: we, too, had expected a certain explanation. Laudisi's derisive laughter ends the play, and we as well as the townsfolk have to accept his statement that the Ponzas' fictitious reality, since it serves them so well, could not be destroyed by documents or reasoned inquiry. The lie, as Laudisi says, has "all the earmarks of reality" (A 98).

It is interesting that *It is So!* is one of the few plays in which the covering fiction remains intact and seems to be efficacious. The other examples come from plays that lie outside Pirandello's main corpus: *Liolà*, an early Sicilian comedy and *Lazarus*, a late quasi-religious play. More generally, Pirandello destroys masks and refuses to reconstruct them, as in *Six Characters in Search of an Author* (*Sei personaggi in cerca d'auttore*) and *As You Desire Me* (*Come tu mi vuoi*). The theater plays, *Six Characters*, *Each in His Own Way* (*Ciascuno a suo modo*) and *Tonight We Improvise* (*Questa sera si recita a soggetto*) explode rather than resolve; there is no final act. The indeterminacy and lack of closure suggests that modernism, in Pirandello, contains the precepts of post-modernism.

The major purpose of Pirandello's work, then, is to observe the process of masking and unmasking and, in examining the reasons for a character's construction of a particular fiction, reveal what happens when it is destroyed. In some works, notably *To Clothe the Naked* (*Vestire gli ignudi*) and *The Pleasures of Honesty* (*Il piacere dell'onestà*), as well as in the novel cited earlier (*The Late Mattia Pascal*), we are explicitly involved with characters who "lie," that is, self-consciously construct fictitious personae. The novel is an extended adventure in the possibilities of self-fashioning. Pascal, who has fortuitously been pronounced dead when a drowned man's body is identified as his, seizes the opportunity to create a whole new persona to free himself from the strains of an unhappy life. Ursula Drie, in *Naked*, believing that she is about to die from the poison she has taken, tells a story to a newspaper reporter that will cover her sordid past with a dignified fiction. Baldivino, in *The Pleasure of Honesty*

(B), agrees to marry the pregnant Maddalena to cover over her lover's adulterous actions.

Each of these fictions, it is interesting to note, results from the desire to alter a previous sexual attachment, a passion gone astray, and each collapses when a new passion intrudes. For example, Pascal has to relinquish his freedom as a dead man, which he undertook because of a loveless marriage, when he finds himself attracted to a young girl and she to him. His lie cannot incorporate others, since it is not attached to life. Ironically he finds that those in "life" can lie easily. Confined in his artificial form, he can no longer yield to life's flux, since the fiction is too fixed to accommodate new circumstances.

Ursula Drie (*Naked*), is a victim of other people's desires. Each of the males in Ursula's life insists that her story be consistent with his picture of himself as protector or lover. Her lie forces each of them to recognize his own desire. Nota, the author who has taken Ursula in after her failed suicide attempt, needs her in order to confirm his own artistic intuition and as a way to reenter life. He feels his isolation as an author, as one who has only lived through the fictions he has created. Laspiga, a young naval officer, wants to believe the romantic myth that she tried to commit suicide because he had deserted her. Consul Gotti wants to deny his complicity in his affair with her and that his sexual passion makes him equally responsible for the death of his child, whom they left unattended in their passion. What none of them is willing to recognize is that Ursula lied to cover her realization that she had acted out of her own sexual needs and that she loves none of them. But while she resists becoming the character each of the males would have her be, she learns that she cannot be what she desires as long as she is caught in the nexus of human relationships. Since each story contradicts the other, Pirandello refusing to amalgamate or arbitrate, the notion of monological plot is critiqued as well as the nature of human passions.

Baldivino (*The Pleasures of Honesty*) is representative of the male Pirandellan protagonist who is (or considers himself to be) intellectually superior to those around him. Like Leone in *The Rules of the Game* (*Il giuoco delle parti*), or Henry in *Henry IV*, he is exquisitely aware of the human condition and hence, like the other characters in this group, he serves as an instrument of Pirandello's self-conscious examination of the nature and power of form and masks. Baldivino cites Descartes in expressing his belief that only the repetition of events allows us to be seduced into believing that we are dealing with something tangible, something we call the "real". Hence, in discharging his promise to clothe the family with a social myth of propriety, he insists on absolute conformity, absolute rigor in their behavior. As a result, while he blossoms into a handsome and confident man within the mask he wears, the others suffocate under the domination that results. Absolute form is killing: it cannot represent all our needs, all our desires, and one man's saving fiction is another's death mask. Finally Baldovino has to give up the security of his fictitious role when he discovers that its basic internal deception is about to give way. He has not acted as husband-lover. But Maddalena has fallen in love with the character he has created, and he is forced to realize that he has prolonged his fiction as a safeguard against his own growing love. Courageously they agree to accept the lie as their truth, well aware that they are entering into a relationship that cannot rely on static fictions and which, in the course of flux and change, will bring pain.

Henry is perhaps the best known and best example of Pirandello's sensitive intellectuals; for this reason *Henry IV* is often read as his *Hamlet*. The play, in all its richness, revolves around a series of appropriations of masks. Henry actually chooses his role three times, initially assuming his historical identity as part of a masquerade. Clearly, he saw in the historical Henry a double of his own suffering and humiliation. When the fall from his horse during the masquerade's pageant causes his "madness," that is when he awakes believing he is the medieval king, he plays his role as a true fiction, one bounded by a static plot. Hence he endlessly repeats the known events of the historical figure's chronicled story. The madman's mask is absolute, and it is an instrument of domination; all those around him must take up roles to satisfy his drama. It is the only way to escape the painful nexus of human interactions. Much like Don Quixote, Henry controls the story and action, since those who believe him to be mad "play along."

Pirandello's play does not follow this linear history; rather the plot involves the audience in the question of the nature and reality of madness itself, the revelation of Henry's lucid play-acting constituting one of the major reversals of the drama. We have been watching a group of people from his former existence attempt to lure him from his presumed madness. Their intrusion into his comfortable fiction forces Henry to make a final choice. The shock therapy that the group plans to administer involves another self-conscious manipulation of time, flux, and fictions. A portrait of his beloved marchioness, in costume, is to be replaced by her living daughter decked out in the same dress. Their hope is that this substitution of life for artifice will bring him into the contemporary world. When he reveals himself in anger to the intrusive group, he accuses them of planning a tactic that could have returned him to madness. As he confronts them he explains the reasons for his assumption of the mask the second time. Better the known pain of his historical character, one he can manipulate and control, than the denials and humiliations of those around him. Conflict rises as Henry accuses Baron di Nolli of having purposely pricked the horse that threw him years ago. As his anger grows, he grabs the young girl, Frieda, thus making a final choice consistent with his intellectual conviction that the only way to assuage pain is to step outside the flux, the change wrought by time, ageing and the conflict of desires. He wants to reassert his authorial control as he has had it ever since he "sanely" took up the mask of "insanity." Since it is Frieda, not her mother, who represents what he lost when he was removed from "the banquet of life," his choice is also consistent with the passion that motivated previous actions—sexual jealousy.

But Henry's freedom to choose is ended when he kills the baron. Having chosen revenge, he is permanently condemned to his mask of madness, although he is totally aware of his condition. He will stare out forever, with a look of horrified recognition. Henry is one of Pirandello's greatest creations, and may be likened to a modern Orestes, who still feels the need for revenge, even when there is no sanction, no covering paper sky. But the source of his desire is more like that of Dante's Francesca, since she, too, is caught forever by her passion. It is she whom Pirandello uses as an example, in his preface to *Six Characters*, to explicate the difference between art and life. To achieve the fixity of art is to be "embalmed" forever: "hence ... Francesca alive and confessing to Dante her sweet sin" will be there for a hundred thousand times as the pages are turned "repeating the story each time with such living and sudden passion that Dante every time will turn faint" (A 372).

It is interesting that, of the hundreds of Dante's characters whom Pirandello might have recalled, he chooses Francesca and her "sweet sin." But even this short review of his work shows us that it is primarily sexual passion and jealousy that Pirandello explores. For the final scandal of the human condition is our inability to control our passions coupled with our inability to construct the "other" as we would have him or her. Like Strindberg, he realized that the pain of confronting otherness is most vividly experienced in the relation between the sexes. In *Six Characters* Pirandello unites this ongoing concern with an examination of the connection between this conflict and the nature of the theater itself and the act of artistic creation. Just as Ursula had a pre-history before the actual plot events of *Naked*, so, too, does the family of six, the characters, who invade a theater, interrupting a group of actors who are setting up for a rehearsal. As in *Naked*, the characters' stories are revealed bit by bit as the events of the play move forward. It is interesting to note that Pirandello's procedure is much the same as Sophocles' in *Oedipus*, Aristotle's model. Pirandello also uses foreshadowing, irony and revelations attendant on angry, passionate outbursts as moments to reveal that pre-history.

The story, as we come to know it, is again one of sexual passion and the desire for control. The Father, having observed what he takes to be his wife's desire for another man, sends her away with her lover, keeping their son with him. Many years later, as he is about to consummate an assignation with a young woman who has been procured for him by a dressmaker, Madam Pace, his former wife rushes in to reveal that the girl is his step-daughter. The Father, who could control sexual jealousy cannot control basic sexual needs, and the Mother's revelation only narrowly prevents "incest." In a kind of parodic inversion of the Oedipal problem, the Father forgets that one may be sleeping with one's daughter if he sleeps with a younger woman, just as Oedipus forgets that any older woman may be one's mother. But in marked contrast to the Sophoclean drama, knowledge and the avoidance of the sex act itself cannot prevent conflict and pain. In Pirandello's story, the Father then takes the destitute wife and her children, the older Step-Daughter and a young boy and girl to his home. His older son refuses to accept his step-siblings, just as he refuses to cooperate in the creation of the play as one of the "characters."

The denouement of the story coincides both with the end of the attempt to create the play-within-the-play and the play Pirandello has written. The much foreshadowed pistol shot is revealed to be the young boy's action as he shoots himself, when he comes upon his little sister drowned in the courtyard fountain. Pirandello's play enacts the struggle amongst the characters to have their version of the story represented. It is a power struggle, principally between the Father and his step-daughter. Once again, facts are of no importance; the incidents of the "story" are never in dispute. It is a question of character, motivation and intent. What matters is who gets to tell the story. If you are Helen, it matters whether it is Aeschylus or Euripides who is authoring you. The power, then, lies with the authority of the teller, in language and interpretation.

But the struggle is also between the genres, between the power of narration and that of mimetic representation. Mary Ann Frese Witt explores both the modal and sexual tensions implied by this struggle in what she calls "The Battle of the Lexis," noting that, in *Six Characters*, this contest "has a psychoanalytical basis in that the female code parallels the mimetic, and the male code parallels the diegetic in the painful struggle to represent certain primal scenes" (402). This clash of codes is to be found throughout Pirandello's work, Witt says, and it is through this opposition of showing (drama) and telling (narrative) that he joins Brecht as an anti-Aristotelian modernist (397). Witt examines this particular play because, as she puts it, it is his most "radical." She might have noted that it is his most radical because it is his most overtly self-conscious play; theater, itself, is its true subject. The possibility of the co-existence of the codes is what is dramatized, and the format allows Pirandello to break the cardinal rule of authorial remove in the dramatic. He is on stage himself. The theater company is rehearsing one of his plays when the six characters intrude. But more than that, and ironically, it is his absence, or abstinence, his refusal to dramatize them that has brought the six to the theater "in search of an author."

The theater setting presents another level of confrontation, one that cannot be covered by Witt's linguistic examination. Half of the staged battle occurs between the characters and the troupe. It is not simply that the drama cannot cover the inchoate narrative, or as Witt puts it, "the impossibility of purely showing what must be told" (397), but how the theater works through artifice, through images which are themselves distanced from "reality." Here it is helpful to recall Nietzsche's opposition between the Dionysian and the Appollonian. The pure suffering pre-linguistic Dionysian always resists the constraints of the Apollonian image maker, but, without those constraints, the experience cannot be communicated. It is one of the deepest ironies that the central protagonists cannot accept the direction or choices of the people of the theater. The Step-Daughter, in her frenzy over the fateful room's decor, is being the positivist, refusing to accept the distinction between the object or gesture as experienced and the object or gesture as signified. It is her refusal to have the actress "play" her rather than "be" her that constitutes this struggle. If, as is usually true, we experience the character of the Step-Daughter to be more vital, more "real," than the character of the actress, we have been seduced to Pirandello's vision of theater as the site of passionate struggle. Both, of course, are, characters, both created by an author, both portrayed by actresses whose own pre-stories have nothing to do with what we are watching. But Pirandello has more highly imaged the painful need to be represented in the character of the Step-Daughter than he has the actress's need to be able to portray the Step-Daughter. Like Francesca, the Step-Daughter will always be there to scream her pain and scoff at the figure of her father as long as there is an actress to play her. However, if she stands ready to proclaim the plight of the female victim, frequently inarticulate as is the Mother and her little sister, so too does the Father stand ready to reenact the shame of his failure, his inability to construct a protective, rational cover for very basic emotions. He will forever declaim on life, art and be "too literary," as the theater people say of him. His very excess of language is a mark of the failure of the body's performance. As Shoshana Felman puts it, in analyzing the relationship between the erotic and the speech act in J. L. Austin's work and Molière's *Don Juan*, "The act of *failing* thus leads, paradoxically, to an *excess* of utterance. . . . It is precisely this excess of energy that is continually discharged through humor" (113, emphasis in original). Hamlet's wit and constant verbal play can also be seen as the product of the same failure.

Pirandello's refusal, in *Six Characters*, to plot the story, or rather to choose between the Father's version and the Daughter's, is a refusal to take sides in this battle of the sexes. He does not take his Orestes to Athens to have his story adjudicated, find expiation, and be released from his furies. Pirandello's refusal subverts not only Aristotle's distinction between genre and modes, but also defies his cardinal observation that the act of playwriting is the act of selecting and ordering events chosen from the story. But this does not mean that telling triumphs over showing in *Six Characters*, for although a story does get told, it is as partial and as multiple as the characters' perspectives. Further, not all of the story is narrated. Ironically, again, the culminating act is that of the young boy's pistol shot, and the chaos that ensues demonstrates that his story has not been told and none of the other characters can tell it, caught as they are in their own subjectivity. As the Step-Daughter says, "Idiot! If I'd been in your place, instead of killing myself, I'd have shot one of those two, or both of them: father and son" (A 238). That, of course, reflects her own desire for revenge. We will never know what the suicide represents as intent, since all action ceases with it. Thus explosive, direct action kills narration.

But the shot also kills playwriting. The hazard of the game that Pirandello is playing is that, if the last irony is not perceived, and much of the thematic criticism of the play indicates that it escapes many, then the victory is Aristotle's. A story cannot be staged; reality must be shaped to be represented. That final moment in which the violent act, the pistol shot, catches the acting troop in the illusion of reality—"Is he dead?"—confirms the power of representation. It is ironic that the actors are furious at being caught by the very command they have over us, the usual audience. But the deepest irony, and the contrast with Aristotle, is that Pirandello has indeed written a play, the one we are watching. He has found a way to dramatize the abstract questions that are the sub-text of all his work. The conflict between life and art, flux and form, the chaos of experience and the limiting and limited statement of form, the philosophizing that is a passion versus the passion that is expressed in direct action are the material out of which he orders the incidents of this play. And he exerts complete authorial control over this impossible conflict. Although it is the most self-conscious of his work, or for that matter among all the overtly theatrical modern plays, it rigorously adheres to the formal elements of realism, down to finicky directions to the actors. As noted earlier, even the sudden appearance of Madam Pace is self-consciously justified. It is due to this realistic frame that the play works and that all the ironies can evolve. For just as the shot suddenly seems "real," we must be seduced, all along, into believing the reality of the fantastic six characters.

The triumph of *Six Characters* is that it brings together all of Pirandello's observations about the human condition and the nature of his art, demonstrating that his view of the world is, itself, deeply theatrical. We all want to author ourselves, but cannot. We cannot keep either ourselves, our passions, or those of others from changing over time, and if we deny change, we live lies. Nor can we create fictions that will assuage our need for others. Out of this need we will attempt to fix others in their roles and to cover our embarrassment with justifying lies. What happens in Pirandello's plays is that conflicting fictions reveal how we deceive ourselves in defining the objects of our desires. Pirandello's Copernican revolution was to remove that final anchor of the seeming strategies of self-definition and control. Not only are we incapable of fixing the other to our desires, but, as Pascal said, and Pirandello quotes in l'*Umorismo*, "[t]here is no man who differs more from another man more than he differs, with the passing of time, from himself" (136).

WORKS CITED

Bentley, Eric. *The Playwright at Thinker*
Felman, Shoshana. *The Literary Speech Act: Don Juan with J. L. Austin, or Seduction in Two Languages.* Trans. Catherine Porter. Ithaca: Cornell UP, 1983.
Pirandello, Luigi. *Naked Masks: Five Plays by Luigi Pirandello.* Ed. Eric Bentley. New York: E. P. Dutton & Co., 1952. (A)
———. *On Humor.* Trans. Antonio Illiano and Daniel P. Testa. Chapel Hill: U of North Carolina, 1974.
———. *The Late Mattia Pascal.* Trans. William Weaver. New York: Rizzoli, 1984.
———. *To Clothe the Naked and Two Other Plays.* Trans. William Murray. New York: E. P. Dutton & Co., 1962. (B)
Will, Mary Ann Frese. "Six Characters in Search of an Author and the Battle of the Lexis." *Modern Drama* 30.3 (1987): 396–404.

FROM *MARIANNE* TO *VENDREDI*: TWO *HEBDOMADAIRES DE GAUCHE* OF THE POPULAR FRONT

Steven Ungar

The End of an Order, the End of a World

The 1936 election of the Popular Front government in France marks the end of a social order held together by the differences of class and culture evoked throughout Marcel Proust's *A la recherche du temps perdu*. For some, that end is welcome and long awaited. Lasting less than two years at the end of France's longest Republic to date, the Popular Front is a period of intense political, social and cultural reform. Despite its brevity and its evident failures, it remains the object of joyful remembrance: "The Popular Front myth, historically and culturally, draws much of its pervasive and continuing power from the way in which it acts as an imaginary resolution of political contradictions."[1] Beyond popular memory, critical inquiry into the Popular Front might well be organized around a number of major questions involving object, method and aim. How does the Popular Front appear and disappear within the 1930s? How might it provide us with a better understanding of interwar France? The questions are so vast and complex that some selectivity is required.

My choice of the interwar period stems from a view that its role in the cultures of modernity has yet to be determined. Historians and political scientists such as Eugen Weber, H. Stuart Hughes, Zeev Sternhell, Robert Soucy and Ezra Suleiman have written on the period with insight and sensitivity. But most literary and cultural studies seldom forsake the "higher" realms of the fine arts and letters; little has been done to explore the institutional and industrial aspects of interwar French culture. The following pages are part of a longer project setting the 1936-1938 Popular Front period within a wider ("denser") configuration linking art and culture to historical processes.

At the start of his history of French film of the 1930s, Jean-Pierre Jeancolas notes how description, analysis and interpretation are preceded by more elementary concerns of time and period: "Moving forward, I realized that the thirties did not end in 1940. They did not end at all. From 1937 or 1938 on, they are caught up in a vague time during which the Popular Front dissolves while the spectre of a war nobody wants anything to do with takes shape on the horizon. The war begins before the war." [2] Taking Jeancolas at his word but in the opposite chronological direction, I want to begin my account by suggesting that the thirties begin . . . before the thirties.

Through the late 1920s, Surrealism is the notorious offshoot of a generation of educated French youth discontent with its cultural legacy (*patrimoine*). But even here, what passes for avant-garde in literature, painting, theater and film smacks of privilege and elitism. André Breton, Philippe Soupault and Louis Aragon call their prototype Surrealist journal *Littérature*, but any irony conveyed by their title also affirms a tie to established practices which—presumably—they intend to subvert. Likewise, Breton's attempts to mobilize Surrealism into a revolutionary force are sincere, but most readers of the *Surrealist Manifestoes* of 1924 and 1930 remain at a comfortable distance from working class struggles. When Breton joins the French Communist Party in 1927, the brevity of his affiliation is as telling as any declaration of solidarity. To the extent that it can be taken as a revolutionary doctrine, Surrealism resolutely affirms its independence from party allegiance.

Breton's zigzags should be seen in the context of the instability of French politics in the 1925–40 period. Such instability is not, however, always identified with change. For Germaine Brée, it is more apparent than real: taken as a whole, the years 1920–36 witnessed a fairly consistent alternation between governments of the Left and Right; 1920–24, Bloc National 1924–26, Cartel des Gauches; 1928–30, Union Nationale; 1936, Front Populaire. Furthermore, until the acute governmental crisis of the thirties, the French economy seemed to run fairly smoothly and even to be improving. A trend toward increased prosperity between 1924 and 1930 spread to the lower-middle and working classes, giving people an impression of being better off.[3] My own perception of the period is somewhat different, with an emphasis on the conflict between a mentality of polarization and what Brée sees as the overriding continuity of political forms. But even in Brée's model of consistent alternation, difference is cumulative and thus visible only over an extended duration. For the interwar years, a progressive devaluation of established political forms and institutions imposes an urgency to the call for reform and change which, in France, comes to full expression between 1932 and 1938.

From the Defense of Culture to Everyday Life

The 1930–35 period in France is marked by a wave of transitory movements, fronts, unions and coalitions promoting visions of a politically ambitious culture. Typically, these groups are united by a shared opposition: they are anti-Communist rather than conservative, or anti-Fascist rather than liberal. On Friday, June 21, 1935, André Gide is keynote speaker at the First International Congress for the Defense of Culture, held at the Palais de la Mutualité in Paris, with some twenty to thirty speakers over five days. Here, in part, is his sense of what is at stake at the Congress: "Literature has never been more alive. Never has so much been written and printed, in France and in all civilized countries. Why then do we keep hearing that our culture is in danger?"[4] Gide's remarks point to the tone of immediacy surrounding cultural debate in the context of spiritual and political crisis. At the same time, they illustrate the inability of Gide's literary generation to move beyond the attitude of sympathetic fellow travellers. Eloquent as they may be, Gide's words are no longer in tune with the militancy imposed by the times.

When direct political action is blocked, it is replaced by symbolic resistance in the form of alternative forms and practices. In *Teachers, Writers, Celebrities*, Régis Debray writes a critical history of the intellectual function from the Third Republic to the present. For Debray, a period of influence for publishing between 1920 and 1960 straddles the Third, Fourth, and Fifth Republics as an intermediary phase between a university cycle dominating French cultural institutions from the start of the Third Republic to 1920 and a post-1968 media cycle from which we have not yet emerged. Adapting Debray's model to the post World War I period, I want to focus on the transition from a traditional academic environment toward a literary culture dominated by the figure of the publisher, the institution of the publishing house and the industry of the book trade.

In nineteenth-century France, the notion of word as commodity already extends traditional literary culture toward popular forms such as the newspaper:

> The daily paper was arguably the *first* consumer commodity made to be perishable, purchased to be thrown away. It became the most ubiquitous example of the habits of consciousness and of socioeconomic practice which, in more explicit, thematic forms it sought to impart to its audience—or, as we might say, within its market. In selling a transformed perception of its culture, it sold itself first of all. The disenchanted intelligentsia, the alienated writers, reacted predictably. For them, the newspaper became the quintessential figure for the discourse of their middle-class enemy, the *name* of writing against which they sought to counterpose their own. . . . In the 19th century, the daily had not yet retreated into the transparency of dailyness.[5]

The newspaper is a highly accessible form of the written word capable of serving as chronicle, forum and marketplace. When viewed as a composite of texts, it illustrates how what we refer to as news derives from a plurality of evolving cultural practices, both high and low. The notion of news as an interplay of event and text bears directly on issues of representation I want to address in the specific instance of the left-wing weekly. At the level of cultural practice, it also affects the relation between journalism and literature: "Much of 'literature' defines its conditions of existence as counter-discursive. Its status as 'literary' *marks* it as oppositional. For this reason, any attempt to seize dominant discourse leads *outside* the high cultural realm and into areas which might almost seem drearily down to earth" (Terdiman, 117).

Over the final decade of the Third Republic, a proliferation of political and literary journals emphasizes the format of the weekly. Because my inquiry involves a good amount of description, I want once again to characterize it through a series of working questions. Why did these publications flourish when they did? Why is the interwar period in France often called the age of the weekly? How is the proliferation of weeklies—that is, their genesis, financing, format, marketing, personnel and editorial policies—determined within the cultures of the word from literary publishing to advertising? In sum, what follows is based on the assumption that an understanding of the successes and failures of *Marianne* and *Vendredi* can, in turn, promote a clearer sense of the Popular Front as a historical and cultural phenomenon. The major Parisian weeklies of the 1930s grow out of the daily. On the eve of World War I, *Le Petit Parisien* and *Le Petit Journal* lead Parisian newspapers with respective circulations of 1,550,000 and 600,000. Both are creations of the mid-19th century. Of the two, *Le Petit Journal* is the older. Started in 1865, it is soon directed by Emile de Girardin who, in 1836, had founded the first wide-circulation Parisian daily, *La Presse*. Girardin has a shrewd sense of marketing and uses the *roman-feuilleton* to cater in particular to female readers. At the turn of the century, publicists of *Le Petit Journal* boast that their paper has five million readers.[6]

By the mid-1920s, competition from technical, trade, and specialty periodicals pushes the large Parisian dailies to create specialty sections—known as *pages magazines*—which always appear on the same day each week. These sections are often highlighted by splashy layouts and column headings; they range in subject from sports to theater, fashion to home improvements. While the news content of the specialty sections is minimal, their commercial function is evident: "The magazine pages addressed both reader and advertiser, appealing to the former in order to attract the latter. Such was, at least, the principle presiding over their birth in the high-circulation dailies where no serious expenditure was made without an eye toward profit" (Manevy 223).

Case Studies: Two Independent Weeklies

October 26, 1932: At a moment when its prestigious literary monthly, the *Nouvelle Revue Française*, seems locked into an outmoded and apolitical modernity, the Editions Gallimard launch *Marianne* ("grand hebdomadaire littéraire illustré"). Directed by Emmanuel Berl, *Marianne* is a large-format sixteen-page weekly mixing social and political commentary under the column headings "Le Monde comme il va" and "Les Caprices de Marianne" with reviews of literature, theater and film by Pierre Mac Orlan, Colette, Eugène Dabit, Ramon Fernandez, Jean Giraudoux, Emmanuel Mounier and Roger Vitac. In a throwback to the strategy of the 19th century daily, each issue contains a page of serialized fiction or work in progress by established writers such as Marcel Aymé, Roger Martin du Gard, Antoine de Saint-Exupéry and Georges Duhamel.

Marianne exudes the literary tone of the *NRF*, with Berl using his personal ties at the Quai d'Orsay to add political coverage to the cultural features. The result is singular: "By the quality and diversity of its contributors, by its makeup where arts and letters dominate politics, *Marianne* sets itself from the start on a plane apart from that of militant journalism."[7] Gaston Gallimard's motivation for financing the weekly is openly commercial: *Marianne* is created to compete with *Candide*, *Je suis partout* and *Gringoire*, highly successful weeklies of news and opinion which draw readers from the politically conservative Action Française. What *Candide* and *Je suis partout* had done for the Editions Fayard and *Gringoire* for the Editions de France, Gallimard wants *Marianne* to do for his publishing house. The new weekly is not Gallimard's first venture into popular journalism. As early as 1922, *la presse* becomes the third component of the "*NRF*, revue et édition mêlées" formula when Gallimard launches *Les Nouvelles Littéraires*, "le journal des gens d'esprit!" This early literary weekly is primarily a publicity vehicle, providing Gallimard with visibility for his writers as well as advertising space for his catalogue. Additionally, it allows him to promote lesser-known properties for the literary prizes which make or break the reputations of both writer and publisher.

Six years later, Gallimard consolidates his journalistic division when he establishes ZED Publications to cover his financial interests in publishing, printing and advertising. ZED allows Gallimard to pursue additional projects without risking the *NRF*'S finances and reputation. Soon, he launches two wide-circulation weeklies, *Détective* and *Voilà*. Where the former flaunts sensationalist coverage of crime and *faits divers*, the latter bills itself as "l'hebdomadaire du reportage" and features full-page pin-ups to illustrate the ghost-written memoirs of reputed *femme fatales*. Far removed from both the *NRF* and the literary aura of the "Collection Blanche," both weeklies enjoy wide circulation (up to 350,000 for *Détective* through 1936), allowing Gallimard to offset losses incurred by specialized periodicals such as *La Revue musicale*, *La Revue juive* and *La Revue de cinéma*.

At first, the strength of *Marianne*'s literary coverage overrides Berl's desire to promote his pacifist views. But by 1936, *Marianne* is out of line with the partisan sensibilities of the Popular Front. Even a peak circulation 120,000 is only half to a third of those of its conservative counterparts. 60,000 regular subscribers are not enough to keep the journal afloat. Berl stays on as director until January of 1937 when Gallimard sells *Marianne* to Raymond Patenôtre who wants to adopt a more profitable news and photo format ("another *Match*"). By 1939, Patenôtre's wish comes true: *Marianne* becomes *Marianne-Magazine*, a glossy weekly without serious political content. In August of 1940, it sets up shop in Lyon and supports the "revolutionary" Pétain government. Later the same month, its editorial section is completely shut down and *Marianne-Magazine* disappears.

While *Marianne* never becomes a serious commercial rival of *Candide*, its role as a liberal forum allows Berl to publish and commission texts by Gide, André Malraux, Pierre Drieu La Rochelle, and Léon Daudet.[8] In this, he follows the example of the *NRF* where independents and internal exiles from party politics alike are welcome:

> From the start, *Marianne* is marked politically: moderate Left, non-militant, antifascist, favorable without great enthusiasm toward the Popular Front. The journal defends peace, Briand against Poincaré. In foreign policy matters, Berl does nothing without getting the opinion of Saint-Léger. Before each editorial, he takes his orders at the Quai d'Orsay. And when Bernanos breaks noisily with the extreme Right and Action Française, he chooses to do it with *Marianne*. All of which favors an image, a tone, a tendency wished for by Gallimard so that his weekly might be the *Candide* of the Left.[9]

Berl's politics set *Marianne* at a commercial disadvantage to its conservative rivals. Yet his support of neutrality culminates a spirit of non-partisan idealism found in other interwar journals such as *Clarté*, *Europe* and *Commune*. Less than three months after the February 1934 riots, a nucleus of writers including occasional contributors to *Marianne* such as André Chamson and Jean Guéhenno sets out to establish a new weekly. In November of 1935, they bring out the first issue of *Vendredi*, "hebdomadaire littéraire, politique et satirique fondé sur l'initiative d'écrivains et de journalistes et dirigé par eux."

More than any other weekly of the period, *Vendredi* marks the ambitions and complexities of the Popular Front. From the start, it operates as an antifascist collective. Its three directors—Chamson,

Guéhenno, and Andrée Viollis—form a precarious union of the Radical, Socialist and Communist constituency that is to elect the Popular Front government in May 1936. Like *Marianne*, *Vendredi* mixes reportage on literature and the arts, fiction in progress and political editorials. And in the tradition of *Le Canard enchaîné*, it features satirical commentary and cartoons. *Vendredi* develops directly out of the events of February 1934 and their aftermath. As recalled by Chamson's widow, Lucie Mazauric, the events between February 6 and 12, 1934 were so complex that immediate understanding was impossible: "In order to come up with a perfectly exact idea of events and their causes, I used to read tons of newspapers every day, from *L'Action Française* to *L'Humanité*, reading every article closely, following the strict practices of textual criticism, *à la chartiste*."[10]

November 11, 1935: *Vendredi*'s first issue is most promising. *A la une*: a presentation by Chamson, short polemic on "Les Trois Affaires Stavisky" and a table of contents announcing contributions by Gide, Jacques Maritain, Benda, Jean Giono and Paul Nizan. Soon, however, support turns to criticism. By the Popular Front's first anniversary, *Vendredi* denounces Blum's economic reforms of March 1937. On the international front, an excerpt from Gide's "Retour de l'URSS" (29 January 1937) and coverage of the Moscow Trials by Jean Guéhenno (5 February 1937) illustrate growing disenchantment with the Soviet government.

On another front, *Vendredi*'s coverage of the Spanish Civil War is extensive and openly sympathetic to the Republican cause. The February 26, 1937 issue alone carries two human-interest articles: "Visages de la Révolution espagnole: Barcelone" and "Commissaires de Guerre." Less than two months later, Paul Nizan denounces French non-intervention. Responding to those who favor negotiating a peaceful protection of Catalonia in exchange for the rest of Spain, Nizan openly expresses the impatience of the hard-line Communists who militate within *Vendredi* for a more aggressive foreign policy: "The Italian and German officers who get together at the Hotel Cristina in Seville have particular liking for this phrase: 'Next year, in Toulouse . . .' I wonder if allowing them to achieve this goal really promotes peace and if it is wise to uphold a policy which, under the pretext of defending the original revolution of Catalonia, is a hypocritical policy of betrayal in relation to an entire nation."[11] Fifty years after the fact, Nizan's article reads as an accurate forewarning against a mentality of conciliation which—by 1940—will have led to the Munich agreement, the phony war and the fall of France. Through the end of 1937, *Vendredi* follows the marketing formula of its competitors. Increasingly, however, its editorials are strident and oppositional. On the front page of *Vendredi*'s December 24, 1937 issue, an editorial by Andrée Viollis carries the ironic title, "Paix sur la terre" while Jean Renoir contributes a short piece on "Le Cinéma et l'état" and the right column offers a polemical exchange between Gide and Guéhenno. At the bottom, a cartoon entitled "Nuit de Noël" shows three Magi dressed in military gear hovering over an infant while a protective figure of Liberty holds a hand over the Christ child. The caption reads, "Vivra-t-il, le divin enfant?" The same issue carries a review of Malraux's *L'Espoir* and an ad by the Editions Denoël for Céline's *Bagatelles pour un massacre*, "Pour bien rire dans les tranchées."

By 1938, *Vendredi*'s continuing differences with the Blum government's foreign policy force a change within the weekly. Chamson, in particular, faces yet another crisis of conscience: "We were the journal of the Popular Front's hopes, the journal of its coming to be. Today, we are sorry to have become the journal of its setbacks." That spring, a joint statement signed by the directors announces that *Vendredi* is to join forces with the *Nouvelle Revue Française* in order to promote "all forms of free and creative thought." In fact, the change is an evasive action on the part of the directors who opt for a more disengaged stance rather than risk seeing their weekly become the object of an unfriendly takeover. Less than six months later, Blum is no longer in power and the Munich agreements further undermine *Vendredi*'s pacifism to a point where circulation drops below 5,000. As of November 17, *Vendredi* becomes *Reflets* and adopts the format of a weekly removed from serious political commentary. But even this ploy fails and *Reflets* disappears in mid-December after only five issues.

Closing and Reopening Statements

The lifespans of *Marianne* and *Vendredi* seemingly equate brevity with failure; both publications illustrate the delicate balance between doctrine and reform characteristic of the Popular Front's constituency. If, as Roger Shattuck contends, a sense of shame today surrounds the failures of that constituency, we should learn from those failures in preparation for the future. My case is still, however, partial. For while I hope to have argued for the inherent historical interest of *Marianne* and *Vendredi*, their documentary function does not yet tell the whole story. Where a time-filled analysis aspires to complete description with a concern for historical specificity, other concerns emanate from the conditions of writing and utterance. These latter concerns have their own specificity, tempering the emphasis on accurate and full description with a healthy consideration of what Hayden White refers to as the formulable aims of *understanding*.[12] In this sense, my account of *Marianne* and *Vendredi* is meant to open onto at least two additional inquiries. The first might be a typology set forth according to difference: the daily opposed to the weekly, the bi-weekly and the monthly, the independent opposed to the party organ. Study of *Marianne* and *Vendredi* should lead to similar assessments of their conservative rivals and of other monthlies ranging from the *NRF* to *Esprit* and *Combat*.

A second inquiry might extend toward other kinds of symbolic resistance. *Marianne* and *Vendredi* can be set alongside groups such as the Association des Ecrivains et des Artistes Révolutionnaries and Comité de Vigilance des Intellectuels Antifascistes, known as the AEAR and CVIA, respectively. In the area of film production, the idea for an Alliance du Cinéma Indépendant grows out of the AEAR in 1933. Three years later, it leads to the creation of Ciné-Liberté: a "true cooperative of film workers, technicians and actors, united in a single purpose, that of making popular newsreels, documentaries and fiction films."[13]

On its own, the historian's project of full and accurate description allows for indefinite supplementation, remaining more or less open-ended in a negative sense unless it moves toward modes of explanation or comprehension. My approach to *Marianne* and *Vendredi* is meant to relate them as both documents and texts. Systematic concern for the latter function lends itself to what I want for now to term the project of critical poetics. A poetics of culture? of Popular Front culture? Yes, so long as it contends with questions of definitions, method and aim such as those described by James Clifford:

> When is a gap in knowledge perceived, and by whom? Where do problems come from? It is obviously more than a simple matter of

noticing an error, bias, or omission.... The epistemology this implies cannot be reconciled with a notion of cumulative scientific progress, and the partiality at stake is stronger than the normal scientific dictates that we study problems piecemeal, that we must not overgeneralize, that the best picture is built up by an accretion of rigorous evidence. Cultures are not scientific "objects" (assuming such things exist, even in the natural sciences). Culture, and our views of "it," are produced historically, and are actively contested. There is no whole picture that can be "filled in," since the perception and filling of a gap lead to the awareness of other gaps.[14]

A *poetics* of culture? of Popular Front culture? Yes, so long as that project recognizes its implied epistemology and politics. In proposing this, I do not look to the historical or the political as absolute determinants. Instead, my choice of object and period means to illustrate that one cannot move from the literary to the political as though the latter were somehow "out there" rather than always already inscribed in the text as an enabling condition and inevitable circumstance.

The common fate of *Marianne* and *Vendredi* points to the problems of redirecting standard cultural forms toward activist practices without falling prey to party doctrine. Where *Marianne* remains more or less a cultural weekly expressing the pacifist vision of its editor, *Vendredi* is tied at the levels of direction and readership to constituencies with defined political and social programs. For the sake of a final comparison, I want to set the two weeklies against an independent group of the same period—The Comité de Vigilance des Intellectuels Antifascistes (CVIA)—which mobilizes journalistic forms toward militant activism. From the start, however, I want to emphasize that while many names associated with *Marianne* and *Vendredi* reappear in connection with the CVIA, it is the reconfiguration of the latter which is meaningful for any understanding of the period.

Like *Vendredi*, the CVIA appears after the February 1934 riots as a response on the part of writers, journalists, teachers and tradeunionists united by a common fear of the threat to peace represented by fascism at home and abroad. A manifesto, "Aux Travailleurs," sets forth the group's ambitions in the second issue of its publication, *Vigilance*. (See my translation of the manifesto in the appendix). It is signed by Paul Rivet ("Professeur au Musée"), Alain ("Ecrivain") and Paul Langevin ("Professeur au Collège de France"), a trio whose respective affiliations with Socialist, Radical and Communist parties form a union of the Left emulated by *Vendredi* a year and a half later. "Aux Travailleurs" also carries the signatures of Benda, Breton, Fernandez, Gide, Giono, Guéhenno and Martin du Gard. When Rivet is elected deputy for the 5th *arrondissement* of Paris on United Front anti-fascist platform, solidarity between intellectuals and workers is suddenly to be more than a pipe-dream. With Rivet's success, intellectuals are finally learning how to organize in order to oil the wheels of political discourse.[15]

The spirit of solidarity between intellectual and worker built on by the CVIA is the stuff of popular myth. Suitably, it has an apocryphal origin. Several days after the February 6 riots, a construction worker is reputed to have remarked that a swift response by the workers needed to be made against the right wing thugs who had stormed the Place de la Concorde: "We ought to have rifles and go down to the rich quarters . . . then we need a man to march at our head, a leader . . . a fellow of Gide's type." "Aux Travailleurs" asserts the ambitions of the CVIA as a preventive action against a perceived threat of homegrown fascism. But what exactly is fascism in France in the spring of 1934? As it appears in the manifesto, the term is ambiguous, designating the regimes in Germany and Italy as well as those groups opposed to the ideal of a parliamentary republic in France.

References to national revolution in the manifesto set the theme and the tone for the debate over pacifism which divides the CVIA under the Popular Front. The call to defend against a "new Middle Ages" extends an association of fascism and capitalism toward an authoritarian and bellicose social order. In 1934, the fascist menace is embodied at home by the thugs who opt for violence in the name of loosely defined notions of monarchy and rootedness. Over the next four years, the internal menace yields to debate prompted by international politics: the Spanish Civil War, Hitler's annexation of Austria and the Munich agreements.

When the final issue of *Vigilance* appears in July of 1939, the Popular Front no longer exists and the *drôle de guerre* promises to bear out the CVIA's worst fears. The pacifism it had staunchly upheld and which had alienated its Communist adherents turns out to be ineffective against Hitler. In retrospect, the pacifists' act of conscience (*prise de conscience*) sets the ethical impulse into disrepute. Like the AEAR and the Amstersdam-Pleyel movement, the CVIA has ideological roots in pre-World War I attempts to find diplomatic solutions to Franco-German differences. Through 1935, the stand against fascism responds to a perceived domestic menace and a potential threat which is closer to a mentality than to a political movement. After 1935, the political menace is all too real, operating on an international scale against which the CVIA is powerless.

As with *Marianne* and *Vendredi*, final assessments of the CVIA tend to be harsh, even on the part of former participants who remain sympathetic to the spirit of the group: "It is the story of a disaster. We had come together to battle fascism and war, and we wound up having both, with the defeat thrown in as a bonus."[16] Despite such reservations, the CVIA between 1934 and 1936 rallies disparate factions on the Left into a political force: a "front" in the positive sense of the term. Furthermore, this very spirit of solidarity sets the tone for a nonpartisan Leftist activism that extends toward the resistance movements of a decade later. Finally, the CVIA typifies the virtues and the pitfalls of an independent political movement led by self-avowed intellectuals who respond to the force of *l'histoire vécue à chaud*. Along with the more literary orientation of *Marianne* and *Vendredi*, it remains an example from which subsequent movements will learn and—hopefully—benefit.

Jean Renoir, The Popular Front and "Le Crime de Monsieur Lange"

Jean Renoir's *Le Crime de Monsieur Lange* was shot in the fall of 1935 and released in January 1936, at the height of the mentality of *rapprochement* leading to the Popular Front victory four months later. From an idea suggested by the painter and set designer, Jean Castanier, Renoir completed the draft of a screenplay entitled "Sur la cour" before calling Jacques Prévert to help write a new dialogue. Other early titles for the film included "L'Ascension de M Lange," "Dans la cour," and "Un Homme se sauve." The original screenplay reprinted in André Bazin's study of Renoir suggests the importance of Prévert's contribution. In fact, it is often held that credit for the final screenplay and production ought rightfully to be shared between Renoir, Prévert and the Octobre group.

Where Renoir's *Toni* had portrayed the conditions of unskilled peasant laborers in the South of France, *Lange* focuses on urban industrial workers. The film is less about individuals than about institutions and social forces represented within the physical space of the courtyard and its various functions as printing plant, laundry and living quarters. Jules Berry's Batala is a smooth talking capitalist who seduces creditors and employees with a charm that is alternately laughable and treacherous. Arizona Jim is Amédée Lange's cowboy alter ego, but Lange himself is less of a heroic figure than a messenger of the cooperative mentality. His "crime" is not merely that of killing Batala, but that of evolving from a dreamer totally exploited by the modes of capitalist production toward a moving force of the cooperative. As with the Popular Front, if an idealized egalitarian society is to become a reality, initial euphoria must be followed by concrete acts. When Batala returns to claim ownership of an enterprise he had abandoned on the brink of bankruptcy, he literally spoils the party. Since his false death permits the printing plant to reform as a collective in his absence, the only way for the cooperative to survive once he returns is for Lange to kill him for real. Fully in keeping with the irony Prévert brings to the revised screenplay, Batala dies as a false priest whose call for a true priest is echoed by the drunken concierge.

The film's ending is uncertain. After Valentine finishes her account at the inn, she and Lange go off across the beach toward a symbolic exile reminiscent of Orestes's departure from Argos at the end of Sartre's *Les Mouches*. More to the point, where Arizona Jim might ride off into the sunset, Lange and Valentine head... for Belgium. Thus, if *Le Crime de Monsieur Lange* reproduces the economic and social ideals of the Popular Front, it also portrays their inevitable decline. As Christopher Faulkner notes, the transition from capitalism to collective ownership is promising. But the necessity of capital does not disappear; it only changes hands.[17]

Renoir's film portrays men and women for whom, as Lange tells Valentine before inadvertently shooting Batala, only the present counts. The film operates by metonymy and understatement, with ideology and politics the cumulative consequences of more immediate and personal concerns. The film's political meaning devolves from its portrayal of workers and bourgeois who internalize the conflicts of their social, economic and historical conditions. In so doing, they are seen by today's spectators as symptomatic of the working class and bourgeoisie who are the inevitable victims of forces they never come close to identifying. In this sense, the film, because of the working class and petit-bourgeois society it portrays, is basically apolitical; that is, too enamored of stability and too xenophobic to let itself be attracted by international movements: "No, it was simply conservative.... It spoke through a press with an enormous circulation by *Le Matin* or *L'Echo de Paris*—reactionary, conformist, limited in its outlook."[18]

After the fact, *Lange* holds out the image of men and women creating something that has never before existed. Today, the film's lesson is exemplary. Like the Popular Front it heralds, *Le Crime de Monsieur Lange* shows that *la fête* of revolution is intense, joyous and shortlived. What follows it is more serious, more complex, and often less satisfying, a progression borne out by Renoir's subsequent films of the Popular Front period: *La Vie est à nous*, *La Marseillaise*, and *La Bête humaine*.

APPENDIX

Aux Travailleurs (5 Mar 34) [reprnt. in *Vigilance*, no. 2 (18 May 34)].

United above all divergence against the spectacle of the fascist riots of Paris and by a popular resistance which alone has confronted them, we declare to all workers, our comrades, our resolution to fight with them to save the rights and freedoms conquered by the people from a fascist dictatorship. We are ready to sacrifice everything to prevent France from submitting to a regime of oppression and bellicose misery.

We condemn the corruption revealed by the recent scandals.

We struggle against corruption and against deception.

We will not allow virtue to be invoked by the corrupted or their corruptors.

We will not let the anger brought forth by the money scandals of the banks, trusts, and arms dealers turn against the Republic, the true Republic which is the people working, suffering, thinking, and acting for its own emancipation.

Comrades, under the name of a national revolution, we are being given a new Middle Ages. We must not conserve the present world, we must transform it and free the nation from the tutelage of high capital by siding closely with the workers.

Our first act has been to form a *Committee of Vigilance* available to workers' organizations. Let those who subscribe to our ideas identify themselves.

This manifesto, distributed on March 5, has been signed by more than 1200 scholars, doctors, engineers, lawyers, artists, professors at the Collège de France, professors in the university and secondary systems, grade school teachers, students, educators at every level, intellectuals of every category. The signers constitute the *Committee of Antifascist Action and Vigilance* which takes on a double task: *vigilance in regard to fascism and intellectual struggle against fascist demagoguery.* The committee will publish a series of scientifically researched brochures edited in simple terms on the principal problems relating to fascism. It is organizing a lecture campaign across the country so that its mandated representatives may tell everyone what fascism is, where it rules, and what it might be here if we were to let it take hold.

NOTES

1. Keith Reader, "Renoir's Popular Front Films: Texts in Context." In Ginette Vincendeau and Keith Reader, eds., *La Vie est à nous: French Cinema of the Popular Front, 1935–1938*, (London: British Film Institute, 1986) 40.
2. Jean-Pierre Jeancolas, *15 ans d'années trente: le cinéma des Français 1929–1944* (Paris: Stock, 1983) 7.
3. Germaine Brée, *Twentieth-Century French Literature* trans. Louise Guiney (Chicago: Univ. of Chicago Press, 1983) 11.
4. Quoted in Roger Shattuck, "Having Congress: The Shame of the Thirties." In *The Innocent Eye: On Modern Literature and the Arts* (New York: Washington Square, 1986) 4.
5. Richard Terdiman, *Discourse/Counter-Discourse: The Theory and Practice of Symbolic Resistance in Nineteenth-Century France* (Ithaca: Cornell University Press, 1985) 120.
6. The figure is potentially misleading. Five million readers does not mean five million copies sold, since it is likely that each copy had several readers. (Raymond Manevy, *Histoire de la presse, 1914–1939* [Paris: Corréas, 1943] 149n).
7. Claude Estier, *La Gauche hebdomadaire, 1914–1962* (Paris: Armand Colin, 1962) 96.
8. Herbert Lottman astutely notes that generosity toward disenfranchised conserva-

tives such as Marcel Jouhandeau, Paul Léautaud, and even Georges Bernanos often transcended the bitter rivalries between publishing houses: "Gallimard and Grasset, even the *Nouvelle Revue Française* and *Marianne*, offered a no-man's land where they and their counterparts on the left could rest their swords" (*The Left Bank* [Boston: Houghton Mifflin, 1982] 73).

9. Pierre Assouline, *Gaston Gallimard: un demi-siècle d'édition française* (Paris: Seuil "Points Biographie," 1985) 237.

10. Lucie Mazauric, *Vive le Front populaire* (Paris: Plon, 1976) 37.

11. "L'an prochain, à Toulouse... " *Vendredi* (2 April 1937) 1.

12. *Tropics of Discourse: Essays in Cultural Criticism* (Baltimore: Johns Hopkins Univ. Press, 1978) 20.

13. *Commoedia*, 14 July 1936. Quoted in Pascal Ory, "De 'Ciné-Liberté' à 'La Marseillaise': Hopes and Limitations of a Liberated Cinema (1936–1938)." In Vincendeau and Reader, 9.

14. "Introduction." In James Clifford and George E. Marcus, eds., *Writing Culture: The Poetics and Politics of Ethnography* (Berkeley: Univ. of California Press, 1986) 18.

15. David Caute, *Communism and the French Intellectuals, 1914–1960* (New York: Macmillan, 1964) 114.

16. "Témoignage de M. François Walter." In Anne Roche and Christian Tarting, eds., *Des Années Trente* (Paris: Editions du Centre National de la Recherche Scientifique, 1985) 69.

17. Christopher Faulkner, *The Social Cinema of Jean Renoir* (Princeton: Princeton Univ. Press, 1986) 66.

18. Jeancolas, "French Cinema of the 1930's and its Sociological Handicaps." In Vincendeau and Reader, 62.

HABERMAS'S THESIS OF INTERNAL COLONIZATION: RECONSTRUCTED OR DECONSTRUCTED MARXISM?

Wolfgang Sohlich

If one could baldly paraphrase the critical dilemma of postmodernism, one might draw on Derrida's analogy of writing to playing chess on a bottomless chessboard. It is a game that has no ground to support it, no finality, and no meaning beyond itself. Understanding is entrapped in a web of language and has only the web to unravel the forms of its own groundlessness. There is no knowing without presupposing and no presupposing without arbitrarily uncoupling a sign from the endless signifying chain and positing it as an origin. Interpretation that lays claim to meaning becomes a gesture of mastery. In this certainty of epistemological uncertainty, interpretation which stubbornly persists that it wants to make sense must justify itself—even when it has scuttled metaphysics and drifts precariously in the changing tides of history. The choice of Marx and Habermas today cannot be justified by claiming that historical materialism has a privileged view of history. But one can shift terrain from the condition of knowledge to the effect ideas have on everyday consciousness and to an assessment of their effectiveness in combatting the power of the master. Deconstruction discovers that the master of Western discourse is reason and that he serves male, white power. The implications of such sweeping revelations are troubling at best. By equating reason with mastery, theory must be content with living in the lacunae and deferrals of reason without being able to specify the what and how of change. It must obliterate all recollections of the emancipatory potentials of Enlightenment reason and it cannot ask whether a capitalist society can absorb a progressive feminist movement or assimilate non-white cultures on terms other than gender and race. Such questions imply that one tries to make sense of the world, and the issues they raise appear to have an urgency which cannot be pacified by an anti-philosophical discourse on philosophical presuppositions.

In an interpretative climate that is permeated by suspicion

toward any theory that still pretends to make sense, I think it is reasonable to return to historical materialism in its constructed and reconstructed forms. The masters have no trouble making sense, and I would think that it suits them when those who oppose them confess their inability to mean anything at all. I have attempted to present Marx's theory of value and Habermas's theory of late capitalist societies in order to show how Habermas restructures Marx and why he proposes a thesis of internal colonization which is so substantively different from Marx's thesis of alienation. I must confess that I feel somewhat like a sectarian autodidact playing chess on a bottomless chessboard when I try to extract not completely unreadable narratives from the encyclopedic scope of the works of Marx and Habermas. I am, of course, aware that I am presenting this essay to an audience which is primarily interested in literature. I am assuming, without verification, that the interpretation of literary texts can be enhanced by a knowledge, however fragile, of the social and cultural horizon in which it is made. If Habermas is correct when he argues that the play of the metropolis and the market can no longer be grasped from the periphery, then theory will once again serve the cause of enlightenment.

***

Cooperative labor is the cornerstone of historical materialism. What and how people produce make them what they are and defines the relations among them. Political institutions, art, religion, and philosophy are reflections of the how and what of labor. They are veiled expressions of the social power of capital. The theory of value primarily explains that market relations are class relations. It tries to show why a private economy based on individual competition and greed does not, as Habermas put it, "produce for the wealth that is needed by society but for the wealth whose needs society must satisfy" (T&P 234). The theory of value is also a theory of human alienation. It deconstructs the fiction of an autonomous and just market and points to the deep structures of the labor process to account for the destruction of national traditions and for the psychological and economic violence suffered by a class whose lives and actions are reduced to mere instruments of capital.

Marx analyzed the relations between capital labor because he saw that bourgeois societies had changed the direct political domination of feudal societies to indirect economic domination, and he adopted the point of view of labor because he thought that the emancipation of all could only be achieved through the revolutionary struggle of the working class. Lukacs's theory of class consciousness would later provide the theoretical foundations of revolutionary practice by assigning a privileged place in the process of production to the proletariat. It fell into disrepute, however, when the inner logic of historical development was brutally contradicted by institutional transformations of late capitalism. Subsequently the Frankfurt School redirected Marxist theory from the base to the superstructure. It wanted to understand why capitalism had such astonishing recuperative powers and it concentrated on those utopian potentials of bourgeois culture which could sustain critique and revolutionary hope. Habermas continues the tradition of the Frankfurt School rather faithfully in *Strukturwandel der bürgerlichen Öffentlichkeit*, although his method is more historical than that of the Frankfurt School. Then, in *Theory of Communicative Action*, he attempts a synthesis of Marx and the Frankfurt School with Weber, system theory, and linguistic theory.

The classical configuration of institutions is most rigorously developed in *Strukturwandel der bürgerlichen Öffentlichkeit*, the first major work by Habermas. The economy and the family make up a private sphere while public opinion and the state apparatus comprise a public sphere. State and economy are called systems in *Theory of Communicative Action* and are internally related by functional or instrumental actions based on interests. The nuclear family and the public opinion sphere are institutions of symbolic reproduction. The family socializes subjects on the basis of preconscious norms whereas the public opinion sphere is subject to a communicative practice. Here social interactions are governed by consensus formation based on norms that need justifying under conditions of justice and equality. During the classical period of capitalism, state and economy remained separated but functioned in the contexts of norms derived from the family and public opinion sphere respectively. In his detailed account of the development of modern institutions during the 18th century, Habermas also presents an outline of what he will later call communicative action. The symbolic order of classical capitalism has the contradictory character of ideology. The bourgeois family is built on property and plays a major role in its reproduction. It guarantees genealogical continuity of individuals and capital through the private accumulation and hereditary transmission of wealth. It also socializes authority-oriented subjects whose attitudes and values tie them to the relations of capital to labor and help reproduce them. The domination of capital over labor is duplicated in the family circle where the father exercises authority over spouse and children. The public opinion sphere is made up of private, male property owners and male members of the liberal professions who serve property. They succeeded in transforming the character of power with a legal revolution which imposed limits on state power and protected a specifically capitalist mode of life with constitutional guarantees of human rights and civil liberties. The idea that economic interests rule representations is classical Marxism and Habermas has no quarrel with it. But he also argues that the family understood its own way of life differently. Family members believed that theirs was an intimacy sphere which protected them from economic pressures. It was a privileged realm where they could freely develop their inner life as human beings in an atmosphere of mutual respect and love (SdO 64). The rule of public opinion formation required that the citizens follow the dictates of reason independent of status or particular interests, that ideas be justified according to criteria of reasonableness and justice, and that they be subjected to the scrutiny and approval of autonomous, reasonable men. Since collective self-representations are eventually sedimented in everyday consciousness, they take on a life of their own and cast a spell over systems ruled by interests. Thus Habermas claims that the ethics of responsibility and probity also influenced market relations; and since the citizen is also a father who experiences the family as the site of purely human values, these also find their way into the agenda of public opinion. "*The developed bourgeois public sphere is founded on the fictional identity of the assembled public or private individuals in their role as proprietors and simply as human beings*" (SdO 74, my tr., italics in org. text). This contradiction explains why natural law guarantees human rights and civil liberties along with private property.

Self-understanding and interests comprise the contradictory character of ideology. Freedom, equality, and fairness are universal potentials inherent in the symbolic practices of family and of the public opinion sphere. By separating these potentials from particular interests, Habermas situates himself implicitly in the hermeneutic tradition of Ernst Bloch and the work of Horkheimer and Adorno prior to *Dialectic of Enlightenment*. The theoretical implications of this move are fully discussed in *Knowledge and Human Interests* and in *Theory and Practice* where he argues that Marx's theory of labor cannot account for a theory of reflection or interactions based on speech situations and must reduce the critique of ideology to a positive science (K&HI 52–60; T&P 235–42). The separation of idea from interest is important in several respects. It allows Habermas to preserve the progressive aspects of a tradition that it criticized. It also creates a more flexible relationship between base and superstructure since cultural representations which have also a life of their own can react back on the base. Finally, the universality of self-representations can inspire hope in a better world and release energies for transforming societies. In *Strukturwandel* Habermas merely applies the post-Marxist critique of ideology—that of Bloch and the Frankfurt School—to the public opinion sphere. But the implications of his analysis are much more unsettling than they first appear. The idea that public opinion ought to decide political issues by debating in conditions of fairness, freedom, and equality and by appeal to the universalities of constitutional, natural law is a powerful thought. It is an especially troubling idea to the system elites because in democracies power can only be legitimated by appeal to citizen consensus. Habermas's theory of communicative action is a highly complex theory of linguistic practice and speech situations which draws on a prohibitive body of linguistic theory. Its genesis in *Strukturwandel* helps us understand the more immediate theoretical affiliations and the practical political intent.

Habermas dates the end of the liberal era around the great depression of 1873 (SdO 175). The crisis complex is formed around two major developments: 1. the high concentration of capital power in big industrial concerns; 2. the pressure from labor movements exerted through the political party system following the introduction of universal suffrage (SdO 176). Class relations, which had been exacerbated by economic crisis, could now be pacified through collective bargaining and state intervention. In *Strukturwandel* Habermas still follows Marx and Lukacs since he attributes the advanced division of labor and the bureaucratization of state and industry with their debilitating effect on the human psyche to the growth and concentration of capital (SdO 184). And he implicitly follows Adorno by imputing to a manipulative mass culture which is governed by the laws of the market the role of systematically commodifying communication (SdO 193–210).

The narrative of *Strukturwandel* chronicles the proletarianization of the classical bourgeoisie and the destruction of its institutions and culture. Corporate capital replaces family capital, political parties usurp the public opinion sphere of private citizens, and ideological representations, which masked and disclosed the ambivalent relations between family and economy or public opinion sphere and state, are neutralized when the lines between institutions become blurred. They are replaced by a mass culture which makes domination invisible. The instrumental rationality of money and power—Marx called it abstract reason—penetrates into all aspects of human life. The sense of humanity of the small property owner could be traced back to his real economic independence which, in turn, insulated the family from the vagaries of the market and gave birth to the utopian self representation of the family. He now joins the ranks of an undifferentiated army of corporation men whose work does not belong to them. Functional competence and human indifference define this conformist type whose soul belongs to the company (SdO 186). The exchange of personal property for wages draws the family into the orbit of the market. It loses its power to insulate and protect and with it its self-understanding as a milieu of interiority and humanity (SdO 189). Bourgeois humanism, which according to Habermas originated in the experience of privacy of the nuclear family of the classical period, could not survive the economic and social neutralization of the family. The latter ultimately becomes a peripheral remainder which is drawn into the exchange process as a mere consumer of income and leisure.

During the liberal era political sovereignty rested on the authority of a public opinion which was tested in the give and take of debate. Late capitalism diminishes the role of the citizen and consensus is the product of political compromise among interested and politically dominant factions (SdO 215). The newspapers of the classical era served the public opinion sphere. Today they sell information for profit and increase circulation by adapting the content and form of print to the educational level of an unenlightened mass population (SdO 199). Political debate is replaced with the marketing of political candidates when the political process is alienated from citizens and objectified as media event. The political participation of the former citizen has shrunk to the derisive gesture of choosing by acclamation among depoliticized personalities in commodity form. The world as depicted in *Strukturwandel* is a lifeless and incomprehensible world without freedom. While human misery is no longer predominantly material in nature, economic, political, and social oligopolies have systematically deprived the individual of personal autonomy and political participation. It is a world of commodities writ large. From this perspective the humanistic and political cultures of the liberal era with their utopian energies become beacons projecting their faint light into an uncertain future.

The *Theory of Communicative Action* incorporates Weber's theory of the rationalization of the lifeworld and system theory into Marx's theory of economic domination. I see no fundamental deviation from the core theoretical premise of *Strukturwandel* because Habermas still maintains that advanced capitalist societies reproduce capitalist relations in a different form and that the colonization of the human psyche is caused by the intrusion of the instrumental reason of capital and power into the private lives of individuals. The state guarantees the continuance of the capitalist mode of production by legal and military means and it supports it by, a. o., influencing business cycles and attending to the infrastructures required by capital. "Government intervention," he writes, "has the *indirect* form of manipulating the boundary conditions for the decisions of private enterprise, and the *reactive* form for avoiding its side effects or compensating for them" (TCA 344). This is merely a more precise formulation of the hegemonic character of advanced capitalist societies with their state directed and supported economies and government services in the areas of welfare, unemployment compensation, social and therapeutic services. The modifications are nevertheless far reaching. Habermas's appropriation of system theory makes his model of late capitalist societies unnecessarily schematic. System theory roughly conceives of societies as self-regulating organisms and analyzes how they fulfill self-maintaining functions. Habermas emphatically dissociates himself from the implications of cybernetic social management of system theory. He justifies its use by claiming that he needs to objectify the lifeworld of communicative action methodologically so that, unlike Marx, he can also understand it from the perspective of the observer (TCA 374). But self-critique has always been a requirement of critique. Marx did not write from the perspective of the lifeworld, as Habermas claims, but from the perspective of a classless society. When Habermas stands with one foot in the lifeworld and one foot in systems, his critique implies a view of an order in which systems and lifeworld are separate. The argument is circular. The economy and the state now become systems ruled by instrumental reason in the form of money and power. The departure from *Strukturwandel* is obvious. If the inner logic of the economy is capital and that of the state power, then alienated labor and alienated bureaucratic rule become the inescapable fate of modernity.

The incorporation of Weber further weakens Marx's theory of value because it enables Habermas to differentiate between forms of societal rationalizations which are modern and evolutionary and forms which are capitalistic and regressive. Habermas is convinced that the rationalization which precipitated the destruction of religious world views is irreversible and on balance evolutionary. Occidental rationalism has split reason into its discrete elements and institutionalized them in the disciplines of the sciences, formal law, and autonomous art. The separation of the cognitive element has made possible dramatic advances in the sciences. The separation of the moral practical element produced a morality based on universal principles rather than authority and subjected the power of government to rational, natural law. Finally, the separation of the esthetic-expressive moment of reason produced an autonomous art freed from the imperatives of work and the norms of everyday experience (TCA 397). According to Habermas this aspect of modernization is not inherently colonizing. The problem is that modernization follows a highly selective pattern because it confines expert cultures to institutions which are removed from everyday experience yet does not create the conditions in which they could be reconnected to our lives (TCA 328). Habermas thinks that the separation of culture, society, and personality is also progressive. When the cultural heritage is transmitted through educational institutions, or when democratic will formation occurs within the boundaries of norms which have become reflexive, it is subjected to a communicative rationality (TCA 145). Norms that are no longer accepted as a second nature must withstand the power of critique. The human personality which is shaped by a self-conscious appropriation of the cultural heritage is no longer subjected to the preconscious representations of family, church, or nation (TCA 145). In modern societies the cultural tradition, the political process, and personal conduct must be justified in the context of a communicative practice which is governed by the fiction of fairness, equality, and justice (TCA 150).

The communicative ethic is rooted in the utopia of Enlightenment reason. It is not to be confused with the sexually repressive vocational ethic of Protestantism which was a private morality separated from legal norms (TCA 304). The communicative ethic which Habermas develops contains the moral-practical and esthetic-expressive moments of reason and does not establish sovereignty over desire (LC 89). Communicative action is an idea which recalls the unfulfilled promises of the bourgeois revolution. Within the boundaries of fairness, equality, and justice it lays claim to the right to decide under what kind of laws we want to live, what kind of society we want to be, and what kind of lives individuals want to choose. But modernization has also excluded the creation of institutions of freedom which would protect communicatively structured private and public spheres against the debilitating influence of economic and administrative systems (TCA 328). The absence of such institutions and the separation of the institutionalized moments of reason from everyday experience insure that capital maintains its predominant position within the hegemonic order. These conditions—not the mass media as Habermas suggested in *Strukturwandel*—make colonization possible because they guarantee that everyday consciousness remains fragmented and thrown back on outdated traditions. These conditions, Habermas suggests, meet the functional requirements of the ideologies of the liberal era by fulfilling the negative requirement of not allowing holistic interpretations to come to the fore (TCA 355).

Habermas can now distinguish between necessary and unnecessary forms of rationalization. System and lifeworld are both rationalized but according to different criteria. Those intrusions into the lifeworld which are designed to protect it as a communicatively structured domain are not colonizing. The rationalization of systems according to the criteria of instrumental reason and of the lifeworld in accordance with communicative reason are also necessary. But when instrumental reason intrudes into the lifeworld as capital and as bureaucratic rule, it becomes a colonial master whose pacification program leads to spiralling increases in reification. Alienated labor is compensated for by increased consumption; but this trade-off only draws the individual further into the orbit of exchange relations. The political disenfranchisement of the citizen is exchanged for bureaucratically dispensed social security measures. Here too political powerlessness is compensated for by administered provisions for life. Only sustained economic growth can keep the arrangement alive because prosperity gives to capital what capital demands and to the vast majority what is required to keep them pacified. Yet increased growth also means increased consumerism and intensified bureaucratization. Because the problem is insolvable, Habermas is persuaded that the crises of advanced capitalist societies crystallize around the roles of voter and consumer.

It would be difficult to argue that historical materialism should not be submitted to rigorous reexaminations under the conditions of late capitalism. These conditions have so dramatically expanded the scope of capital and bureaucratic power and so effectively contained revolutionary movements that Adorno and the Habermas of *Strukturwandel* harbored no or very little hope for change. Habermas has given a historical account of the development of late capitalist societies and identified the forms of alienation which result from shifting power relations from the market to systems. These are remarkable achievements. But critical theory has always bound critique and self-critique to practice. It must identify crises and show how they can be overcome through action. This is essentially what Habermas tries to accomplish in *Theory of Communicative Action*. How then does he reinscribe critical theory into an apparently seamless web of power and what, if anything, remains of Marx's theory of labor?

Marx's theory of labor comprises the elements of cognition, ethics, and esthetics. Since relations of production are determined by the mode of production, a unitary concept would ideally mediate human relations in a society which is free from the independent dynamics of capitalist accumulation. Habermas deconstructs this comprehensive scheme on two fronts. He separates mode and relations of production into independent practices of instrumental and communicative action and he argues that the rationalization of the lifeworld is irreversible and on balance progressive. I believe that he is right in pointing out that Marx never developed a theory of reflection which could establish the critique of ideology on firm theoretical footing (K&HI 44). Human interactions are regulated by language in speech situations. The knowledge derived from such contexts cannot be scientific. The truth of speech situations is at best based on consensus reached in accordance with the criteria of communicative action. A connection to the mode of production is nevertheless affirmed since Habermas suggests that the rules of communicative action develop in reaction to changes in the base, although they also follow their own logic (RdHM 163). But this still does not explain why he separates system and lifeworld and instrumental and communicative action so ideally or why he should appeal to the authority of Marx when he reduces humankind's relation to nature to instrumental action (K&HI 35). He actually does this by dividing Marx into the realist of *Capital* and the theory of value and the hopeless romantic of the pre-*Capital* period (TCA 341). Aside from the fact that such arbitrary divisions rob Marx's theory of its utopian energies, Habermas appears to reduce Marx's references to useful labor in *Capital* to instrumentally useful labor. At the very least, his assertion needs to be supported by textual evidence. If communication needs the fiction of utopia as a condition for speech situations, then one is permitted to ask why the fiction of a reconciled world which does not exclude nature and work should not be a necessary condition for transforming a world in which work is alienated and nature brought to the brink of extinction. Marx's vision of reconciliation can only be anachronistic if we fully accept Habermas's ontogenetic theory of history which roughly establishes homologous relations between three types of human societies and Piaget's stages of development of moral awareness and interactive competence (RdHM 183-94). On these assumptions the separation of systems from lifeworld and the rationalization of the lifeworld are progressive. But I think Habermas misses the point. Objects of labor become commodities because they are products of labor by private individuals or corporations who work independently of each other for profit (C 1: 165). There can be neither solidarity nor respect for nature when the means and end of labor are profit. Rationalization itself is not the problem but the reduction of labor to labor power and the reduction of nature to resources.

By separating the economy and the state so irrevocably from human life and by arguing essentially that instrumental relations be confined to systems and not spill over into the lifeworld, Habermas gives the impression that he would like to resurrect an attenuated version of the heaven/earth duality of the political state of the liberal era with its abstract promises of autonomy, community, and universality sedimented in constitutional law and the realities of civil society where the eternal combats between the Gargas and Shlinks go on unabated (OJQ 220). Even when he tries to rescue the utopian potentials of Enlightenment reason from the flotsam of bourgeois ideology, Habermas curiously ignores the utopian potentials of universal suffrage which Marx formulated in a provocative question: "Is not private property abolished in an ideal sense when the propertyless come to legislate for the propertied?" (OJQ 219). In short, Habermas appears to leave the entire apparatus of state and economy fully operative qua systems and thus leaves himself open to the charge of appropriating Marx for conservative ends.

I do not believe that this charge would be just. Habermas has never renounced Marx's insight that capitalist societies are founded on the domination of capital over labor. When he channels the utopian energies of Marx's theory of labor into communication and disengages it from systems, he certainly deconstructs Marx. Yet I believe that for Habermas the practical consequences override considerations of theoretical purity. The only hope for a political practice that does not regress to totalitarianism and cannot be easily neutralized by the scopic power of state and economy is a practice that understands itself as free from system imperatives and which is rooted in the legitimation of democratic sovereignty itself. Capitalism and democracy are contradictory realities of modern societies. So far capitalism has succeeded in eroding democratic processes by transforming public opinion formation into commodified media events. Habermas attempts to reconquer an expropriated public opinion sphere and to pit the constitution against a legal apparatus that guarantees the continuance of capitalist power. At one point he mentions that the forces of a communicative ethics have been gathering since the sixties in the experimental complexes of countercultures and this reference alone indicates that Habermas is not just attempting to dust off an outmoded and idealized concept of political participation (LC 90). In another context he corrects Marx's theory of labor by arguing that value is not only produced by exploiting labor power, but by organizational changes. While he concedes that the power of consumption is still restricted by antagonistic class relations, he proposes this hypothetical exception: "but a political regulation of relations of distribution would not be irreconcilable, under the presuppositions of a revised theory of value, with the conditions of a production oriented toward the maximization of profits. This possibility and the success of a conscious policy of crisis management then depend on whether the forces pressing toward democratization of society succeed in penetrating the total complex of production . . ." (T&P 231). A theory which envisions democratic sovereignty over wealth can also accommodate the idea of democratic governance of economic priorities. In this context, the rationalization of the lifeworld is not as final as it appears. If the knowledge acquired in separate disciplines can flow back into a community that is free from the dual imperatives of capital and bureaucracy, then science might no longer serve the arms race, ethics might transcend national boundaries, and art might just contribute to the development of social relations that resemble creative play.

WORKS CITED & CONSULTED

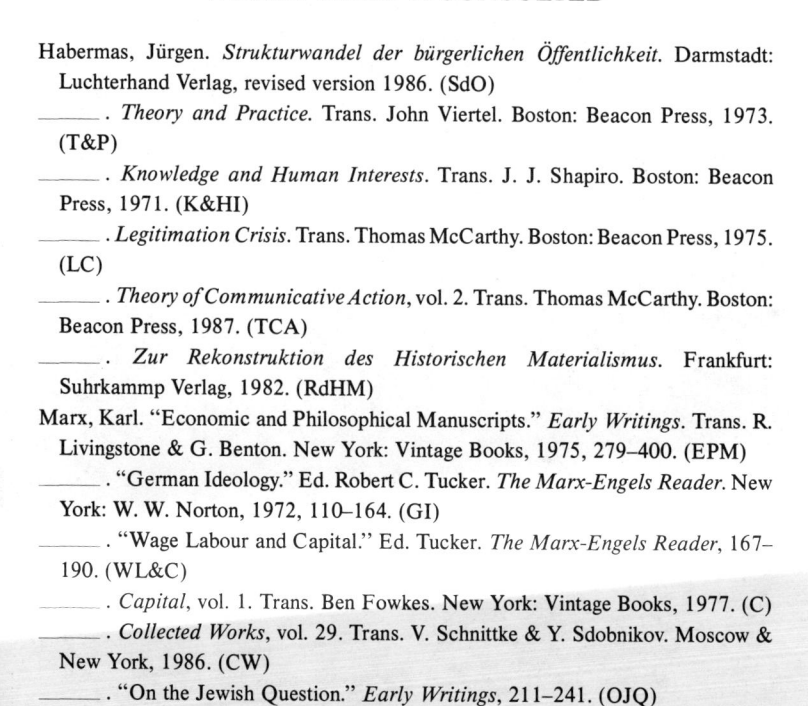

Habermas, Jürgen. *Strukturwandel der bürgerlichen Öffentlichkeit.* Darmstadt: Luchterhand Verlag, revised version 1986. (SdO)

———. *Theory and Practice.* Trans. John Viertel. Boston: Beacon Press, 1973. (T&P)

———. *Knowledge and Human Interests.* Trans. J. J. Shapiro. Boston: Beacon Press, 1971. (K&HI)

———. *Legitimation Crisis.* Trans. Thomas McCarthy. Boston: Beacon Press, 1975. (LC)

———. *Theory of Communicative Action*, vol. 2. Trans. Thomas McCarthy. Boston: Beacon Press, 1987. (TCA)

———. *Zur Rekonstruktion des Historischen Materialismus.* Frankfurt: Suhrkammp Verlag, 1982. (RdHM)

Marx, Karl. "Economic and Philosophical Manuscripts." *Early Writings.* Trans. R. Livingstone & G. Benton. New York: Vintage Books, 1975, 279–400. (EPM)

———. "German Ideology." Ed. Robert C. Tucker. *The Marx-Engels Reader.* New York: W. W. Norton, 1972, 110–164. (GI)

———. "Wage Labour and Capital." Ed. Tucker. *The Marx-Engels Reader*, 167–190. (WL&C)

———. *Capital*, vol. 1. Trans. Ben Fowkes. New York: Vintage Books, 1977. (C)

———. *Collected Works*, vol. 29. Trans. V. Schnittke & Y. Sdobnikov. Moscow & New York, 1986. (CW)

———. "On the Jewish Question." *Early Writings*, 211–241. (OJQ)

SCHEHERAZADE AND NOZDREF'S COOK: THE ROLE OF THE FEMALE STORYTELLER IN ISAK DINESEN'S *SEVEN GOTHIC TALES*

Tiina A. Kirss

When Isak Dinesen's first collection of stories was published in the United States in 1934, the American publishers suggested the title *Seven Gothic Tales*, with a view to a readership given to a taste for tales of the strange and marvellous. Upon the enthusiastic reception of the book, American critics were hard put to find a precise classification of the nature of these highly wrought and intricate stories that combined the bizarre and the elegant. They were further puzzled by the identity of the author, whom, judging from the name Isak, they presumed to be male. Over a period of years spanning the publication of *Out of Africa* and two other short story collections, *Winter's Tales* and *Last Tales*, the Baroness Karen Blixen gradually and reluctantly emerged from behind her literary mask, and became a much sought-after guest in American literary circles. She also began translating her own stories into Danish, where they were much less enthusiastically received, and often greeted with cold and hostile reviews. In the last ten years of her life she was more warmly welcomed and rewarded by her countrymen.

The importance of the seventeen years she spent in Africa to her storytelling is apparent from literary biographies of Dinesen, from her autobiographical works, *Out of Africa* (1942) and *Shadows on the Grass* (1960), and from the shrewd and at times harsh critiques of the "colonialist" mentality some see in her writing. Dinesen began writing stories in Africa to "collect her energies" during the long rains, but serious writing did not start until she was forty-six, after she had returned to Denmark following the death of her lover Denys Finch-Hatton and the financial collapse of the coffee plantation in East Africa that she had managed first with her husband, and then, following their divorce, alone for seven years. Before beginning the stories that were to become *Seven Gothic Tales*, she had written very little, apart from a few short tales in her twenties and copious correspondence. Weed has suggestively noted that Africa provided Dinesen with direct experience of an oral storytelling tradition, as well as with a perspective on the Danish traditions of folk-tales and sagas that she had absorbed in her childhood. While the complexity of framing, the number of narrators, and the highly crafted detail of the prose point to a carefully reworked oral text, there is little reason to mistrust Dinesen's statements that most of the stories in the first collection got their start from an oral "performance." An intriguing passage from *Out of Africa* also provides a clue to the personae in which Dinesen cast herself as storyteller:

> I had been making up many while he had been away. In the evenings he made himself comfortable, spreading cushions like a couch in front of the fire, and with me sitting on the floor, cross-legged like Scheherazade herself, he would listen, clear-eyed, to a long tale, from when it began until it ended. He kept better account of it than I did myself, and at the dramatic appearance of one of the characters, would stop me to say, "That man died at the beginning of the story, but never mind." (242)

Both the film *Out of Africa* and J. Thurman's literary biography have romanticized Dinesen's storytelling to Denys Finch-Hatton, perhaps neglecting the subtler implications of the persona of Scheherazade. This figure offers an entry to the feminist dynamics of Dinesen's work as well as a suggestive emblem for the female storyteller. Scheherazade told stories to the Caliph to defer rape, mutilation, and death, as Dinesen, by a similar procedure, told tales with their roots in personal loss; tales that are perhaps parables for the deferral of tedium and grief. More precisely, the narratee of Scheherazade's tales was her sister, whose presence was a ruse to induce the Caliph to listen. It is tempting to speculate about the absent female narratee of Dinesen's tales, the hearer of the almost faultlessly concealed narrator's voice. Was it her younger sister Elle, whose husband helped popularize her work in Denmark, and who was herself a writer? Was it her Aunt Bess, a dominating presence in her childhood and a sparring partner in feminist issues throughout the spirited African correspondence? Or was the narratee her closest girlhood friend Daisy Frijs-Dinesen, who married the Danish ambassador to Italy and who committed suicide when Dinesen was twenty-four? A set of masks and alibis may be crucial for the female storyteller, who, under the partial protection of these masks can begin the angry and self-healing work of telling and remembering. The highly constructed and reserved autobiographical works, *Out of Africa* and *Shadows on the Grass*, are thus a conjunction in a "fiction" of the urges to pose and to protect the self by means of a chosen mask. As Langbaum suggests, the more transparent autobiographical first-person in the African memoirs may be a justification of "the ageless and authoritative voice behind the stories, the voice of the archetypal storyteller who knows all the stories and has therefore all the memories and wisdom of the culture" (130).

As a storyteller, Dinesen bears affinities with Boccaccio, which are a matter both of her historical situation and the nature of her craft. In *Out of Africa* she refers to the literary and cultural situation of Europe in the 1920s and 1930s as not given to oral storytelling: "For I have always thought I might have cut a figure at the time of the plague of Florence. Fashions have changed and the art of listening to a narrative has been lost in Europe" (OOA 241). She alludes here also to the political turmoil and catastrophe in Europe during and in the wake of World War I, analogous to the 14th century plague-ridden cities of Italy. Her insight concerning the cultural situation of Europe resembles that of Walter Benjamin, who evoked the dying tradition of oral tales in Europe in his 1936 essay "The Storyteller." Dinesen also shares with Boccaccio a highly constructed and layered narrative technique, and the ordering of stories in cycles. Perhaps this mannered and literary transposition of storytelling is an especially apt and symptomatic response to a situation of cultural crisis.

Thematically, Boccaccio and Dinesen share a concern with gender relations, a topic that has been a source of critical debate in scholarship on the latter, particularly in terms of the force of her feminism. Else Cederborg, in her introduction to the freshly-translated *On Modern Marriage and Other Observations*, a piece Dinesen wrote in 1926 when her divorce was impending, suggests that Dinesen's feminist journey was more rich and complicated than it looks from the vantage point of the essays in *Daguerreotypes*. *On Modern Marriage* was part of an ongoing dialogue Dinesen had with her brother Thomas on male-female relations, and it is upbeat, optimistic, calling for the bold acceptance of the death of institutions that are no longer fired by an ideal. She places great emphasis on the need for a dimension of play in love relationships that are "recovering" from the impact of a tired institution: "So one can imagine the possibility that as humanity gradually relieved itself of the heavy yoke of 'the ferocious necessity, mistress of men and gods' . . . love between a man and a woman would represent the most beautiful and bold thing in life, its best game" (79). Cederborg traces Dinesen's feminist thinking through the material in the *Letters from Africa* (1914–1931) on Somali women and the notion of "love of the parallels," a notion Dinesen found in Aldous Huxley's novels as a model for an egalitarian relationship, and a term that was to undergo ironic shifts as she used it in essays and fiction. Cederborg contrasts the feminist impulse in Dinesen's fiction with her disillusionment with feminist practice toward the end of her life: "Whereas her fiction is radiant with indignation at women's conditions in a double-standard society, her essays seem detached and even a little tired of the whole thing" (26).

The statements in the "Oration" are conservative by present feminist standards. The 1953 article received much hostile criticism by feminists in Denmark and Germany. It may seem surprising at first that feminist critics in the last few years have chosen Dinesen's story "The Blank Page," from *Last Tales*, as a parable for female creativity, not only on the scale of the individual woman artist, but on the level of a broad feminist project of recuperative scholarship and literary criticism. What may be at stake is the ideological gesture of designating one's enemies with the honorary title of a "guest in the house," at the price of ignoring embarrassing reactionary statements that merely indicate that their authoress was a "child of her Zeitgeist." In a less cynical vein, such inclusion of "anti-feminist" writers in a feminist canon is a recognition of tensions and ambivalences in their work, and perhaps of a deliberate strategy of indirection in their representation of possibilities for women. The adoption of Virginia Woolf as a paradigmatic feminist writer by critics has reflected this latter process, and the way "a room of one's own" has become a (code-)emblem of female artistic creativity is similar to the appropriation of Dinesen's "Blank Page."

While there are certainly parables of female creativity in several of Dinesen's stories, it is more suggestive to examine them in the wider perspective of generic subversion, what Susan Hardy Aiken calls "a countertextual thematics of female authority and creativity" (172). The widest frame for these explorations of narrative strategies and subversive use of genre is the figure of the female storyteller as Scheherazade. Women's compulsion to tell a story may indeed be a survival tactic, a metaphorical way to defer rape, mutilation, and death. To theorize about the female storyteller is to extend Benjamin's ideas concerning the cultural function of the storyteller. The woman artist haunts Benjamin's essay, whether as the maternal righteous man of Leskov's tales, the silkworker in the quotation from Valéry, the Muse of epic remembrance, or the resourceful Scheherazade who begins fresh stories under the Muse's tutelage. In Scandinavian cultures women have been the guardians and transmitters of rich folkloric traditions, yet another example of Dinesen's claim that "above the righteous judgments of Odin stood the decisions of the Norns" (84). It is also intriguing to consider the "figural" connections of Scheherazade and Boccaccio in relation to other story cycles compiled or written by women, such as the Japanese *Tale of Genji*, Marguerite de Navarre's *L'Heptaméron*, Marguerite Yourcenar's *Nouvelles Orientales*, and Julia Voznesenskaya's *Women's Decameron*.

In a 1959 interview with *Atlantic Monthly* editor Curtis Cate, Dinesen suggested what she had meant by the word "Gothic" with respect to her own stories: "When I used the word 'Gothic,' I didn't mean the real Gothic, but the imitation of the Gothic, the Romantic age of Byron, the age of that man—what was his name?—who built Strawberry Hill, the age of the Gothic revival" (quoted in Langbaum, 54). A first approach to Dinesen's relationship to Gothic traditions and genres must take into account the problematics of "imitation" implicit in her claim. By her own admission, the casting of her stories in exotic and historic settings gave her a kind of aesthetic distance and imaginative space to explore issues that were in fact quite modern: changes in sexual politics, class relations, and literary affairs, such as the dominance of the psychological novel over the story in European fiction of the 1920s and 1930s. The contrived form of the Gothic tale, with its abundance of inset tales and digressions, reflects the preoccupation of Gothic works with their own artificiality. Sybil James, in an article on Dinesen's transformations of the Gothic, subtly suggests the tone of Dinesen's self-consciousness:

> Dinesen makes an indirect presentation of her message through inset tales; through a more symbolic use of events ... and through witty conversation. This last method relates to her speaking of the Gothic she drew on as imitation or artificial Gothic. The very modernness of the treatment lies to a great extent in just this awareness of the artificiality of the Gothic trappings, in a self-consciousness that is part of the wit yet does not mock or parody the Gothic. (141)

Self-reflexivity and consciousness of imitation extend also to the narrative communicative situation, especially to the position of the narrator. The deliberate archaism of the diction of the stories is one layer of the intricate masks through which the author's/narrator's voice speaks as both storyteller and sage, able to transmit transvalued ideals of the past into the changed climate of the present. As Benjamin has noted, the combination of anonymity and experience constitutes the authority of the storyteller. Yet the real key of the storyteller for Benjamin is closeness to oral traditions, and I have already suggested the ambiguities and antinomies in Dinesen's relationship to oral storytelling. Dinesen's narrative anonymity is self-created and self-reflexive, and thus "imitative" of the figure of the storyteller whom she holds up as an ideal.

Dinesen experimented with the Gothic repertoire and sensibility in various ways, including a Gothic novella, *Ehrengard* (1963), and a Gothic novel, *The Angelic Avengers* (1946), written under the pseudonym Pierre Andrezel in the apparently long hiatus of fifteen years between *Winter's Tales* and *Last Tales*. Except for the occasional suggestion of an analogy with Jane Austen's parodic *Northanger Abbey*, this novel has received scant critical attention, and has usually been dismissed, presumably in accordance with Dinesen's own public disclaimer in a 1956 interview with the *Paris Review* that it was her "illegitimate child," an improvisation that she dictated to pass the time in the tedium of the German occupation (quoted in Langbaum 197). These critical dismissals seem to be unaware of the complicated game of cat-and-mouse that Dinesen carried out to preserve the mask of Pierre Andrezel, and the possibility that her remarks in the interview were one more decoy in the series. In view of her unfinished second project for a novel in 100 pieces, Albondocani, of which seven tales form the first part of *Last*

Tales, *The Angelic Avengers* deserves a closer look, impossible within the scope of this paper. The *Seven Gothic Tales* are more fantastical or marvellous than they are frightening, and horrible effects are presented very lightly or avoided altogether. The fantastic tales of the Continental tradition, such as the tales of E. T. A. Hoffmann or Gogol, are a more suitable intertext for their interpretation than British Gothic novels. In the tales of Hoffmann the emphasis is less on the accumulation of marvellous happenings than on clever narrative structure, using inset tales and doubled characters. The most pervasive quality of the tales is wit—a light, ironic, sometimes wry humour investing what one would expect to be hairpin turns of horror in the plot. Dinesen herself referred to several of her tales as "entertainments" in the style of marionette comedy. A marionette play, *The Revenge of Truth*, which turns out to be a coy reference to one of Dinesen's youthful attempts at drama, is performed as an episode in "The Roads Round Pisa." Elsewhere marionette comedy serves as a metaphor for quest-dramas of identity and power, as in the last two tales, "The Dreamers" and "The Poet." In "Carnival," one of the tales intended for inclusion in *Seven Gothic Tales* but rejected by Dinesen because it was unfinished and too light in emotional tone, the entire action of the story is mapped out like a commedia dell'arte performance, with characters attending a theatre supper still costumed for a masked ball.

A clue to the serious burden of the *sprezzatura* quality of the stories can be found in Paul Johannesson's observation that though the tales fulfill a need for amusement in readers, they also deal with characters who have need for amusement, individuals who are "trapped in one way or other, by sex, by class, by history" (59). Further, Johannesson notes Dinesen's particular interest in trapped women, women "who are forced by social conventions to live on the edge of life." Punter agrees with the judgment that the Gothic tales are fundamentally "feminist" in impulse, although their resolutions may seem reactionary:

> Dinesen is above all a feminist writer in the sense that for her the problems of society are filtered through a pervading and ironic female self-consciousness. . . . The feminism in the writing is not a mere question of attitude or opinion: it is the very fabric out of which her tales are woven, and it is present even when the

apparent opinions being expressed are—as they frequently are—deeply and committedly reactionary. (378)

These suggestions highlight both important affinities and divergences between Dinesen's tales and the "female Gothic." The entrapment of women in convent and castle is an important thematic and formal feature of the Gothic, and, as feminist critics have pointed out, in the hands of women writers the construction of the Gothic heroine becomes a fictional resource to represent women's entrapment and subtly subvert it. Speaking of Ann Radcliffe's novels, for example, Ellen Moers goes so far as to say, "In Mrs. Radcliffe's hands, the Gothic novel became a feminine substitute for the picaresque, where heroines could enjoy all the adventures and alarms that masculine heroes had long experienced, far from home, in fiction" (126). Dinesen's imitation of the Gothic draws on the empowerment of the Gothic heroine, but she goes much further, extending the problem of women's entrapment to an ironic questioning of sexual politics in general, and of the way social conventionality stifles both sexes. Her male characters are transformations of melancholy Romantic heroes, as much in quest of sexual and societal identity as her women.

I suggest that the core of the Gothic for Dinesen lies in the resources and possibilities for her characters' movement from entrapment through amusement to subversive imagination: for both the characters and their author the relief (if not release) of constraint is bound up with the act of storytelling and with a complicated and "contrived" narrative structure that can be likened to a Gothic house. While they are entertainments for the imprisoned, the tales are also teaching pieces, where conventional stereotypes about women are discussed directly in conversations and illustrated by inset stories. This "training in sensibility" is revealing if not invigorating for the characters, but it is especially directed to the reader, calling for an imaginative response to the issues of the story and inviting the telling of new tales. Sybil James suggests that imagination replaces Gothic moral sentiment in Dinesen's stories dispensing with "the direct authorial Gothic preachiness, the self-important solemnity that we find in [Ann] Radcliffe's passages on St. Aubert's efforts to train Emily in the proper brand and degree of sensibility" (James 141). The teaching in Dinesen's tales often occurs in the last line of the story, where the storyteller turns to the audience with an epigram or motto, a mode for which Dinesen herself had much respect and delight (see her essay "On the Mottoes of my Life," in *Daguerreotypes*). Dinesen places her female characters in the situation of the traditional Gothic heroine, as the objects/victims of the plots of adoration, seduction, and domesticity woven for them by a patriarchal society. The women are almost without exception engaged in resistance to these plots, and bear the marks of resisting in their odd strength of character and their mythic proportion, often tinged with the grotesque. As a result, In Dinesen's tales there is little trace of the traditional Gothic heroine, the persecuted and passive victim, nor even of the heroine of Ann Radcliffe's Gothics, where the young woman keeps her virtue by means of her wit and marries at the end of the story. Instead, Dinesen deploys a cast of "odd women" modelled on the goddesses Athena and Diana, gypsies, witches, and crones, whose plots end ambiguously in the play of possibilities evoked by the enigmatic pronouncement or laconic motto of the tale's last sentence.

The patriarchal plot, the resistance of female characters, and the prevalence of odd female characters can be easily recognized in the most obviously Gothic of the tales, "The Monkey," which is also the story most often cited by critics. The popularity of this tale for close readings probably results from the number of Gothic devices on the surface levels of setting and plot—the tale comes complete with castle, convent, sinister metamorphosis, and seduction scene. The old Prioress of a lay convent for elderly single women attempts to arrange a marriage for her nephew Boris, who faces a scandal in Court for his homosexuality. The bride she chooses is Athena Hopballehus, whom Boris has known since childhood, and the daughter of a neighbouring castellan. Athena's unusual physical appearance—her size and strength—derive from her hybrid origins, her giant father having been a lover of the most beautiful woman of the time, the Princess Pauline Borghese, an incarnation in his eyes of the goddess Venus Anadyomene. True to her own name, however, Athena has no intent of marrying and rejects Boris's suit, foiling even the Prioress's seduction supper by putting up a brutal fight in the bedroom, where she has the physical edge. The story ends with a coup de théâtre, a stroke of the marvellous, as the Prioress's strange pet, a monkey from Zanzibar, returns from his autumn ramblings, and in hot pursuit the two change places in a sudden metamorphosis: "Where she had been, a monkey was now crouching and whining, altogether beaten, trying to take refuge in a corner of the room. And where the monkey had been jumping about, rose, a little out of breath from the effort, her face still a deep rose, the true Prioress of Closter Seven" (162). The monkey leaps up to his perch on the bust of Immanuel Kant, and the Prioress watches as the two young people forge a strange unity effected by Athena's gaze, which still bears the memory of the fight of the night before. The old woman seals the story with the enigmatic command: "Discite justitiam, et non temnere divos" (Obey the law, and do not anger the gods).

This tale, the most often quoted and analyzed of the *Seven Gothic Tales*, contains many examples of Dinesen's transformations of Gothic conventions: scenes of the heroine's imprisonment, the castle and the convent, the Prioress's magic love-potion, Count Hopballehus's interminable lawsuit, premonitions, and good and tyrannical parents (James 143). The elusive track of the monkey certainly raises issues about Dinesen's narrative use of the marvellous, but in a more significant departure from and exploitation of the Gothic, this story is an important instance of Dinesen's "doubling" of old and young women, crones and fierce virgins, who hold a similar "power of existence," and who function as storytellers or stage managers. Critics seldom comment on the fact that the drama of "The Monkey" is carried by the power struggle between two women, each separated from the spheres of patriarchal society, and sequestered in ambivalent places of freedom and confinement.

The Prioress's convent is a place where the values of traditional womanhood are accepted as dogma, and distant rumours of the questioning of these values in the outside world are met by a few valiant old ladies with the reluctance and nostalgia of a "gallant and faithful old general." Athena's ancestral castle is an enclosed place of freedom, where her imagination has been fed with fantasies of the French Revolution rather than the drawing room, but it is also a place of confinement, where her major task is caring for her father and his anxieties about an important lawsuit.

Just as they stand apart from the traditional roles for women in marriage and domesticity, the two women are similar in the energy-charge of their presence, and in the impression of strength they convey to Boris. As he kisses the Prioress's hand in homage, Boris gets "such a terrible impression of strength and cunning that it was as if he had touched an electric eel." He reflects that women "when they are old enough to have done with the business of being women, and can let loose their strength, must be the most powerful creatures in the world" (119). Athena, at the moment of the Prioress's crowning assault upon her virginity, seems to Boris to have in her "the magnet, the maelstrom quality of drawing everything which came inside her circle of consciousness into her own being and making it one with herself," a capacity he thinks to be characteristic of Nero's martyrs (158). Despite, or perhaps because of, the similar order of magnitude of their strength, the Prioress and Athena are evenly matched for Amazon warfare, the Prioress fighting with rhetorical weapons, Athena by the logic of her self-possession. Under the impact of this struggle between two women, the plot of Boris's destiny seems to shade off into a sub-plot. The narrative dynamics of "The Monkey" are played out between two rival female stage managers: the Prioress, who by plotting Athena's marriage becomes a strange mediatrix of the values of beauty and marriage in the community of women she governs, and Athena, who guards her own destiny by the physical power of her refusal, but who is fully capable of plotting other destinies for Boris, were she to comply and marry him. Around the contest of plots between the Prioress and Athena, Dinesen secretes a dense medium of stories, complete, incomplete, and repeated, a virtual hive of women's destinies. As he embarks on the male quest-journey of courtship, Boris becomes a kind of focal point for the old ladies of the convent, both in their gossip and in their memories. As he departs from Closter Seven to court Athena, one of the old ladies hands him three white asters from her winter garden. Boris reenacts for her the departure of her lover, who was killed at Jena thirty years ago: "She felt at the moment the resurrection of an entire destiny, and handed him the flowers as if they had been some part of it, mysteriously come to life in a second round, as if they had been her three unborn daughters, now tall and marriageable, joining his journey in the quality of bridesmaids" (119). The terrain around castle and convent is also saturated with rumours, folktales, and legends—the old gardener's tales of unicorns in the forest around Hopballehus, tales of medieval hangmen—and these condense around Boris as he makes his way through the landscape, combining with his memories of the ritual of Walpurgis night that he witnessed with his fellow-travellers.

The sexual politics of the Gothic tales are bound up with the power dynamics of storytelling—who tells whose story, and who becomes the object or brunt of a story. Older women are the storytellers and stage managers for the destinies of their younger counterparts, and, like the Prioress, they receive varied degrees of opposition to their schemes. Rarely, however, is the confrontation of the women as direct or as intense as the "face-off" between the Prioress and Athena. Only in "The Caryatids," written later than the *Seven Gothic Tales* and left unfinished, is there a power struggle of as great a magnitude, and, as in "The Monkey," it involves a marriage plot. Childerique, the central female character, is allied by an incestuous marriage to her half-brother, Philippe, the son of her mother by the neighboring lord. She is not aware of the incestuous connection, but has transferred or projected the dynamics of incest to her stepbrother, son of her legal father and his second wife. Just as "The Monkey" is haunted by the path of a marvellous creature, "Caryatids" is shot through with the fear and fascination of the uncanny gypsy world. As Childerique tries to prevent her stepbrother's marriage to the gypsy widow Simkie, she discovers her own powerful gravitation to Simkie's witchcraft, which not only reveals her past to her, but releases her from the assumed role of caryatid (supporting female figure) in a noble household to her fantasies of an independent sexual identity. "Caryatids" warrants a close analysis in terms of Cixous' rereading of Freud's "Uncanny," and it is the tale that most directly reveals Dinesen's intuition that witchcraft is a mode of empowerment for women.

Pairs of women characters appear in relations of friendship or sisterhood, as well as in the crone/virgin or noblewoman/witch pairings. Sometimes, as in the pastoral idyll that forms the outer frame of "Caryatids," the pairing is a painterly device in composing a tableau, and one of the women (in this case Childerique's friend Delphine) soon disappears into the narrative tapestry. In other stories the doubling is a more important sustaining structure in the narrative. In "Supper at Elsinore," the tale revolves around two elderly spinster sisters, who have made similar choices, and whose destinies are almost identical, resulting in the same degree of freedom. Fanny and Eliza are presented much as in fairy tales, with distinctive or opposing physical characteristics, but with an underlying symmetry of attitude that suggests that they are doubled terms, modulations of the same trait or position. The narrator alternates the sisters' position center-stage in a delicate dance, giving just enough nuance to allow their maximum degree of difference to emerge as if refracted through their relation to their pirate brother whose ghost appears as their dinner guest at the end of the story.

Tiina A. Kirss

In "The Roads Round Pisa," the two young women Rosina and Agnese are friends, "blood sisters," and allies, but their polarity emerges in a more complex kind of chiaroscuro. Though they never appear together in the same frame, except as part of the grandmother's narrative, they act as comic foils for each other. While in "The Supper at Elsinore," Fanny and Eliza both fit their brother's estimation of women who have no price and who "ought not to have been women," Agnese, who is younger than Rosina, actively carries out her own fantasy of female freedom and adventure, including crossdressing as a man: "This girl had been allowed to grow up wild and had become a real child of her age. She got into her head the wild notion that she looked like the Milord Byron . . . and she used to dress and ride as a man, and to write poetry" (174). Agnese is single while Rosina is trapped in a marriage to the impotent Prince Pozentiani, an alliance arranged for her by her step-grandmother to prevent her sharing her mother's fate of death in childbirth. Agnese uses her greater freedom to act as her friend's courier, and substitutes for Rosina in bed during Rosina's clandestine visit to her lover. The surprise appearance that night of Prince Pozentiani's substitute, Prince Nino, by whose agency he is to conceive his heir, binds Agnese to an even more complex destiny than the intrigue of her friend. Agnese's success depends upon her cross-dressing, her imitation of the male role, even to the point of serving as a second in a duel, and upon her adeptness at telling stories. In the sixth section of the tale, where the marionette show is revealed as both a replica and pivot of the interlaced narratives, Agnese "followed the development of the plot in the spirit of a fellow author." A few pages later, still disguised as "Daniele de la Gherardesci," she consents to play the part of Prince Nino's second in the marionette comedy of the duel, and tells Prince Nino the story of Joseph and Potiphar's wife from the perspective of Potiphar's wife as an old woman. The story both maintains and reveals her disguise: she, not Rosina, is the woman Nino slept with, and the duel will release both Agnese and Nino from the symbolic stasis of the moment when they recognized their mutual love and consummated it without confessing it.

Cross-dressing is an important issue in "The Roads Round Pisa," and it is a curious feature of the third important woman in the story, Carlotta, Rosina's step-grandmother, that she appears initially as a man. Carlotta is the first to release the narrative momentum of the tale when she appears on the scene as the victim of a carriage accident. At first glance she appears as "a bald old man with a refined face and a large nose," but, replacing her bonnet, inside which was fastened "an abundance of silvery curls," she becomes "a fine old lady of imposing appearance" (169). Late in the story, after the birth of her great-grandson, she again appears in a male role in a tiny inset tableau of the Nativity: "the young father [Mario] came in and was introduced to the guest; but he played no greater part in the picture than the youngest Magus of the adoration, the old Countess having taken for herself the part of Joseph" (215). For Dinesen these miniatures, whether they are theatrical scenes or tableaus, or narrative cameos like Agnese's story, retell a traditional story from the woman's point of view.

Carlotta, who is desperately plotting to prevent Rosina from bearing a child by her lover Mario, is both a storyteller and a stage manager. It is she who tells Rosina's story to the central character of the outer frame, the melancholy Augustus von Schimmelmann, and assigns him a mediating place in its denouement. Unlike the aged and faithful housekeeper Madame Baek in "Elsinore," who first receives the strange visitation of the dead son of the household and goes to bring the sisters from Copenhagen to the ghostly supper, Carlotta is unable to mediate her plot directly because of her injuries in the carriage accident. Her story, which forms the third section of "The Roads Round Pisa," is a deathbed confession, and the addressee, Augustus von Schimmelmann, is a stranger to her. The motivation of the tale is in part confessional, and in part pragmatic. She needs a nobleman to carry out her errand, and she enlists Augustus's services to see it through.

It is interesting that Carlotta, both a prohibitive and protective presence in the life of her step-granddaughter Rosina, is the one who tells Rosina's tale as well as her own. At no point does Rosina appear to tell her own story. One wonders about the narrative strategies behind this indirection, and we will therefore need to examine more closely the power dynamics between the older and younger woman in this pair. Rosina is by no means a conventional character, though she is caught up in the traditional roles of wife, lover, and mother. At every step of her apprenticeship to traditional roles, she has offered up her defiance along with her extraordinary beauty. Upon the announcement of her betrothal, she appears before her grandmother "as lovely as the young St Michele commanding the heavenly hosts" to tell her that she is in love with her cousin Mario and would marry no one but him. Carlotta describes her own counteroffensive, which includes the Gothic device of shutting up the young virgin in a castle, but the reader learns nothing of Rosina's actual response to her imprisonment. The reader does learn that she sabotages the marriage by publicly proclaiming the impotence of her husband Prince Pozentiani, turning him into a public laughingstock, and by applying to the Pope to annul her marriage. Rosina desires the traditional benefits of marriage and family, but she is willing to use unconventional means to receive them on her own terms.

Carlotta's solution to the dilemmas of womanhood is the radical one: she is terrified of childbirth, and "trades" in her wealth and beauty for the promise that her widower husband, whose first wife died in childbirth, would give her no children. Carlotta's fear marks her tutelage of her step-granddaughter (Rosina) in whom she affirms the attitudes of the goddess Diana toward men: "I did not want her to marry, so I was for a long time well pleased to see the hardness and contempt that the child showed toward all men, and especially toward the brilliant young swains who surrounded her with adoration" (172). Carlotta's role in orchestrating and narrating Rosina's destiny, and in organizing the whole tale around the germ of her fear, is a fascinating example of the female storyteller's power. It is perhaps most interesting that where her radical (feminist) pedagogy fails with Rosina, whose story ends happily contrary to Carlotta's designs and expectations, Carlotta succeeds in teaching Augustus, whose own search for truth and identity occurs in the context of an unhappy marriage to a beautiful and jealous woman. Carlotta's mediation places Augustus, as he journeys toward Pisa, in a position to witness the unfolding of the "marionette comedy" acted by all of the main characters in Carlotta's story. In the course of events he speaks with Agnese and comes to question the dogmatic kernel of social opinion about women, the dogma that Carlotta herself believes in and resists: "a woman's beauty is the crowning masterpiece of God..." (171). Carlotta teaches Augustus at least to imagine the viability of the way she herself has completed the ellipsis: ". . . and [a woman's beauty] is not to be given away." Carlotta envisions a nominally celibate but deeply subversive female freedom to complete her destiny by means of other resources than her socially valued commodity of beauty. The last frame of the story closes around Augustus as he receives from Carlotta a smelling bottle that he recognizes as the companion piece to the one given him by his maiden great-aunt. The talisman, imprinted with the words, "Amitié sincère" seems to evoke the possibility of new relations of genuine friendship between the sexes, which is not governed by the successes or vicissitudes of the sexual politics of reproduction.

"The Roads Round Pisa" is a teaching tale with a male narratee, as well as an entertainment. Augustus is, after all, in need of entertainment as well as instruction and guidance in his state of melancholy—he is one of the trapped people who in Dinesen's judgment are badly in need of fun lest they die from their earnestness. Tantalizing questions remain, however, concerning Carlotta as a storyteller, telling tales about another woman. What are the silences in Carlotta's story? Why does Rosina not tell her own tale?

These questions become even more fascinating in "Deluge at Norderney," the first story in *Seven Gothic Tales*, where Malin Nat-og-Dag, the eccentric spinster noblewoman, tells a younger woman's tale. In the hayloft that Malin has turned into a salon, the four refugees from a sudden tidal wave tell their stories to pass the time before the rising waters claim them. The Countess Calypso von Platen Hallermund is Malin's sixteen-year-old goddaughter, who has fled from her homosexual uncle's castle, a kind of male counterpart to the convent in "The Monkey," where she has been imprisoned. Malin herself tells the story of Calypso's escape: Calypso, convinced that her femaleness cut her off from the only companionship possible within her uncle's "fiefdom," was prepared to cut off her breasts with a hatchet. As she prepared for her ritual in her great-grandmother's attic, she noticed a painting of nymphs on the wall, and recognized a beauty companion to her own. After this sexual awakening, she proceeded to her uncle's bedroom, but found it unnecessary to kill him with the hatchet, for he was not half as threatening as he once had seemed. Instead she escaped to the seaside resort of Norderney, accompanied by Malin, where the destinies of the hayloft refugees converged.

It is interesting that though Calypso has broken free from a classically Gothic situation of imprisonment, she remains silent throughout the "Deluge at Norderney." She is the only one of the characters who does not tell a story, and she submits unquestioningly, though perhaps with a twinkle in her eye, to the mock wedding that Malin and the false Cardinal celebrate between herself and the melancholy young "hero" Jonathan Maersk. The relationship between Malin and Calypso echoes that of Carlotta and Rosina in

"The Roads Round Pisa," one of many examples of such interlacings between the separate Gothic tales.

The important difference, or heightening of the powers of the female storyteller, is the explicit evocation of Scheherazade at the end of the tale. As dawn breaks with the floodwaters reaching the floorboards, Malin interrupts a story she has just begun telling to the Cardinal about her childhood freedoms with the words, "à ce moment de sa narration . . . Scheherazade vit paraître le matin, et, discrète, se tut" (79). Indeed, Malin has aligned herself with Scheherazade's narrative situation earlier in the tale: Calypso is the narratee of her tale, just as Scheherazade told tales to the Caliph with her sister as the silent narratee. Implications abound for the narrative dynamics of "Deluge" in the importance of Scheherazade, disguised as an elderly spinster. The curiously late unmasking of the picaro/false Cardinal, and the function of pauses and silences in this story are particularly fascinating issues for further exploration.

I have already suggested in connection with "The Roads Round Pisa" that storytelling is an important teaching device with respect to the broader sexual politics that govern the social sphere of the Gothic tales. I return now briefly to "The Monkey" to suggest further ways in which the tales function as "didactic entertainments" for educating heroes as well as heroines. Boris is an example of Dinesen's rather passive and melancholy male protagonists, who generally govern (as in "The Roads Round Pisa") the outer frame of the tale but who need the energies of some kind of female manipulation to get them moving toward the destinies they seek. Often this energy is gathered from observing a drama unfold between two women, and in Boris's case, the face-off between Athena and the Prioress becomes catalytic. For Boris, watching the drama, the effect of the struggle is humorous, reflecting his well-developed theatrical taste for parody and burlesque. Earlier, when his aunt revealed her unusual choice of a bride for him, Boris reflected on how it might be "an extravaganza of the first water" for Athena to accompany him to Court. Likewise, in the last scene, as Athena refuses to be beaten by the Prioress's threats of pregnancy, Boris cannot help laughing at her undauntedness. The quality of his laughter seems to be a combination of the enjoyment of watching a good adventure unfold, and a marvelling, just short of fascination, at a being totally alien to himself. There seems to be no trace here of the sinister, of sarcasm or uneasiness. Instead of solving his worldly dilemma, the drama of Athena's seduction becomes an entertainment that Boris watches and participates in as a variety of fool, and he seems to laugh gently at his own expense as he imagines the possible plots that Athena might weave around him:

> Here, just as the conquering old woman and her young man had believed the situation to be closing around her, the girl was about to ride away from Closter Seven, like to Samson when he lifted upon his shoulders the doors of Gazi . . . And if she should really become aware of him, would the giant's daughter, he wondered, carry him with her upon the palm of her hand to Hopballehus, and make him groom her unicorns? (159)

Boris's role in the Prioress's plot as the seducer and young romantic hero cannot hide the fact that his worldly situation and sexual inclination place him outside the pale of the conventional social order. On his way to propose to Athena he thinks sadly of young men, "perfect in beauty and vigor—young pharaohs with clean-cut faces hunting in chariots along the Nile, young Chinese sages, silk-clad, reading within the live shade of willows," who had been forced into roles of "supporters of society, fathers-in-law, authorities on food and morals" (122). His marriage is an alliance of convenience, not of desire, and thus he stands in a position to ask open questions about married life, and the real problems of living with a wife such as Athena. At Hopballehus, he imagines his life married to Athena, and asks himself how the story might end: "If she marries me . . . she will be susceptible to my tricks; but is my married life to be an everlasting fair? And if I ever drop from my rope, will she pick me up, or just turn her back and leave?"

Both the heroine and the hero fit with difficulty into the conventional sex roles that apply in the world outside the territory demarcated by the castle and convent. In the last section of the story Dinesen implies a kind of bond between them because of this social alienation, but the possibilities as to its nature and future are left tantalizingly unclear. Just as the first discussion Boris has with his aunt was carried out by means of maxims and riddles, the last sentence of the story is a motto, leaving open which gods the young people are to avoid angering, and which law they are to obey. The answer seems closer when we consider that the metamorphosis of the monkey and the Prioress carries more than a hint of the dangers of polarizing the

Apollonian and the Dionysiac—the powers of reason and rhetoric on the one hand and the vital energies of sexuality on the other. The monkey, bearer of terror and the marvellous, a species of Gothic monster, forces the tale onto a new symbolic level, and the two young people are given a dazzling object lesson in imaginative wisdom. Sharing the lesson, it is questionable whether they can equilibrate the two extremes anywhere else than in the seclusion of the convent, the forest, and the castle.

The last sentence of the story bears the impact of a judicial verdict, and leaves the reader in the baffling interval between an event on the level of the fantastic and the beginning of a new story. As Walter Benjamin points out, a storyteller has counsel for her readers, oriented toward the practical interests and survival skills that the reader needs: "After all, counsel is less an answer to a question than a proposal concerning the continuation of a story which is just unfolding. To seek this counsel one would first have to be able to tell the story" (86). The effect of the proverb is both prospective and retrospective, pointing at the same time to past stories that have been told and forgotten, including the stories in the dense atmosphere around Hopballehus, and new stories that might be told, as continuations of Athena and Boris's destiny, or in the interstices of life-stories of the women in the convent. The link with the past appears perhaps more easily for the reader who does not understand the Latin and cannot situate the quote. As Benjamin puts it, "A proverb, one might say, is a ruin which stands on the site of an old story, and in which a moral twines about a happening like ivy around a wall" (108).

It is characteristic of the narrative situation of Dinesen's Gothic tales that they call on both characters and readers to design destinies and tell stories, using the imaginative energy provided by the shock of a marvellous event that ruptures the narrative order. The transformation of the Prioress and her "familiar" of a monkey is interpreted by the new Prioress's maxim, but the interpretation is deferred as far as Boris and Athena are concerned, as the tale does not resolve in the manner of a traditional marriage plot. The tale solicits rereading, but its parting counsel seems also to invite new stories tracing the elusive track of the monkey, who stakes his territory across both the convent and the castle, leaving no register of the scene or the story immune from his influence.

I have mapped out the terrain for an inquiry into Isak Dinesen's strategies of female storytelling, and pursued the elusive track of

Scheherazade through a few of the Gothic tales. The range of narrative possibilities, silences, and pauses reminds us of the aptness of Dinesen's own early title for what was to become *Seven Gothic Tales*: "Tales of Nozdref's Cook." Nozdref's cook, a character in Gogol's *Dead Souls*, could compose a soup from whatever ingredients he was given, and he is perhaps a kind of "double" of the deformed Kikuyu servant Kamante, whose life Dinesen saved in Africa, and who showed exceptional ability as a cook, imitating to uncanny perfection the European cuisine in which he was trained (OOA chapter I). Dinesen's Gothic tales also combine, tastefully and exotically, all sorts of thematic and generic ingredients. I have suggested that one of them is the "female Gothic," particularly in Dinesen's variations on narrative complexity. Much further work is in order on how Dinesen constructs and "instructs" her heroines, on what may be the nature of the uncanny and the fearsome in the atmosphere of the tales, and on the structure of the inset tales as dreamwork. The most suggestive relation between Dinesen and the female Gothic is narrative form, an issue left virtually unexplored in the essays in Fleenor's anthology, though in her definition Fleenor states that the female Gothic "frequently uses a narrative form which questions the validity of the narration itself." Perhaps the most strikingly Gothic and imitative feature of Dinesen's *Seven Gothic Tales* is their complexity of framing, with inset tales, witty conversations and embedded narratives.

The figure of Scheherazade haunts the margins of the most sensitive male critics of storytelling. I have already mentioned Walter Benjamin. Michel Foucault, in his essay "Language to Infinity," offers Scheherazade as the inverse image of "Diderot's blunder," the point that reveals the faultline in his text where the mirror of death is concealed. Foucault hardly touches the gender implications of this opposition, and tantalizes the feminist critic to explore further the deferral of rape and death in the tales of Scheherazade.

Dinesen's tales offer a fascinating opportunity to beckon Scheherazade closer and to entice her into unmasking herself. Dinesen herself was both complicit and resistant to casting herself as Scheherazade: the utter opacity of her narrative voice and the mask-game she played with editors and critics are facets of the seductive appeal for her of the role of the female storyteller. Late in her life Dinesen tended to act the role of Malin Nat-og-Dag, but she often lacked a Calypso. It is in pursuit of the silent female narratee, who is perhaps also the figure of the reader, that I suspend, for the space of a pause, my quest for Scheherazade in the Gothic tales of Nozdref's cook.

WORKS CITED

Aiken, Susan Hardy. "Dinesen's 'Sorrow-Acre': Tracing the Woman's Line." *Contemporary Literature.* XXV (1984), 156–186.
Benjamin, Walter. "The Storyteller." in *Illuminations.* Transl. Harry Zohn. New York: Schocken Books, 1968.
Cixous, Hélène. "Fiction and its Phantoms: A Reading of Freud's 'Das Unheimliche' ('The Uncanny')." *New Literary History.* VII (1976), 525–48.
Dinesen, Isak. *Anecdotes of Destiny and Ehrengard.* New York: Vintage, 1958.
———. *The Angelic Avengers* (under pseudonym Pierre Andrezel). New York: Random House, 1946.
———. *Carnival: Entertainments and Posthumous Tales.* Chicago: U of Chicago P, 1977.
———. *Daguerreotypes and Other Essays.* Chicago: U of Chicago P, 1979.
———. *Last Tales.* New York: Vintage, 1957.
———. *Letters from Africa 1914–1931.* Transl. Anne Born. Ed. for the Rungstedlund Foundation, Frans Lasson. Chicago: U of Chicago P, 1981.
———. *On Modern Marriage and Other Observations.* Transl. Anne Born. Intro. Else Cederborg. New York: St. Martin's Press, 1986.
———. *Out of Africa and Shadows on the Grass.* New York: Vintage, 1985.
———. *Seven Gothic Tales.* New York: Vintage, 1934.
———. *Winter's Tales.* New York: Vintage, 1942.
Fleenor, Juliann E. "Introduction: The Female Gothic." in *The Female Gothic.* Ed. Juliann E. Fleenor. Montreal: Eden Press, 1983.
Foucault, Michel. "Language to Infinity." in *Language, Counter-Memory, Practice.* Ed. and Intro. Donald R. Bouchard. Trans. Donald R. Bouchard and Sherry Simon. Ithaca: Cornell UP, 1974, 53–67.
Freud, Sigmund. "The Uncanny." *The Standard Edition of the Complete Psychological Works of Sigmund Freud.* Trans. and Ed. James Strachey. Vol. XVII. London: Hogarth, 1955, 217–256.
James, Sybil. "Gothic Transformations: Isak Dinesen and the Gothic." *The Female Gothic.* Ed. Juliann E. Fleenor. Montreal: Eden Press, 1983, 138–152.
Johannesson, Eric O. *The World of Isak Dinesen.* Seattle: U of Washington P, 1961.
Langbaum, Robert. *The Gayety of Vision: A Study of Isak Dinesen's Art.* London: Chatto and Windus, 1964.

Moers, Ellen. *Literary Women.* Garden City: Doubleday, 1976.

Punter, David. *The Literature of Terror: A History of Gothic Fictions from 1765 to the Present Day.* New York: Longman, 1980.

Weed, Merry. "Marchen and Legend Tradition of Narrative in Two 'Tales' of Isak Dinesen." *Journal of Folklore Institute.* XV (1978), 23–44.

PSYCHOANALYSIS AND FEMALE IDENTITY: THE ADOLESCENT DIARIES OF KAREN HORNEY

John Neubauer

Questions about the traditional assumption that literature is clearly distinct from other texts has led to a recent interest in the margins of literature, including the "autobiographical margin" of letters, travelogues, memoirs, and diaries, where truth and fiction, *Dichtung und Wahrheit* mingle. It is perhaps at this border territory that one may get the best sense of what lies on either side.

The urge to display oneself, warts and all, and the corresponding existence of a large reading public interested in such displays on paper, is a distinctly modern media phenomenon, whose beginnings may be dated with the appearance of Rousseau's *Confessions* (1762). The flood of autobiographical retrospectives in the nineteenth century has been stimulated to no small degree by the rise of a reading public with ever greater appetite for the private life of great men. The expectation that one's personal letters and intimate diary (*journal intime*) will one day be published, has changed their tone, as the correspondence of Goethe clearly demonstrates. A tension between privacy and public stance informs the diaries of such writers as André Gide, and Paul Valéry.

That people with established reputation should consider all of their writings, even the most intimate ones, ultimately a matter for the large public is perhaps not too surprising, in light of the power of modern media. More surprising is the emergence of journals and diaries written by people with no public reputation, such as adolescents, which are designed, secretly or openly, for posterity. Anne Frank was assuredly not aware that she cultivated a genre, but her diary was in fact preceded by adolescent diaries designed for public consumption that reported of personal or general crises.[1] Its prototype was Marie Bashkirtseff's *Journal* (1887), written between the ages of 12 and 24, in the shadow of death but in search of an eternal glory. As Marie wrote in the preface, she hoped to survive as a eternal glory. As Marie wrote in the preface, she hoped to survive as a great artist, but she wanted to have her journal published if she was to die young (5),[2] for she dreamt "of glory, of celebrity, of being known everywhere!" (17). The realization that the journal would still her hunger for fame only posthumously (207–208) gave her style a special charm. Hugo von Hofmannsthal remarked in a review when he himself was only nineteen: "It is written like a coquettish and heartfelt letter to some unknown person" (121).

Such diaries and other autobiographical writings that are addressed to some public must be distinguished from the bulk of adolescent diaries that neither responds to extraordinary events nor was written with a public in mind. In the identity crisis of adolescence diaries open the possibility of self-dialogue and may point the way towards resolution by aiding the search for expression. While these private documents of personal development do not survive in most societies, many of them did get into print in western cultures since the end of the nineteenth century, not because of their literary merit or their portrayal of extraordinary events, but because of the professional interest that psychologists and psychoanalysts take in them. Thus *A Young Girl's Diary* was published and analyzed by Viennese psychoanalysts in 1921, and many others were published and analyzed by the prominent psychologist Charlotte Bühler, who believed that "unrehearsed" adolescent diaries may be the best raw material for the study of the adolescent psyche. More recently, nineteenth-century adolescent diaries have been published in France.

Bühler could have made good use of Karen Horney's adolescent diaries, for they intelligently and sensitively record a young girl's reactions to her world and the emotions welling up in her. Since she wrote for herself only, with no reader in mind, she never poses. Their posthumous publication is justified both because of her later fame as a psychoanalyst and their value in portraying feminist issues and the history of psychoanalysis in the early years of this century.[3] In addition to five diaries (written at the age of 13–15, 15–17, 18–19, 19–22, and 25–26 respectively), the book also contains Karen's letters to Oskar Horney, written at the age of 21–22. She married him shortly thereafter, in 1910. These letters partly bridge the gap between the last two diaries, and, more importantly, they assume some of the diary's functions. The last diary was written past Karen's literal adolescence, but it records responses to her psychoanalytic treatment, which revaluated her adolescent problems. The book allows thus to compare the immediate adolescent records with their later analytic reassessment. The continuity between the early diaries, the letters to Oskar, and the responses to the analysis is graphically displayed in a remark to Oskar (Little Hornvieh): "I'm just writing away, whatever comes into my head, hardly realizing that someone else is to read it. Little Hornvieh functioning as Karen's diary!" (October 6, 1906: 169). A few months later Karen added, probably responding to Oskar's comments on his "diary role": "Yes, I find it highly sensible, letters in diary form. The business has only one hitch: assume I am in a very pronounced mood one day and write it down. When I go at the letter again, perhaps I read over what I wrote. And the letter strays into the waste-basket. Anyway that's the way it will be mostly, and the more, the more unreservedly I had put down everything in the sense of my mood, i.e., the more valuable the letter was as a letter . . . ?" (March 24, 1907: 190). Though two weeks later she felt "almost safe just writing to you" (April 10, 1907: 199), the awareness of a reader clearly functioned as a censor.

Karen started her diaries simply to remember better the days of her youth in later years (3). The sporadic entries of the first two years reflect a naive, well-intentioned "Backfisch" with typical crushes on her male as well as female teachers. Although she chided herself occasionally for the lack of religious sentiments and she violently rebelled against her authoritarian father, her values were decidedly middle-class and deeply embedded in her cultural tradition. From a late-twentieth-century perspective, she is both naive and emotionally undeveloped at age 13–15.

The tone of the diary changes, however, at seventeen, when a conflict develops between her inherited middle-class principles and her adolescent desire for personal and natural values. If her first moral law, "thou shalt not lie," reaffirms the parental world, her second one enjoins her to seek a personal identity: "thou shalt free thy self from convention, from everyday morality, and shalt think through the highest commands for thy self and act accordingly. Too much custom, too little morality" (82). Now she writes poetry, copies poems into the diary, is enchanted by the erotic poetry of Marie-Madeleine, and reads Max Halbe's successful drama *Jugend* on adolescent rebellion.

But the voice that demands the right of self-determination incorporates the parental voice of the superego: the injunction against lying is both part of her heritage and a condemnation of conventions that often foster insincerity. Karen—like her fellow-adolescent Kafka—often seems to oppose not traditional beliefs and rules but their undermining through hypocrisy. First she rejects her father for disobeying his own religious values within the family, then she condemns the "utilitarian morality" of her brother Berndt (98), and finally she gets disillusioned by her much adored mother, when the latter does not want to receive Karen's Jewish boyfriend in their home (124).

Yet Karen does not reject her parental world only by means of those principles that it ostentatiously upholds and surreptitiously undermines. She also rebels against these principles under the banner of authenticity, freedom, and naturalness. She is an adolescent of her age, part of the turn-of-the-century generation that turned against its parental world by seeking the authenticity of instinct and spontaneous emotion, the fresh air of outdoors, the freedom of the naked body, the simplicity of folklore, and the magic of exoticism.

Her case shows how deeply this rhetoric of freedom and authenticity was rent by contradictions. What Karen seeks is no libertine freedom from all constraint, but submission to the "higher," "purer," and more personal laws of her own femininity. But these laws do not manifest themselves in a "natural" way; they are elusive and the source of much inner turmoil. Just what do they demand of her?

At nineteen, Karen is inspired by the Swedish feminist psychologist Ellen Key, the "lustrous star" towards which her soul directs its way, the source of her "sacred flame of enthusiasm" (92). Key wants to balance the individual's demands for happiness with a concern for the species" (92 f), and Karen learns from her that a woman's "individual freedom of mind" is circumscribed by the "demands of nature," i.e. the raising of children which necessitates stable marriages. The diary notes: "we want this freedom for our emotional life and for its expression, freedom not license, for we feel bound to the demands of Nature. We want to achieve a new morality" (102).

This "new morality" is not just a warmed-up old one, for it is meant to safeguard in a particular way the emancipation of women. How wanton sexuality can endanger that emancipation is shockingly brought home to Karen when she accidentally comes upon the following passage in a book: "Force me to my knees, dearest. For I am a woman. No good, shy little girl of the humble womanliness described in books—no, on the contrary. But just for this proud, free independently thinking woman there is no sweeter lot than to be allowed to worship, to bow down in love. Oh, dearest—will you be my master?" (73). The corny crudity of the passage did not temper its relevance. For Karen was a "proud, free, independently thinking woman," who blazed the feminist trail by attending Gymnasium and medical school—and she was fully aware of it. But she could not achieve full independence and freedom if, like the fictional female, she remained a slave of sexuality and therefore a servant of her male masters. The only solution that seemed open to her, the "new morality" of Ellen Key and others, demanded that she suppress the elemental sexual desires that repeatedly welled up in her. In crucial ways this "new morality" was even more coercive than the old one: Ellen Key, the Wandervogel, the adolescent teetotalers, the vegetarians, and all the other moral reformers and prophets of a "new humanity" spoke of liberation but demanded abstinence. Their moral rigor appealed to the idealism of youth.[4]

Karen wished to accept the rigor of the "new morality" though she could not live up to it. Occasionally she rebelled against it and thought that the debased physical craving had a beauty and justification of its own, but most of the time she accepted its principles and accused herself for "sinning" against it, so much the more since there existed a direct line from the bourgeois to the "new moral" condemnation of sexuality. Karen's fear of her own sexuality appears already in her early adolescence, prior to her reading of Ellen Key. When reading the erotic poems of Marie-Madeleine her senses exult "in unbridled delight" but her intellect "turns away in disdain" (63), she feels compelled to conclude: "In my own imagination I am a strumpet!" (64). In a poem a few months later she celebrates her "success" of liberating herself from one of her first dominating lovers: "My pride has conquered love. . . . He treated me like a strumpet" (77).

Ellen Key's emancipatory program reinforces Karen's intellectual disdain for sexuality, and she notes two years later under the influence of Key, on March 29, 1905:

> To be free of sensuality means great power in a woman. Only in this way will she be independent of a man. Otherwise she will always long for him and in the exaggerated yearning of her senses she will be able to drown out all feeling of her own value. She becomes the bitch, who begs even if she is beaten—a strumpet. . . . Otherwise eternal battling. And every victory of the senses a Pyrrhic victory, bought with loathing, ever deadly loathing afterwards. (104)

Were we unfamiliar with the source, we could trace Karen's sexual philosophy to Christian morality or Schopenhauer. Though she was familiar with Nietzsche, she did not adopt the Nietzschean protest against their self-debasing consequences, and her late-adolescent years became "eternal battles" between the intellectual demands of the "new morality," which she accepted but could not obey, and her "base" sexual cravings that either conquered at the price of lowering her self-esteem or threatened her moral principles. Unable to live up to the principle of purity she accepted, she was given to periodic self-castigations. Possessed by Ellen Key's "deep moral earnestness," she could not understand, why "the most brutal naturalism" seemed equally "intelligible" to her (91). As a result, Karen's adolescent love-life pathologically reenacts a Tannhäuserian conflict between the higher and the lower, the heavenly and the earthly, the pure and the debased.

On the one hand one finds the deep, pure, and intellectually satisfying relations that Karen wishes to keep sexually "uncontaminated": her friendship with Rolf (the Jewish boy), which had a decisive influence on her development (recorded in a lengthy retrospective: 120–46, 150–60), and her epistolary courtship with Oskar Horney.

The first entry on Rolf in the diary on August 11, 1904 foreshadows everything:

> I love you like a sister, Rolf, like a friend who only wants the best for you. You say that my love gives you peace. See, I come to lay my hand on your poor tormented heart. I am too young for other feelings not to be mixed in with this pure love. Then a consuming longing for you comes over me, a wild turmoil of my senses. But that is just like a foreign element that doesn't belong to me, and it soon disappears. (89)

Sexuality seems like an alien intruder into her "true" self, a contamination of her pristine love for an intellectual and moral tutor (129). When Rolf kisses her "quite gently, quite uncertainly" for the first time, Karen is "disconcerted and sad": "I had the feeling that now a shadow had fallen across our delightful relationship as friends" (133). First, his kisses leave her cold, later she accepts them "with a sort of passive well-being" (137), but when she becomes sexually aroused she resents it and blames him as well as herself: "all the hours in which our senses spoke loudest seem to me somewhat ugly, like a foreign body that had entered in and did not belong there. And that lies not only in the matter itself, but I believe that the spiritual part involuntarily appears higher and nobler than the physical" (143). When Rolf, who "did not kiss well" (143) "danced horribly" (135), suddenly reappears in Karen's life, she writes to Oskar Horney that Rolf "will now have understood that the sensual incident was a foreign body in our relation, because sensually we do not suit each other" (223).

What surfaces here in connection with the man who brought Karen's "spiritual awakening" (185) was person-bound sexual incompatibility but part of a larger pattern. A review of the year 1906 notes the painful end of the relationship with Rolf but marks also a new beginning (on Bastille day!):

> Correspondence with the little Hornvieh and the start of a friendship with him. And with that the taking up again of a thread that ran luminously through a year of my life, the friendship with Rolf. What Rolf awakened in me is being brought to life again by Hornvieh. How shall I say it briefly? The reflecting about myself perhaps, about the deeper springs of my ego, the search within. (149)

The theme of repetition and continuity appears already three weeks earlier, in a letter of December 11–12, 1906 to Hornvieh himself: the "finer language" of his letters reintroduced the possibility of "a life of a higher sort" that Rolf had shown to her in her "petit-bourgeois family" (175 f). It is an ominous sign, however, that she must confide on February 13, 1907, "perhaps there is a bit of the hussy in all of us" (187).

For a while, there seems to be no danger of sexual "contamination." When Karen gets acquainted with Hornvieh she is in love with a man called Losch (148), their paths depart, and only the correspondence remains, in which Karen rather freely analyzes her amours (e.g. 209–11, 228) and Hornvieh (inasmuch as this can be deduced indirectly from her letters) reciprocates. But once the "epistolary episode" in the relationship with Hornvieh is over, a few entries during her marriage to Hornvieh and her analytic treatment indicated that Hornvieh inherited not only the idealistic, noble role of Rolf, but also its disturbing sexual contamination: "In Oskar I found everything I consciously wished for—and behold; my instinctual life rebels.... Oskar is always self-controlled. Even when he forces me to submit to him—it is never savagery or animal brutality—he is at all times controlled, he is never elemental. For living together certainly ideal—but something remains in me that hungers" (April 18, 1910, 238 f). In the following January Karen notes that she has an increased capacity for sexual enjoyment (247) and that her "relation with Oskar has become sexually harmonious" (249), yet the diary ends with somber and perplexed remarks about her neuroses.

"Animal sensuality" (106) not only "contaminates" Karen's "higher" relations with men, it is also a source of self-accusation when she is strongly attracted to men she does not respect morally or intellectually. In her relationship to Ernst and Karl, as in her "contaminated" pure ones to Rolf and Oskar, the intrusion of something uncontrollable lowers her self-esteem and disturbs her emotional balance.

She got to know Ernst, who "kisses well" (107), at the end of her friendship with Rolf, and "senses ran ahead of love" (November 17, 1905: 107). The short-lived romance leaves her perplexed: the moments of passion with Ernst ("the man I really loved!") appear to her in retrospect often as "beautiful and precious," but she feels compelled to add immediately that this may be due to the fact "that with him I did not have the finer feelings, but was blindly craving a sacrifice for my senses" (April 1906: 143). By the end of the year, the image of Ernst and her attachment to him becomes unequivocally negative: "out of the blue sky I was seized by a senseless passion for someone else, who was built of a coarser stuff (than Rolf)" (letter to Hornvieh, December 11–12, 1906: 176). "Now at least I am free of him and at rest, for I have seen him too clearly for what hie is. Him in his good-citizen's pettiness and cowardice, in his mendacity, and his brutality and his egoism. How could I ever have loved him so deeply, so passionately? Forever an open question" (January 3, 1907: 149).

The unanswered question leads to repetition. Karl, whom she gets to know as a philosophizing friend of Hornvieh (224–26), reappears during her marriage as the person to whom her "instinctual life" (not her self!) is drawn "because it scents the beast of prey in him which it needs" (April 18, 238). Seeing him again, Karen has a strong desire to throw her arms around his neck and kiss him (241), but Oskar observes the scene and tells her a few days later that "I had 'thrown myself away' because I had so conspicuously flirted with

Karl" (242). She responds with disproportionate "spasms of sobbing" and a "deep depression," because the remark hit a raw nerve that gets lacerated each time she can not live up to the sexual principles of the "new morality." On these repeated occasions she becomes that fictional intelligent and emancipated woman, whose "animal passion" makes her a slave to male masters. Lest she became a bitch, a hussy, a prostitute, she had to emancipate herself and suppress this animal sexuality, but she repeatedly failed and self-flagellations followed.

Karen Horney's adolescent diary shows that the turn-of-the century "new morality" had extended the reign of bourgeois values by insisting that sexual cravings be suppressed. The demand acquired a special function in the emancipation of women, for, as Karen's diary shows, it claimed that women could maintain their independence from dominating males only by preventing wanton sexual self-abandonment. For Karen at any rate, the theory had disastrous consequences, for she repeatedly "slipped" and bitterly came to accuse herself in the wake of it. Hence her melancholy conclusion that there was a "hussy" in her and perhaps in all women (186). Responding to an article that Hornvieh sent him on the question of emancipation, she wrote: I doubt "that women will *ever* be able to achieve intellectually what men do. Lies in the nature of the matter—women are too involved in the sexual—children! etc. So that the woman question won't bring any direct advance in the life of the mind (science, art)" (January 13, 1907: 184).

Yet surely, not all voices of turn-of-the-century culture preached this sublimation of female sexuality, and in view of Karen Horney's later career one is particularly interested to know how psychoanalysis helped her in her predicament. After all, it was Freud's central message that neuroses and psychoses result from the repression of sexual urges in modern society.

Yet Freud's theory and therapeutic record in dealing with young women is complicated and hardly emancipatory. His treatment of Dora, for instance, shows not only that he was quite hesitant and inexperienced in treating female adolescents during the early years of the century, but also that he attempted to cover this uncertainty by assuming a paternal attitude that finally led to Dora's decision to terminate her treatment prematurely. As Glenn has shown, Freud was not sufficiently sensitive to the need of adolescents. Furthermore, one of Freud's important insights, namely the "sexual life does not begin only at puberty, but starts with clear manifestations soon after birth" (*Outline* 26), led to a relative neglect of adolescence and therapeutic attempts to cure adolescent problems by tracing the symptoms back into childhood. Freud's only essay exclusively devoted to adolescence, a rather slight contribution from 1914 to the fiftieth anniversary of his Gymnasium entitled *Zur Psychologie der Gymnasiasten*, asserts that affective dispositions toward both sexes are determined during the first six years of a person's life. While later these attachments can be developed and transformed to suit new directions, the early mode of attachment to parents and siblings has deterministic power: all subsequently encountered persons will become substitutes of these first objects of affection, ordered into series that issue from the parents and siblings. Later acquaintances assume an "emotional heritage," they arouse sympathies and hostilities without having given reason for them. "All future choices of friendship and love are made on the basis of memory traces that these first models have left behind."[5] The relevance of this to transference in analysis is evident, and Freud was probably right in surmising that Dora broke her treatment off because Freud became another father figure for her. One may add that Freud was not quite innocent in this because, in spite of his realization that Dora's father and his friend Herr K lied, he took a parental and typically male view of Dora.

Freud's "Transformation of Puberty" ("Die Umgestaltung der Pubertät"), the third part of his *Three Essays on Sexual Theory* (*Drei Abhandlungen zur Sexual theorie* 1904–05) was published almost simultaneously with his case-study of Dora. He defines puberty in this extended, but similarly inadequate discussion as the transition to object-directed and genital sexuality (5: 112). Sexual development occurs in three phases: object-directed infantile sexuality (primarily directed toward the mother's breast) is replaced during the "autoerotic" sexuality of childhood but reestablished in a new form during puberty. The object-attachment of genital sexuality that follows upon the period of autoeroticism is patterned after the infantile attachment to the mother: "It is not without good reason that the child's sucking at the mother's breast has become exemplary for every love relationship. *The object finding is actually a re-finding*" (5: 126 my emphasis).[5]

Thus puberty and adolescence are strongly pre-determined for both sexes; they are particularly problematic, according to Freud, for girls. Since the masturbatory childhood sexuality of the little girl is clitorial and of "a thoroughly masculine character" (5: 123), female puberty signifies no affirmation of sexual identity but the suppression of a masculine clitoral sexuality. The shift in erogenous zones and the related suppression of a restant male sexuality is so painful that Freud sees in it the source of a female predilection to neuroses and hysteria and a fundamental negative feature of femininity (5: 125).

This theory of female sexuality, which has rightly become the target of many attacks, forms the background to Karen Horney's first exposure to psychoanalysis, and her disappointment must have played an important role in her later psychoanalytic work. Could psychoanalysis help to convince her that accepting her sexual urges would be part of her emancipation and the foundation of a more "natural" and secure self-image? The diary shows that this was not the case, even though she was treated by Karl Abraham, the pioneering Freudian analyst in Berlin and one of the outstanding leaders of the movement in general. Whether the dark, somber mood of the last diary from 1910–1911 is attributable to disturbing matters that the analysis made her face, whether she entered therapy for professional or for personal reasons is unclear. The undeniable fact is that during her illness and self-doubt, psychoanalysis addressed her with the same ego-destructive voice as her father and the "new morality." Commodore Berndt Wackels Danielsen, who thought that a girl need not go to Gymnasium, Ellen Key, who thought that women must sublimate their sexuality in order to emancipate themselves truly, and Karl Abraham, who thought that Karen's secret "prostitution wish" was normal because all middle-class women took interest in prostitution (242)—all these paternal voices could not fail to humble her self-image, because they belittled or ignored matters that were inextricable parts of her personality.

The very first entry from Berlin, on April 18, 1910, picks up old problems and offers old answers couched in a new language. When Abraham considers Karen's great attraction to "brutal and rather forceful men," her "wanting to blend in with the will of a man who has set his foot on my neck," her "overly strong attraction" to Ernst, "that clumsy, brutally egotistic, coarsely sensual fellow" (238), he concludes that this was due to Karen's Oedipal love for her father—and therefore inescapable. Karen, who hoped to kill her passion for Ernst and his likes through analysis, learns only:

all his inferior characteristics, which I kept before my eyes, did not in the least quench my passion; no, on the contrary: the instincts in me wanted such a man—and my conscious I, seeking a man of fine intelligence and discerning kindness, resisted against this in vain. In Oskar I found everything I consciously wished for—and behold: my instinctual life rebels. It feels itself drawn to a Karl U. because it scents the beast of prey in him, which it needs. (238)

When Oskar accuses Karen of conspicuously flirting with Karl, Abraham cites Karen's old self-image as a "hussy," and she claims, "I had taken it so hard because the rebuke had hit upon a repressed wish, namely the very wish to throw myself away, to prostitute myself—give myself to any man at random.... In the prostitution wish there is always a masochistic wish hidden: to relinquish one's own personality, to be subject to another, to let oneself be used by the other" (242). While psychoanalysis, unlike the "new morality," did not say that the prostitution wish and the related sexual urges had to be suppressed or sublimated, it placed these in such light that their acceptance inevitably weakened Karen's self-image.

Abraham's ego-destructive analysis was reinforced by Karen's psychoanalytic readings and foremost among them the writings of Alfred Adler. Finding herself still fatigued several months after the beginning of the therapy, she interprets her shyness and her fear of not being able to do first class work in terms of Alfred Adler, who claims that "the masculine protest is developed in every women and makes her inwardly unfree" and she concludes that "every woman feels herself to be primarily, as such, inferior to men" (251).

The last date in the *Adolescent Diaries* is to be found on a letter to Abraham, which Karen left in her diary and did not send off. On July 9, 1911, five months after the death of her mother and four months after the birth of her first child, she laconically remarks "it is not going well at all," and hesitantly suggests to continue the analysis. Whether this happened is unclear. One may only say that her adolescent crisis ended and her true emancipation started beyond that date, when she turned against the father figures of Freud, Abraham, and Adler, by working towards an alternative psychoanalysis of female sexuality.

NOTES

1. Nelly Ptashkina's diary, for instance, reported her experiences while fleeing revolutionary Russia.
2. Marie's hope for the journal rested primarily with the extraordinary Rousseauistic honesty with which she wanted to endow it: "This journal is the most useful and the most instructive of all writings that have been or will be. This is a woman with all her thoughts and her hopes, disappointments, meannesses, beauties, chagrins and joys" (59).
3. The publication of Horney's diaries received little attention. The few responses include a rather insubstantial article by Yvon Brés (*Adolescence* 60–62), which regards the diaries as irrelevant to psychoanalysis and Karen's later theories.

    In spite of repeated attempts, no German publisher could be found to publish them in their original version.
4. It may be added that a similar rebellion in the name of a new discipline made nazi ideology so attractive to many adolescents a generation later.
5. Freud 4: 239. Accordingly, Freud sees high school teachers as father-substitutes and the peer group as a sibling-substitute. But among these two forces shaping adolescence the "in-group" tensions and fighting take a secondary position to the generation-conflict that Freud redramatizes as the Oedipal conflict.
6. Freud modified his original statement by adding in a later footnote that sexual objects are found either by imitating the early infantile models, which is actually a re-finding, or by seeing and finding narcissistically one's own self in the other. The later is a frequent source of pathological developments (5:126).

WORKS CITED

Adolescence. vol. 4, no. 1. Special issue entitled *Ecrire* (spring 1986).
Bashkirtseff, Marie. *Le Journal de Marie Bashkirtseff.* 2 vols. Paris: Charpentier, 1887.
Bühler, Charlotte. *Jugendtagebuch und Lebenslauf.* 3rd ed. Jena: Fischer, 1932.
―――. *Das Seelenleben des Jugendlichen.* Jena: Fischer, 1921.
――― ed. *Zwei Knabentagebücher. Mit einer Einleitung über die Bedeutung des Tagebuchs für die Jugendpsychologie.* Jena: Fischer, 1925.
Freud, Sigmund. *Studienausgabe.* 10 vols. Frankfurt/M.: Fischer, 1969–75.
―――. *An Outline of Psychoanalysis.* Trans. James Strachey. NY: Norton, 1949.
Glenn, Jules. "Freud's Adolescent Patients: Katharina, Dora and the 'Homosexual Woman.'" *Freud and his Patients.* Ed. Mark Kanzer and Jules Glenn. NY: Aronson, 1980. 23–47.

Hofmannsthal, Hugo von (Loris). "Das Tagebuch eines jungen Mädchens." 1893. In *Prosa*. Frankfurt/M.: Fischer, 1950. 1: 121–28.
Horney, Karen. *The Adolescent Diaries of Karen Horney*. NY: Basic, 1980.
Journal de Geneviève Bréton. Paris: Ramsay, 1985.
Le Journal intime de Caroline B. Enquête de Michelle Perrot et Georges Ribeill. Paris: Montalba, 1985.
Kristeva, Julia. "Le Roman adolescent." *Adolescence* 4.1 (1986): 13–28.
Ptashkina, Nelly. *The Diary of Nelly Ptashkina*. London: Cape, 1923.

A CONTEMPORARY QUEST FOR A NEW KABBALAH

Thomas J. J. Altizer

Walter A. Strauss has largely given his life to a quest for a "New Kabbalah," a Kabbalah which will be traditional and new at the same time, and a Kabbalah which is already present in a new imagination and a new world. Of course, that Kabbalah is invisible and inaudible to our given forms of understanding and analysis, but it is indubitably present, and above all so for one like Strauss who is an authentic son of Israel. If Israel exists in an eternal covenant with God, a covenant which can be suspended or abated but not annulled by its Lord, then that covenant transcends the actualities of history, and does so even when those actualities embody the silence or death of God. Israel was the first people in history to deeply know such actualities, and this occurred in that Exile which gave birth both to Judaism and the Bible, as the silence of God became embodied in the new silence of Scripture, a scripture which was the first full writing in history, and a scripture giving birth to an oral Torah which itself is inseparable and indistinguishable from Scripture. Strauss himself understands Scripture as the invisible Truth made visible or finite, therefore Scripture is a necessary distortion, since it is the Incomprehensible made comprehensible, and therefore paradoxical. This is the paradox that Strauss finds demonstrated throughout all of Kafka's work, and he can even affirm that it is the condition of all writing.[1] Writing itself therein and thereby becomes manifest as Scripture, and the silence of writing can thereby be understood as the silence of Scripture, a silence which is a truly and a purely paradoxical silence, for it is the silence of the revelation of God.

This is the silence which Strauss would unearth in Writing itself, but in a pure writing, a writing now present in a "New Kabbalah," and a writing which for Strauss is most purely present in the writing of Kafka. All too significantly, Kafka's writing in all its forms seldom mentions the word "God," but God is nevertheless present in that absence, and present not only by way of a Jewish reticence to pronounce the divine Name, but also present in the very fullness of that absence, an absence or silence evoking and embodying a paradoxical presence, and a paradoxical presence of the silence of God. Kafka and Strauss would teach us that this is the silence of revelation, a silence present in our world as it has perhaps never been present before, and therefore a silence demanding a new hermeneutic, a hermeneutic which may well be a Kabbalistic hermeneutic, but nevertheless a hermeneutic at a seemingly infinite distance from the mystical hermeneutics of the past. So it is that it is the literary scholar and critic who in our world is most in search of such a hermeneutic, a quest now being prosecuted in multiple forms, such that the literary scholar is becoming a priest or rabbi of the imagination, and is doing so in a time of ultimate crisis not only in Judaism but in all of our established religious traditions.

Even as our art museums have become sanctuaries in the modern world, so likewise our fullest writing has been responded to as revelation, and most particularly so by Walter A. Strauss. Strauss's second book, *Descent and Return*, is a theological or religious assessment of modern Orphism. Here we learn that the Orpheus myth, in losing its classical and neo-classical grounding, becomes *the* myth of regeneration. Yet this is a regeneration issuing in a nihilistic dissolution, a nihilistic dissolution occurring in a new aeon of radical immanence, a radical or total immanence necessitating a reverse Orphic process, a reverse process or progress which is a fulfillment of the progressive attempt at a liberation from Being as defined and exercised by the post-Renaissance world. The new way of Orphic creation, as present above all in Mallarmé and Rilke, presupposes a "new way of being," and even if this new act of creation always implies the "obverse of being," a modern Orphic resurrection is always a resurrection out of death and Nothingness, and might well be identified with a new immanence which is a reversal of Being. Now nothing is more significant about modern Orphism than its creation of a new speech and language, thereby it decisively differs from ancient Orphism, and thereby it realizes a new Orphic immanence, an immanence which is the consequence of a uniquely modern descent into death and nothingness. Modern writing itself is here identified as a fundamentally Orphic writing, and therefore of the transmutation of silence into song, and of our dark center into radiance.

But Strauss concedes in this book that for Kafka the Orphic ideal is utterly meaningless, and one might surmise not only meaningless but totally blasphemous, and a blasphemy issuing in a truly nihilistic dissolution. Perhaps it is against this very blasphemy that Kafka can most deeply be understood, and thereby Kafka can be understood not only as a rebirth of Israel's prophetic reversal of ancient religion and society, but also a rebirth of prophecy in that its utterance cannot finally be silenced or forgotten, and nothing is more dramatic in ancient prophecy than the Israelite prophets' struggle against the prophetic call, a struggle most manifestly present in the Book of Jeremiah, and a struggle which is reenacted by Kafka himself. Kafka's dread of writing can be no less than this, just as the self-laceration of that writing echoes the self-lacerations of a Jeremiah or a Paul. For the prophetic calling is not unlike a Shamanic or Orphic descent; it, too, is a descent into chaos or nothingness, a descent uprooting and shattering every given identity, and a descent effecting a total alienation of the prophet from his society and world. But the prophetic descent issues in no resurrection or rebirth, and the return from the descent is not into radiance but rather into an all too human world, and a world now even darker and more terrible for the prophet as a consequence of his prophetic call.

No modern writer has known such darkness and terror as deeply as did Kafka and no other writer has so despaired over his own work, and if that work does embody a new Kabbalah, it no less embodies a truly prophetic darkness. All too significantly, Strauss's most recent book, *On the Threshold of a New Kabbalah*, exhibits little if any traces of the voyage of *Descent and Return*, it as though the very presence of Kafka's writing forecloses the possibility of an epiphany of radiance, an epiphany ending in Kafka just as it did in the ancient prophets of Israel. Or, rather, those prophets could know radiance only in the glory of the Lord, and even if that glory ends the radiance of the world, it is a glory negating and transcending all worldly or earthly radiance, and so much so that in comparison with that glory all worldly glory is as nothingness. In Kafka, all worldly radiance has likewise disappeared, and so much so that no other radiance is visible or audible, thus necessitating a new silence, and a new silence which speaks the name of God. But that silence is just as forceful, at least for us, as is the prophetic utterance of the divine Name, and even as the prophetic oracles evoke and embody the divine presence as does no other writing, so Kafka's writing evokes and embodies a divine absence and silence as does no other writing in our world.

Seemingly nothing could be more perverse than to seek a new Kabbalah in that writing, for who could imagine a more prolific vision of God than is found in Kabbalistic traditions, traditions which as Gershom C. Scholem declares can actually envision God by way of the images of man:

> The Biblical Word that man was created in the image of God means two things to the kabbalist: first, that the power of the Sefiroth, the paradigm of divine life, exists and is active also in man. Secondly, that the world of the Sefiroth, that is to say the world of God the Creator, is capable of being visualized under the image of man the created. From this it follows that the limbs of the human body . . . are nothing but images of a certain mode of spiritual existence which manifests itself in the symbolic figure of Adam Kadmon, the primordial man. For, to repeat, the Divine Being Himself cannot be expressed. All that can be expressed are His symbols. The relation between En-Sof and its mystical qualities, the Sefiroth, is comparable to that between the soul and the body, but with the difference that the human body and soul differ in nature, one being material and the other spiritual, while in the organic whole of God all spheres are substantially the same.[2]

Perhaps the world of the Sefiroth is envisioned in Kafka's writings, but if so now the world of God the Creator is a dark and terrible world, or is so to us, and the very actuality of the world can only be known through grace with silence.

In Kafka that silence becomes writing, and the very clarity and economy of Kafka's style make that silence immediately present, and that presence is a disrupting presence, a disruption every bit as effective as that created by the prophetic oracle, and yet a disruption which is in full continuity with the solidity and facticity of our all too human world. Nothing is more baffling in Kafka's style than its full conjunction of a primordial abyss with a fully contemporary and prosaic world, a world that is here more prosaic than it is in any other writing, and yet a world that is indistinguishable from chaos. Something very like this is also present in the pre-exilic prophetic oracle, an oracle that is an oracle of judgment and doom, and yet that doom is now inseparable from world itself, a world only now realized to be under total judgment. In the pre-exilic oracle, world can be evoked only to be submitted to the wrath of God, and to the total wrath of God, a wrath wholly removed from any possibility of not being realized here and now, and immediately here and now. But thereby the human world gains an immediacy which it had never known before, an immediacy here called forth by judgment itself, a total judgment embodying the end of ancient Israel. If ancient prophecy issued in the end of ancient Israel, and ultimately in the end of the ancient world itself, may we not surmise that modern prophecy issues in the end of modern history, and perhaps the end of Western history itself?

While the style of the prophetic oracle is very different from the style of Kafka's prose, each embodies an immediacy that is indubitable, and each evokes or calls forth a total response, a total response that is inseparable from the full and actual presence of world itself. Yes, that world is under total judgment, but that judgment can be heard only in the context and in the horizon of the very worldliness of the world, a worldliness that is the reverse side of judgment itself, and hence a worldliness that is indivisible from that judgment. So it is that the full conjunction of abyss and worldliness is called forth both by the prophetic oracle and by Kafka's prose, for each can call forth a human and all too human world only by realizing its end, an end that is present and fully present in that human world itself. Speech can fully speak only by speaking ending, an ending inseparable from the fullness of speech itself, for the fullness and the finality of speech is realized in its very ending, an ending indistinguishable from the actuality of speech. Such ending is present both in Kafka's language and in prophetic language, and it is spoken in each with a power and a uniqueness not found elsewhere in their respective worlds, for here pure judgment is present, and a judgment that is released by the very actuality of the world. Both the Orphic singer and the prophet can sing or speak only as a consequence of an interior voyage through darkness and death, an abysmal darkness effecting an interior ending, and an ending that is spoken in Orphic song and prophetic utterance alike. Yet the pre-exilic oracle, unlike the Orphic song, is not an ecstatic celebration, except insofar as it celebrates the power and the glory of the God of judgment, a celebration that passes into a literal silence in Kafka, who is incapable of pronouncing the name of God.

It is for this very reason that many would deny the prophetic identity of Kafka, but it is to be noted that the modern Orphic singer also does not pronounce the name of God, and not even in his most ecstatic celebration, a celebration seemingly foreclosing the very possibility of the presence of God. That foreclosure was first fully present in Nietzsche, and Nietzsche was an Orphic singer and a prophet of judgment at once, so that if it was Nietzsche's language which first fully embodied the ending of our Western history, that language was Orphic and prophetic simultaneously, a simultaneity which was lost in the twentieth century. In Kafka's language the very finality of prophetic judgment would seem to end the possibility of celebration, an ending perhaps bringing to an end the possibility of a prophetic pronunciation of the divine Name, or ending it in our time and world. If so, the absence of that pronunciation in Kafka would be a positive rather than a negative prophetic sign, and therefore a prophetic sign for us of the impossibility of God language in our world, a world in which the name of God can be pronounced only in an all too literal silence. Strauss would lead us into the center of that silence, for Kafka's "kabbalah" is the paradigm of a quest for truth that can be spoken only in silence, a silence straining to find its way back to the lost authority, unity, and inviolability of the Word (24). And this is a new Kabbalah in large measure because it is neither mythical nor hermetic, but rather pure fiction or parable, a parabolic fiction which "deconstructs" allegory and myth into a written act of presence in a pure moment of articulation (116). So it is that the ground of the new Kabbalah is in the literal or in language itself, but in language whose words are infinitely distant from the Word, hence there is no key to this Kabbalah, and it can be spoken only in silence.

Strauss dares to suggest that Kafka's new Kabbalah is pure fiction or parable becoming *tsimtsum* (126). *Tsimtsum* is a technical kabbalistic symbolic term meaning the contraction of the Godhead, a contraction which was necessary for the creation of the world, and a contraction that is reversed by the Kabbalistic voyage. But what can *tsimtsum* mean in relation to Kafka's language? Does his language contract from all mythical and allegorical language in order to give birth to a new vision of God? And does this necessitate the dissolution of all God language, and beyond that the dissolution of all language which has spoken or evoked the name of God? Or is Kafka's language itself a contraction of the divine Word of revelation? Thence Kafka's language might be construed as a Kabbalistic commentary upon and reenactment of Scripture which contracts the words of Scripture into the prose of a Godless world, a world which therein and thereby becomes charged with the presence of God, but now a presence of God necessitating the silence of God. This would be a new silence of God and a new silence of language itself, and a new silence necessitating a new listening and response, for it would be a new silence which must be resaid and reenacted in the hearer. Strauss is in quest of such a silence, and he would find it in the very language of Kafka, and above all in the parabolic language of Kafka, a language which is a labyrinth of words, and a labyrinth reversing or contracting all Scriptural words.

Torah may well be the most paradoxical of all sacred languages, for it is centered in the Word of God, and even centered in Scriptural words for God, yet it profoundly forbids the actual pronunciation of the divine Name. Moreover, it is the most radically iconoclastic of all scriptures, even while being the richest and most prolific embodiment of words, and of language itself, of any scripture in the world. For the language of Torah is itself a silent language, and not simply because of the silence of writing, but also because this is a writing which is writing alone, and even the oral Torah is known and celebrated as being written in Talmud. Nowhere else in the world has revelation so fully passed into writing, so it is that reading itself or pure reading was born in exilic Israel, a reading liberated from every sacred source outside of scripture. While Kafka himself was certainly not a Talmudic scholar in any save the most indirect sense, and probably only had a minimal acquaintance with the written Torah, he nevertheless was imbued with Torah, as demonstrated again and again in his prose. And it is not only that he frequently calls forth Scriptural personages and events, but far rather that those events recur, and recur again and again, in the most prosaic moments and movements of his fictional and parabolic language. Thus that language is Scriptural and contemporary at once, and so much so that its contemporary and Scriptural poles are indistinguishable.

Thus there is very good reason to believe that God is present in Kafka's language, and present in the very absence of the name of God, an absence which is a paradoxical absence to be sure, for in no other modern writer is the name of God so profoundly and so pervasively present. Yes, that presence is manifest in judgement, a judgment so terrible as wholly to lie beyond any possible human or natural source, and yet a judgment so immediately present that it activates and directs every presence and moment in this all too human and modern world. Now judgement is all, even as it is in the pre-exilic prophetic oracle, an all or totality which is a total presence, and therefore a presence comprehending the ultimate ground of presence. If that ground itself is now groundless, it is nevertheless all the more real for that, for now ground and groundlessness are indistinguishable, and in that indistinguishability presence itself becomes overwhelming. Even as at this very time Proust and Joyce were creating fictional and epic worlds which are indistinguishable from the deeper moments of our history, so Kafka, too, was creating a fictional world which is simultaneously an historical world, but an historical world that would become an actual world only after Kafka's death. No writer has been more prophetic than Kafka of the horrors of the twentieth century, and yet the horror embedded in his prose is an all too realistic horror, and a horror which was apparently never absent when Kafka wrote.

That horror, too, provides good reason for the absence of the name of God, for God is the Creator, and this also is God's world, a world that literally would be meaningless if it were not for either the presence or the memory of God. And a literal meaninglessness is precisely what is most missing in Kafka's fiction, and missing here as it is in no other modern writing, an absence which is the inevitable consequence of Kafka's style. If that style finally transcends all literary and scholarly analysis, therein it parallels the multiple styles of Scripture itself, and even as those styles in all their multiformity are the most realistic styles in all the ancient world, so Kafka's is the most realistic style in our world, and realistic above all in that here there is no distinction whatsoever between form and matter. Accordingly, there is also here no real distinction between God and world, and while this is in no sense true in a traditional pantheistic sense, it is all too true in a modern atheistic sense, for here it is the absence of God which is the presence of God, and a totally godless world which is the full and final embodiment of the judgment of God. That judgment, and that pure and total judgment, is now indistinguishable from world itself, and therein and thereby world itself is indistinguishable from God.

Is God fully and finally silent in Kafka's writing? And did Kafka's writing culminate in a reverent silence, as Strauss believes? If this is a silence of judgment, is it a silence of redemption as well? Strauss believes that it is:

> Kafka is by virtue of his rediscovery of parabolic speech at the same time Scriptural and Talmudic and Kabbalistic: Scriptural because he would like language to penetrate to the very source of speech itself; Talmudic because this speech is identified with the Law and thus marks the distance between itself and the Law by

> infinite commentary; and finally Kabbalistic because it envisions a new deliverance through a hermeneutic that includes myth, a moral order and spiritual truth. The modern Kabbalist, Kafka seems to have recognized, must pass from the broken vessels to the final redemption through silence; and the instruments of this passage cannot be metaphorical or symbolical or allegorical, because they would attest to the plenitude of verbal relations. The Way (in Tao's sense) must be charted as *parable*. Allegory elucidates by proliferation, parable *represents* the silence and makes it available for meditation, which is still another kind of silence. (154)

Perhaps we can only be silent in facing this claim of a final redemption through silence. But is this a uniquely modern or post-modern redemption? And, if so, is it truly Scriptural, Talmudic, and Kabbalistic? No doubt Kafka himself could not have answered such questions, if he ever answered any questions at all, and yet when he willed that his precious manuscripts be destroyed, perhaps he was willing yet another Kafkaesque silence, and a silence that no writing can erase. But if paradox and deep paradox is the condition of all writing, is such paradox present in a final redemption through silence, in which case would redemption be indistinguishable from its very opposite?

NOTES

1. Walter A. Strauss, *On the Threshold of a New Kabbalah* (New York: Peter Lang) 61. Parenthetical references are to this edition.
2. Gershom G. Scholem, *Major Trends in Jewish Mysticism* (New York: Shocken Books, 1954) 215.

WALTER A. STRAUSS
Bibliography

Books

Proust and Literature: The Novelist as Critic, Cambridge: Harvard University Press, 1957.

Descent and Return: The Orphic Theme in Modern Literature, Cambridge: Harvard University Press, 1971.

On the Threshold of a New Kabbalah: Kafka's Later Tales, New York: Peter Lang Publishing, 1988.

Articles

"Turgenev in the Role of Publicity Agent for Flaubert's *La Tentation de Saint Antoine*," *Harvard Library Bulletin*, II, 3 (Autumn, 1948), 405–10.

"Albert Camus' *Caligula*: Ancient Sources and Modern Parallels," *Comparative Literature*, III, 2 (Spring, 1954), 160–73.

"Twelve Unpublished Letters of Marcel Proust," *Harvard Library Bulletin*, VII, 2 (Spring, 1953), 145–71.

"Giraudoux: The Tragedy of Disharmony," *The Emory University Quarterly*, XI, 1 (March, 1955), 18–29.

"A Poet in the Theater: Paul Claudel," *The Emory University Quarterly*, XII, 4 (December, 1956), 206–19.

"Saint-John Perse, Poet of Celebration," *The Emory University Quarterly*, XIV, 2 (June, 1958), 100–11.

"Dante's Belacqua and Beckett's Tramps," *Comparative Literature* XI, 3 (Summer, 1959), 250–61.

"Franz Kafka: Between the Paradise and the Labyrinth," *The Centennial Review*, V, 2 (Spring 1961), 206–22.

"Literature and Reality," in *Truth, Myth and Symbol*, ed. by T. J. J. Altizer, W. A. Beardslee, J. H. Young (Englewood Cliffs: Prentice-Hall, 1962), 51–60.

"Criticism and Creation," in *Proust*, ed. by R. Girard (Englewood Cliffs: Prentice-Hall, 1962), 53–68.

"Albert Camus, Stone-Mason," *Modern Languages Notes*, LXXVII, 3 (May, 1962), 268–81.

"Sense and Nonsense in Censorship," *Emory University Quarterly*, XX, 3 (Fall, 1964), 183–86.

"New Life, Tree of Life: The *Vita Nuova* and Nerval's *Aurélia*," *Books Abroad*, May 1965 (Special Issue: A Homage to Dante), 144–50.

"Vida nueva, árbol de la vida: la *Vita Nuova* y la Aurelia de Nerval," *Dante en su centenario*, Madrid, Taurus, 1965, 344-62.

"Gérard de Nerval," *Emory University Quarterly*, XXI, 1 (Spring, 1965), 15–31.

"The Reconciliation of Opposites in Orphic Poetry: Rilke and Mallarmé," *The Centennial Review*, X (Spring, 1966), 214–36.

"The Humanities in the College," *Emory College Today*, I, 4 (March, 1966), 1–7.

"Existentialism," *Encyclopedia of World Literature in the 20th Century*, Vol. I (New York: Ungar, 1967), 362–65.

"Fellini's Historical Science Fiction," *This Issue*, 4 (1971), (McKee Publishing Co., Atlanta, Georgia), 147–51.

"Nonrecognition and Recognition in Proust," *Nineteenth Century French Studies*, IV (Fall-Winter, 1975–1976), 105–23.

"Siren-Language: Kafka and Blanchot," *Sub-Stance*, 14 (1976), 18-33.

"Le Belacqua de Dante et les clochards de Beckett," *L'Herne* (Beckett issue), October, 1976, 269–80.

"Turning Over an Old Leaf," in *The Kafka Debate*, ed. Angel Flores (New York: Gordian Press, 1977), 17–23.

"Nominative Cases: Proust, Kafka, Beckett," in *The Proustian Novel Reconsidered*, ed. L. Joiner (Rock Hill, S.C.: Winthrop College, 1978), 11–21.

"Proust-Giotto-Dante," *Dante Studies*, XCVI (1978), 163–85.

"A Spool of Thread and a Spinning Top: Two Fables by Kafka," *Newsletter of the Kafka Society of America*, III, 2 (December, 1979), 9–16.

"L'Objet c'est la poétique," in *Rilke: The Alchemy of Alienation*, ed., F. Baron, E. S. Dick and W. R. Maurer (Lawrence: The Regents Press of Kansas, 1980), 63–93.

"Proust," in *Critical Bibliography of French Literature*, Vol. VI, *Twentieth Century*, eds. D. W. Alden and R. A. Brooks (Syracuse: Syracuse University Press, 1980), Vol. 1, 198-350 *passim*.

"Beyond the Human: Georg Trakl and Paul Celan," *Internationales Trakl-Symposium*, 67–77.

"Judenbilder in der französischen Literatur," in *Juden und Judentum in der Literatur* (ed. H. A. Strauss and G. Hoffmann). Munich: Deutscher Taschenbuch Verlag, 1985, 307–37.

"Speculations on Narcissus and Paris," *The Comparatist*, X (May, 1986, 13–29.

"From Mallarmé to Boulez—Some Reflections on Poetry and Music" in the program booklet for the Cleveland Orchestra, November 26–29, 1986, 37–39.

"Trying to Mend the Broken Vessels," in *Kafka's Contextuality*, ed. Alan Udoff (Gordian Press and Baltimore Hebrew College, 1986), 287–341.

"The Agony of Witnessing: Heinrich Böll's Work Viewed from the Perspective of *Gruppenbild mit Dame*," *Postscript*, No. 4 (1987), 39–48.

"Tournier's Quest for Sophia," in *Literature as Philosophy/ Philosophy as Literature*, ed. Donald G. Marshall (Iowa City: University of Iowa Press, 1987), 306–16.

"Exile to Equinox," *Stanford French Review*, Summer 1987, 229–40.

"Toward a Third Testament: Michel Tournier's Attempt to Reappropriate the Sacred," *South Central Review*, 75–83.

"*Le Livre des questions* de Jabès et la question du livre," *Ecrire le livre autour d'Edmond Jabès* (Colloque de Cerisy), (Paris: Champ Vallon, 1989), 295–98.

CONTRIBUTORS

Thomas J. J. Altizer is Professor of Religious Studies at the State University of New York at Stony Brook

Alice N. Benston is Director of Interdisciplinary Studies for the Graduate School and Chair of Theater and Film Studies at Emory University

Richard R. Berrong is Associate Professor of French at Kent State University

Germaine Brée is Kenan Professor of Humanities Emerita at Wake Forest University

Mariana Carpinisan is Assistant Curator at the Cleveland Museum of Art

Ursula Franklin is Professor of French at Grand Valley State College

Lilian R. Furst is Marcel Bataillon Professor of Comparative Literature at the University of North Carolina at Chapel Hill

Tiina A. Kirss is a Doctoral candidate in Comparative Literature at the University of Michigan

Dalton Krauss is Associate Professor of French at Scripps College

Edouard Morot-Sir is Kenan Professor of French Emeritus at the University of North Carolina at Chapel Hill

Marcel Muller is Professor of French at the University of Michigan

John Neubauer is Professor of Literature at the University of Amsterdam

Marshall C. Olds is Associate Professor of French at the University of Nebraska

Randolph Runyon is Associate Professor of French at Miami University

Wolfgang Sohlich is Associate Professor of Comparative Literature at the University of Oregon

Steven Ungar is Professor of French and Comparative Literature at the University of Iowa

Maryann Weber, SND is Associate Professor of French at Notre Dame College of Ohio